Guatemalans in the Aftermath of Violence

THE ETHNOGRAPHY OF POLITICAL VIOLENCE
Cynthia Keppley Mahmood, Series Editor

A complete list of books in the series is available from the publisher.

Guatemalans in the Aftermath of Violence

The Refugees' Return

KRISTI ANNE STØLEN

PENN

University of Pennsylvania Press

Philadelphia

10 9 8 7 6 5 4 3 2 1

Published by
University of Pennsylvania Press
Philadelphia, Pennsylvania 19104-4112

Library of Congress Cataloging-in-Publication Data

Stølen, Kristi Anne.
    Guatemalans in the aftermath of violence : the refugees' return / Kristi Anne Stølen.
        p.   cm. — The Ethnography of Political Violence
    Includes bibliographical references (p.   ) and index.
    ISBN-13: 978-0-8122-4008-5 (alk. paper)
    ISBN-10: 0-8122-4008-1 (alk. paper)
    1. Refugees—Guatemala—La Quetzal. 2. Return migration—Guatemala—La Quetzal.
3. Political violence—Guatemala. I. Title. II. Series.
HV640.5.G9 S76   2007
972.81'84—dc22   2006051919

In Memory of Eduardo

Contents

viii   Contents

Preface

This book deals with three main topics: dynamics of violence, survival strategies in situations of extreme violence, and social reconstruction in the aftermath of violence. It is based on anthropological fieldwork among refugees who returned to the Petén, Guatemala, in 1995 after more than a decade in refugee camps in Mexico. They are survivors of the Guatemalan army's scorched-earth campaign in the early 1980s aimed at destroying the civilian population considered to be the support base of the guerrilla. On the basis of written documents and narratives of the returnees, the book provides a picture over time of the dynamics and escalation of violence in two peasant areas in Guatemala, Western Petén and Ixcán, the latter singled out as a *matazona* (killing zone) by the Guatemalan army. It contests the widely held assumption that the Guatemalan guerrilla movement enjoyed strong popular support among indigenous peasants.

The violence in Guatemala demanded a variety of survival strategies. Some people joined the guerrilla ranks, others joined the so-called self-defense patrols controlled by the army, still others crossed the Mexican border and became refugees. The book aims at capturing the complexities of these survival strategies by drawing on the stories told by the returnees and their neighbors who remained in the country under military control, representing a variety of positions and voices in the conflict. It shows that even though violence is destructive it may also have constructive consequences, engendering community and identity, and that it is simplistic to view those exposed to violence merely as helpless victims, unable to change their circumstances. For many refugees, exile does not mean deprivation and victimization, but instead recognition and even empowerment.

The book depicts how the returnees managed to reconstruct community and identity in a new environment, combining old knowledge with what they had learned through interaction with the international aid and solidarity community during the years of exile. The migration history of the returnees, filled with ruptures and changing social environments, illustrates how poor and extremely exploited people are able, again and again, to mobilize enormous drive and engage in new social experiments when they see possibilities to improve their lot.

A number of people have contributed—wittingly or unwittingly—to the writing of this book. I am most indebted to my own institution the Center for Development and the Environment, University of Oslo, under the leadership of Bente Herstad, for financial and logistic backing during different stages of the project. My colleagues at the Center Oivind Fuglerud, Mette Hallskov-Hanssen and Jemima Garcia-Godos, introduced me to the topic of displacement and generously included me in a comparative research program on forced migration, where we collaborated for a number of years. Jennifer Schirmer, Eddie Robbins, and Mariel Aguilar Støen have read an earlier version of the entire manuscript and have provided suggestive reflections and critical comments.

In Guatemala I am indebted to a number of colleagues at the Universidad de San Carlos, especially Alfonso Arrivillaga, Celso Lara, and Gabriel Moreno, who were counterparts in a program of collaboration between our universities of which my research project was a part. I am also grateful to colleagues at FLACSO (Facultad Latinoamericana de Ciencias Sociales), Instituto de Estudios Interétnicos, and CIRMA (Centro de Investigaciones de Regionales de Meso-América) for support and critical comments underway.

I acknowledge with gratitude the grants provided by the Norwegian Research Council, permitting me to conduct long-term fieldwork in the Petén and to spend several months at the Institute for Latin American Studies and the Benson Collections at the University of Texas, where I found rich material about the armed conflict in Guatemala. Charles Hale, Bryan Roberts, and Margo Gutiérrez contributed to making my stay at UT a very productive one. Part of the book was written during a sabbatical spent in Buenos Aires. I am particularly grateful to Silvina Ramos, director of CEDES (Centro de Estudios de Estado y Sociedad) for offering me very good working conditions at the center.

I am also grateful to a number of people who have read and commented on parts of the manuscript: Santiago Alvarez, Benedicte Bull, Rosana Guber, Laura Golbert, Christian Krohn-Hansen, Stef Jansen, Norman Long, Staffan Löfving, Marit Melhuus, Desmond McNeill, Ingrid Nesheim, Knut Nustad, Finn Stepputat, and Pierre van der Vaeren. The latter has generously allowed me to use the maps elaborated by him and his friend Piet den Blanken. The IT assistance of Kristoffer Ring has been invaluable in all stages of my work. Ryan Anderson and Alida Jay Boye have been helpful in seeing to that my English is presentable. I am indebted to the unknown reviewer of this manuscript for having provided detailed, constructive, critical comments to an earlier draft.

I would like to express my profound gratitude to my informants in La Quetzal for the generosity and confidence that they showed me. I hope that my writing about their lives and experiences is faithful to what they told me and let me observe. It has been my intention to be discreet in telling their stories; therefore, and maybe to some people's disappointment, they will not find their true names in the text. The experience of living with them has been extremely enriching. Without their collaboration this book would certainly not have existed.

Finally, the most precious and constant intellectual, emotional, and moral support during all stages of my work I received from my companion Eduardo Archetti, who passed away before this book was finalized. His enthusiasm, sensitivity, and vast anthropological knowledge have been a constant source of inspiration and encouragement during our more than thirty years of adventure and collaboration. I dedicate this book to his memory.

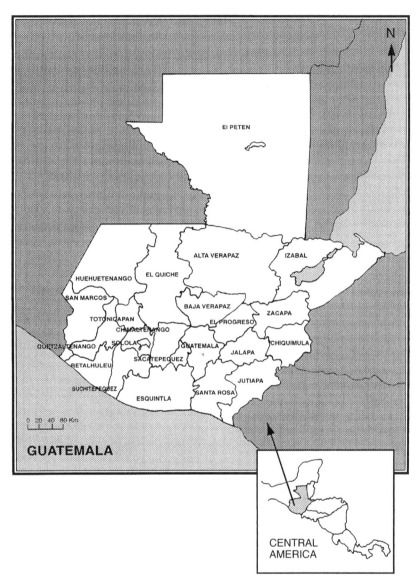

Map 1. Guatemala. From Pierre van der Vaeren, *Perdidos en la selva* (Amsterdam: Thela, 2000).

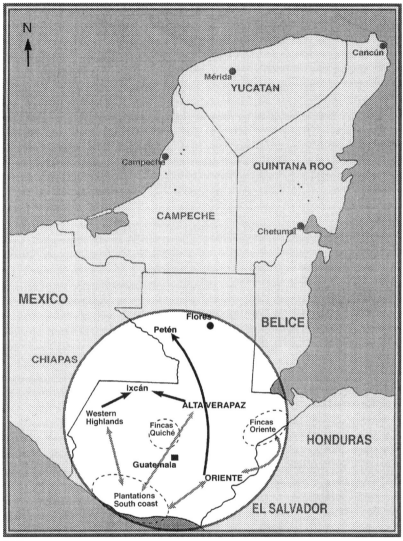

= Temporary migrations from places of origin to export plantations

= Permanent migrations from places of origin to Ixán and the Petén (1970s)

Map 2. Internal migration. From Pierre van der Vaeren, *Perdidos en la selva* (Amsterdam: Thela, 2000).

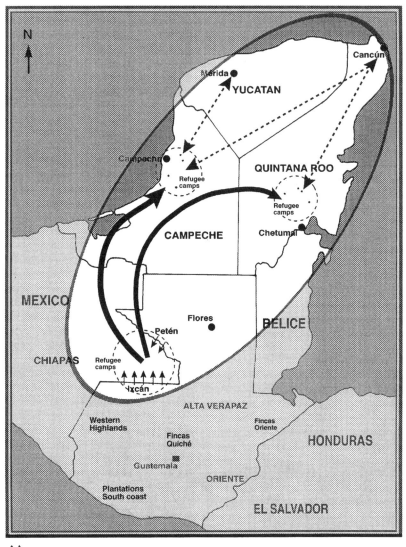

= Flight to Mexico (1981–1983)

= Relocation to camps in the Yucatán Peninsula, Mexico (1984)

- - - = Temporary labor migrations to urban centers

Map 3. Refugee migration. From Pierre van der Vaeren, *Perdidos en la selva* (Amsterdam: Thela, 2000).

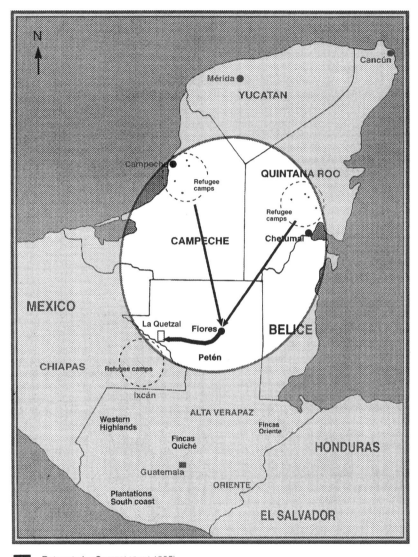

■ – Return to La Quetzal (April 1995)

Map 4. Return migration. From Pierre van der Vaeren, *Perdidos en la selva* (Amsterdam: Thela, 2000).

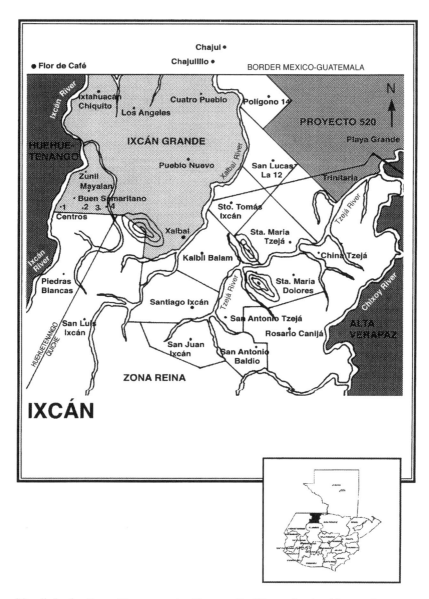

Map 5. Ixcán. From Pierre van der Vaeren, *Perdidos en la selva* (Amsterdam: Thela, 2000).

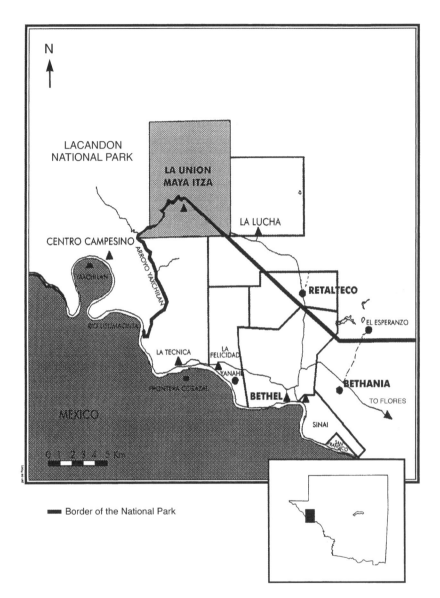

N

LACANDON
NATIONAL PARK

LA UNION
MAYA ITZA

LA LUCHA

CENTRO CAMPESINO

ARROYO YAXCHILAN

YAXCHILAN

RIO USUMACINTA

RETALTECO

EL ESPERANZO

LA TECNICA

LA
FELICIDAD

YANAHE

FRONTERA COROZAL

BETHEL

BETHANIA

TO FLORES

MEXICO

SINAI

SAN FRANCISCO

0 1 2 3 4 5 Km

Border of the National Park

Map 6. Research area. From Pierre van der Vaeren, *Perdidos en la selva*
(Amsterdam: Thela, 2000).

Chapter 1

Introduction: Guatemalan Returnees in the Aftermath of Violence

My first direct contact with the refugee problem in Guatemala was in April 1995 when I visited the Petén as a member of an international consultancy team. When I arrived in the airport of Flores, I observed a chaotic movement of people. The airport was an anthill of journalists, representatives of different international agencies, and a number of young people, most of them foreigners. When I asked what was going on I was told that they were waiting for the arrival of Guatemalan refugees returning from exile in Mexico. The young foreigners were *acompañantes* (accompaniers) who were to escort, as a measure of security, the returnees during their transport to and settlement in La Quetzal, their new home to be established in the Lacandon jungle close to the Mexican border of Chiapas.[1] This was the first collective return of refugees to the Petén (See Maps 4 and 6).[2]

During my subsequent stays as a consultant, I had the opportunity to visit a number of villages in western Petén, located in the same area as La Quetzal. They had been affected by the armed conflict in different ways. In some villages most people had remained under military control during the conflict, because military detachments had been installed in the area. Other villages, which had been the targets of violent repression in the early 1980s, had been abandoned partly or completely by their inhabitants, who for a number of years found a way to sustain themselves in Mexico without being officially registered as refugees. In the late 1980s and early 1990s they had started to return to their home communities. These people were called *repatriados* (repatriated), a label referring to those who returned individually or in small family groups, without the apparatus of international support associated with the collective returns.

The returnees of La Quetzal were a favorite topic of conversation in western Petén at that time. Some of their neighbors considered them dangerous because they believed that they were supporters of, or even worse, actively involved in the insurgency movement, and feared that their presence in the area could contribute to a new flareup of violence.[3] Others characterized the returnees as demanding and spoiled because they had received a great deal of attention and support from national and international aid organizations. Those who had remained in the region under constant fear of military repression had not received such attention or support. The returnees, whom some referred to as cowards for "having abandoned the country and leaving the suffering to those who stayed behind," were perceived as receiving privileges that those who had remained could only dream about.

Through discussions with members of aid organizations, though, a different image of the returnees emerged. They told about the problems and suffering returnees were forced to endure, settling as they did in a previously uninhabited and isolated jungle area. Aid workers described the returnees' heroic struggle to overcome their problems and to construct a new and different community, based on the recognition of human rights, democratic values, and a cooperative economy. Some aid workers even saw returnees as crucial protagonists in the creation of a democratic Guatemala.

What the various spokespeople seemed to agree on was that the returnee community was different in many respects from the spontaneous settlements that had grown up in the Petén in recent decades. La Quetzal was predominantly indigenous, which was not so common in this region—except for some recent influx of Q'eqchi' population—and it was multiethnic, composed of people speaking a number of Mayan languages in addition to Spanish, which most returnees had learned in exile. It was also better organized than the other communities in the area.

What motivated me to convert my emerging interest in displacement and reconstruction processes in the Petén into a research project was the encouragement received from three of my colleagues at the Center for Development and the Environment at the University of Oslo, working on displacement in situations of conflict in Sri Lanka, China, and Peru, and the fact that the Norwegian Research Council was about to launch a new research program on forced migration. We decided to join efforts and develop a program proposal, which in addition to our specific case studies contained some research questions that could be explored comparatively by all of us:

- How do people produce and secure livelihoods under changing and volatile circumstances?
- How do people create or re-create social structures, cultural institutions and forms of organization when confronting fluid, unpredictable situations and possibly opposing the policies of states and other powerful bodies?
- By what processes are social identities shaped and reformulated, and how do they link with struggles over power on the one hand and with livelihood practices on the other?

Within this more general framework of the dynamics of displacement, my project, on which this book is based, also raised a number of specific questions about the armed conflict in Guatemala?[4] What was the nature of the violence that obliged so many poor peasants to leave the country? What was the relationship between the army and the peasants? What was the relationship between the guerrilla and the peasants? And whom did the peasants see as the perpetrators of this conflict?

With these questions guiding me, I decided to conduct fieldwork in La Quetzal among peasant returnees who had spent more than a decade in exile in different refugee camps in southern Mexico. Most of them had fled from Ixcán, El Quiché, where they happened to live in the primary area of operation of the EGP (Ejército Guerrillero de los Pobres), singled out as a *matazona* (killing zone) by the Guatemalan army.[5] They were survivors of the army's scorched-earth campaign aimed at destroying the civilian population considered to be the support base of the guerrilla.

Armed Conflict and Social Reconstruction

A considerable body of literature has been published dealing with various aspects of the armed conflict in Guatemala. Much is either journalistic or written by individuals associated with development NGOs or solidarity groups, and thus strongly partisan. Over the years a number of anthropological and other social science studies have also been published.[6] One common characteristic of these studies is that they have focused for the most part on those who remained in the country during the armed conflict.

I was particularly intrigued by David Stoll's *Between Two Armies in the Ixil Towns of Guatemala*, where he argues, against the dominant view among many scholars/activists that the insurgent movement enjoyed little popular backing except in a transitory and coercive way, and that the Ixil support was primarily a response to government repression (1993). A number of his critics argued that his conclusions were based on a biased selection of informants, mainly people living under strict military control. What would the refugees in Mexico, the people living in the Communities of People in Resistance (CPRs),[7] or the people who were actually fighting in the ranks of the guerrilla tell us, it was asked (Painter 1993; Wilson 1995). The refugees were generally seen as more supportive of the guerrilla and, in contrast to those who remained in Guatemala whose testimony was muted or biased by the army presence, more outspoken. I hoped that my research among returnees would contribute to a more comprehensive understanding of the armed conflict in Guatemala. How had the refugees experienced the armed conflict? What were their versions and visions of what happened and why? And what were the consequences for them? These became guiding questions in my research in La Quetzal.

Most studies of the armed conflict in Guatemala are based on neither participant observation nor direct observation. As in my case, they are based on stories and testimonies narrated after the events took place by people who were involved as victims, perpetrators or witnesses of violence. With few exceptions, this is a common characteristic of such studies worldwide (Daniel 1996; Robben and Nordstrom 1995). This is also the case for Manz's study in Santa Maria Tzejá, even though she labels her work "fieldwork under fire" (Manz 2004).

I had high expectations reading Manz's new book, *Paradise in Ashes* (2004), since it deals with overlapping issues and subject matters and covers part of the same region. Even though her narrative provides a general overview and, at times, moving testimonial, she does not provide enough ethnographic information about the villagers, the army, or the guerrilla to enable informed comparisons based on the material she offers in a piecemeal manner. I share Jennifer Schirmer's view that Manz's paucity of detail on the nature of village life and the repression in the 1970s and 1980s, unfortunately, leads to an oversimplification in describing village divisions before, during, and after the repression and in tracing how and in what ways army violence and guerrilla executions changed relations within the village (Schirmer 2005). My intention is to offer a more systematic and detailed description of the escalating process of violence in the Ixcán and the Petén, demonstrating, among other things, that the role of the guerrilla was far more problematic than the version given by Manz indicates. Moreover, my work places greater emphasis than Manz does on the changes in identity and the roles of ethnicity, gender, and local relations to the state in the return and reconstruction process.

The accounts of violence presented in this book are based on conversations with more than one hundred returnees between April 1998 and March 2001. Most of the events they refer to took place between 1975 and 1982. The time span between the events that caused their flight to Mexico and the collection of the narratives about these events draws attention to the methodological challenges associated with the reconstruction of the past. This goes for anthropologists as well as for our informants.

My informants talked about their past experiences, particularly those related to violence and armed conflict as something that was inscribed in their minds. "Grabado en mi mente" (recorded in my mind) was an expression often heard when people talked about these experiences. But as Kirmayer (1996) and others have argued, memory is far from a photographic register of experiences. First, what is registered is very selective and, thereafter, shaped by interpretation and semantic coding at the moment the experience takes place. What is remembered is therefore constrained and routinely reconstructed with recourse to ideas about what could have happened or must have happened. We tend to construct a processed narrative, and by doing so, our memory about the event will be colored by our narrative about the event.

Thus, reconstructions of the past imply a transformation of the past, because the person who narrates adds explanations and interpretations that he/she may not or could not have given when the events took place. Only afterward do they understand what "really happened," because they have experienced, heard, and learned new things. The latter is particularly relevant regarding the narratives of my informants. They often talk about how the experience of exile has opened their eyes and made them understand things that they did not realize or understand in their previous "state of ignorance." Thus, my informants' narratives are reconstructions of what happened almost twenty years ago, colored by experiences, insights, and knowledge acquired after the events. Since women and men often tell different kinds of stories and put emphasis on different kinds of experience, the voices of both are presented, while attempting to relate their interpretive worlds.

The study of processes of social reconstruction after armed conflicts requires an understanding of the circumstances leading to the displacement and return of the refugees. Within the general context of violence in Guatemala, there is a complex set of factors explaining the outcome of particular resettlement processes. There has also been a wide range of strategies employed to respond to the situation of insecurity and violence. Some people fled their home areas and even the country, while others decided to stay. Some made alliances with the army, some with the guerrilla; others had to flee from both to save their lives. This book aims at contributing to the understanding of the complexities of causes and trajectories of forced migration by drawing on the stories told by the returnees and their neighbors, who represent a variety of positions and voices in the conflict.

The Anthropology of Violence

Violence and violent practices often have been relegated to a secondary place in ethnographic enquiry. On the one hand, they are perceived as either irrational or uncivilized, that is, outside the systems of order regulating social life. On the other hand, they are viewed as a form of instrumental rationality, a means to achieve concrete political or military gains. There has been a focus on structural violence, but this often lacks any discussion of the reasons people give regarding why a particular event sparks the violence, what it means in terms of local values and beliefs, and why some people interpret the violence in one way, some in another (Zur 1998). In a recent attempt to refine the anthropological approach to violence, Schmidt and Schröder (2001) try to bridge the gap between the different anthropologies of conflict, war, and violence. They argue for a strong focus on the processual character of violent practices, linking them both to conflicts and to their cultural imagining. Violence, they argue, and its various forms of social realization represent a highly complex phenomenon that can be reduced neither to a mere mechanical reaction to resource stress or an impulse of human nature, nor to random flexibility of discourse or individual subjectivity. Violence must be understood as a form of practice mediating between the historical boundedness of action and the cultural quest for meaning (19). In other words, they argue for a perspective that comprises the dialectic of practice and meaning, a perspective that is closely related to the notion of violence elaborated by David Riches (1986).

Riches focuses on the act of violence as an interaction between perpetrator and victim and suggests that the understanding of the dynamics of violence is to be found in this interface. For Riches, violence is based on rational considerations by those in competition with each other. The potency of violence lies in the fact that it suits both practical and symbolic ends; it is at the same time a means to transform the social environment and a means to dramatize central cultural ideas (1986: 11). In this perspective violent events can never be neutral or objective, since the different participants—perpetrator, victim, and observer—will be caught up in their own interpretive frames and agendas. One of the advantages in Riches's approach is that it addresses the essential ambivalence of violence as both an instrumental and an expressive action. Acts of violence are not sudden outbursts of aggressiveness devoid of historicity, meaning, and reflexivity. They are imagined and performed by reflexive, socially positioned human beings under specific historical conditions and for concrete reasons. They always express some kind of relationship with another party and do not target someone at random, although the individual victim is likely to be chosen as representative of some larger category (Schmidt and Schröder 2001). This was the case with the peasants in Ixcán, who were considered guerrilla supporters simply because they lived within the area where the EGP had its main base.

One limitation of the focus on the violent act or event, as pointed out by Øyvind Fuglerud (2000), is that acts of violence are often directed by actors and conditions external to the concrete violent arena where perpetrators and victims interact. As in the case of Sri Lanka studied by Fuglerud, the violence in Guatemala cannot be understood if we focus only on the act of violence as mutually defined by those directly involved. The perpetrators as well as the victims were pieces in bigger power games, as clearly documented by Schirmer's study of the Guatemalan military (1998). She reveals that decisions made by political and military leaders, who may not themselves be participating in acts of violence, are decisive for the forms and dynamics of the violence. Based on ten years of fieldwork among Guatemalan officers, she demonstrates in detail that the use of violence was far from arbitrary or irrational. Nor was it a product of evil or madness of bloodthirsty and uncontrolled officers, or of peasant recruits lacking proper military training. Violence and killing were part of a carefully planned military strategy with clear international connections. The same can be said about guerrilla warfare in Guatemala, even though the scale and level of professionalism were much lower. This reminds us that the localized acts of violence referred to in my study tie into the wider processes of the wielding of power.

Bowman (2001) draws attention to another limitation in Riches's approach: his focus on violence as a violative act. Bowman stresses the importance of focusing not only on the violative, but also on the performative aspects of violence and the narratives of violence, which demonstrate that violence not only is destructive but can also be constructive, engendering imagined community and identity. Following this line of thinking, it would be simplistic to view those exposed to violence as merely helpless victims, unable to change their circumstances. Violent crises may constitute positive challenges for some, even if they expect to suffer. In other words, people are not only passive recipients of experience; they may also be active negotiators of it.

I will argue that, in the case of the returnees in La Quetzal, the shared experience of violence has been constitutive in building community in exile as well as after their return, an argument supported by Torres's study among Guatemalan refugees in Mexican camps. She argues that the creation of new communities in exile is based on what she calls a "negative tradition," characterized by actively keeping alive the memories of violence and suffering (1999: 157). The Guatemalan refugees in Mexico certainly built on a negative tradition in the sense that they stressed the shared experience of violence and a common urgency to prevent violence from overpowering them again. However, they brought the negative tradition beyond the personal sphere and into the public one through political action. We will see that the creation of a community based on the shared experience of violence was particularly relevant in the return process.

The importance of giving voice to different actors involved in violent events has been emphasized by a number of scholars (Riches 1986; Krohn-Hansen 1994; Schirmer 2003). My material is comprised of the voices of victims and witnesses as well as the voices of perpetrators. Most of the adults in La Quetzal have been involved in violent actions as victims or witnesses who have been spared or have managed to escape from massacres, and in this way have survived. Their accounts mostly refer to army soldiers killing civilians, individually or en masse. However, the guerrilla is also often part of their accounts, for example, killings of local leaders accused of being guerrilla soldiers or army reprisals following guerrilla actions. Few of my informants have been tortured, but this does not mean that torture was not used. On the contrary, it was a common treatment of people captured by the army, but a treatment few people survived. Unlike their colleagues in other parts of Latin America, the Guatemalan military did not keep prisoners of war.

Some voices of perpetrators will also be heard. However, they did not take part in the same "triangles of violence" as the victims and witnesses, since they are ex-guerrillas who participated in violent confrontations with army soldiers. All of them left the guerrilla at some point and settled in refugee camps in Mexico, where they became part of the collective return movement. For obvious reasons none of the returnees have a past in the army; therefore, no voices of army soldiers are represented.

Place and Identity

The social experience of being a migrant—having to develop practical coping strategies while reworking the experience of migration—is closely connected to identity processes. Refugee studies have suffered from many of the same weaknesses as migration studies, exacerbated by the fact that the object of anthropology has traditionally been bounded systems or units comprised of sedentary people. This sedentary analytical bias in anthropology has unfortunately been transmitted to studies of refugees (Lovell 1998; Rapport and Dawson 1998). It is often taken for granted that the crossing of national borders implies a loss of identity and culture associated with place. Refugees are often described as displaced, misplaced, and uprooted. Underlying these labels is the notion of a naturalized relationship between place and identity. Liisa Malkki (1995) suggests that this notion of identities as rooted in places contributes to the conceptualization of territorial displacement as pathological, as something that expresses itself in different forms, such as terrorism and political crime, broken families, erosion of normal moral behavior, and depression.

Such views of identity have been strongly challenged by social anthropology (Featherstone 1990; Eriksen 1993; Lash and Friedman 1992; Campbell and Rew 1999). Anthropological studies of identity have shown that aspects of the person which have conventionally been held to be inner, private, and fixed are now increasingly held to be public and negotiable. A close relationship has also been demonstrated between social processes and personal identities. Social identities find their definition in relation to significant others, just as people articulate ideas of self or selfhood which are communicated and given meaning through social interaction. Since every individual has several identities such as ethnic, gendered, religious, and national to choose from, the identities communicated depend on negotiations taking place in specific social contexts and according to recognized cultural conventions (Campbell and Rew 1999: 13; Eriksen 1991). In this view ethnicity as well as other social identities are relative or situational to some extent. As argued by Eriksen (1993), even in typical multiethnic societies where cultural differences are pervasive, there are many situations where ethnicity does not matter. Since individuals may have many statuses and many possible identities it is an empirical question when and how ethnic identities become the most relevant ones (Eriksen 1993).

There is now compelling evidence showing that nonethnic criteria for group membership are situationally relevant in every society; in complex societies they proliferate and can be identified as multiple identities. Different forms of group loyalties and membership may largely overlap with ethnic membership, or they may cut across it. I find that the term "social identity," comprising a variety of identities that may be ethnic, gendered, religious, or national, would be more adequate to capture the flux and complexity of social processes, and would allow us to study group formation and alignments along a greater variety of axes than the singleminded focus on ethnic identity allows.

The case of the Guatemalan returnees offers an interesting illustration of identity formation as related to historical processes of social change. Migration, exile, and the return to Guatemala have brought them into contact with a variety of new people and places and this has inspired new perceptions and classifications of themselves and others as well as new models of group formation. In this book I give special attention to ethnicity and gender. We will see that most of the new arenas are not constituted on the basis of ethnicity, and even though ethnicity is still important, its meaning has changed. The same may be said about gender relations and gender perceptions even though the dynamics of change are different.

The idea of a natural link between people and places is also crucial in politics of repatriation (Malkki 1992, 1995; Stepputat 1994; Warner 1994). Repatriation is conceived of as the natural and logical solution to refugee displacement, a restoration of order in the relationship between people, culture, and place. Return is often depicted as an unproblematic reestablishment of the conditions existing before the flight—as normalization for the host country as well as for the refugees. It is seen as the "end of the refugee cycle," to use the terminology of Koser and Black (1994). These notions of repatriation imply not only the physical return to the homeland but also a return to the previous and familiar way of life, culture, and identity, in short, a "transplantation" of the roots to the ground where they belong, to use a botanic metaphor so common when

referring to refugees (Malkki 1995). The case of the Guatemalan returnees discussed in this book, however, reveals that such notions have
little to do with what "return" means to them. Not only have their living
conditions and their perceptions of themselves and "the world" changed,
so have those of the communities and the people they left behind. A return
to the places they came from was therefore unattractive to most of them.
I registered a high level of pragmatism with regard to the location of
land to "return" to. It is also noteworthy that a number of people said that
if they had been offered property rights to land in Mexico, they would
have remained there. This draws the attention to the uncertain and con-
tested meanings of "home" for people whose lives are characterized by
migration related to varying forms of and degrees of violence (Jansen
and Löfving forthcoming).

Migration and Social Change

My study of the returnees is also a study of migration and its enormous
impacts on people's livelihoods. The return to La Quetzal is the end of
a long process of movement that started in the late 1960s and early 1970s,
when thousands of poor peasants from different parts of the Highlands
moved to the almost uninhabited tropical lowlands of Ixcán and Petén
in search of land. This move was part of a colonization program led by
the Catholic Church and supported by the Guatemalan government to
reduce the pressure for land reforms in the Highlands (Morrissey 1978;
Dennis et al. 1988).

A few years after this settlement in the tropical areas, the peasants were
on the move again. Caught in the middle of the gunfire between the
guerrilla and the army, the peasants first tried to adapt to the situation
of terror and violence while remaining in their villages; later, with the
escalation of violence, they hid in the jungle (Falla 1992). When this internal refuge situation became unbearable they crossed the border to
Mexico where they were received by the "international refugee system,"
thus becoming a target group for international aid organizations (Gallagher 1989; Malkki 1995). With the initiation of the peace process in
the early 1990s, a permanent solution to the refugee problem became a
central topic in the negotiations between URNG (Guatemalan National
Revolutionary Unit)[8] and the Guatemalan government. The result of the
peace negotiations made their collective return to the Petén possible in
April 1995. Since that time, they have been in the process of constructing
a new community in the jungle of the Petén.

This process of movement brought my informants into contact with a
variety of social systems and people representing practices, ideas, and

values which were quite different from what they knew in their communities of origin. Common to these situations is that they are characterized by an inequality of power, where the terms of interaction were to a large extent defined by others than the peasants themselves, even though the level of coercion varied considerably. This does not mean that the returnees have behaved as passive victims of their circumstances. On the contrary, they have shown an extraordinary ability to engage in new situations, trying to take advantage of them. Negotiation rather than imposition can be said to characterize much of the interaction. I will examine how different individuals and groups make a living, attempting to meet consumption and production needs, coping with uncertainties and hostilities, but also with a sense of possibilities for the future. I will also examine how people respond to new opportunities and choose between different value positions.

The Returnee Community and Its People

Fieldwork was carried out in La Quetzal, a village with some 1,200 people, belonging to the municipality of La Libertad, in the western part of the Petén (see Map 6). It is located at the end of a narrow gravel road penetrating the jungle to the north after branching off from the main road between the county capital Flores and Bethel on the bank of the Usumacinta River, forming the border with Mexico.[9] The distance between La Quetzal and the border is only 24 kilometers; therefore, contacts with Mexico, especially commercial ones, are close. The distance to the county capital is approximately 140 kilometers; due to the poor quality road, it takes some four hours by car (5–6 hours by bus) to get there. The closest neighboring communities are La Lucha and Retalteco, five and fourteen kilometers away respectively.

The community consists of four neighborhoods, where people have been allocated a piece of land to build their homes and keep their domestic animals, and a so-called *centro urbano* where the community buildings are located. Two of the neighborhoods—Maya Balam and La Laguna—are located on opposite sides of the access road before arriving at the center. Campeche and Cuchumatanes (in that order) are located on the left side of the road that continues to the end of the community. A river runs on the right side, making a division between the village and the land allocated for productive purposes. The neighborhoods are named after the camps where their inhabitants used to live in Mexico, so that most people living in the different neighborhoods are old neighbors.

The *centro urbano* is located in the center of the community. The central buildings are larger than the others and comprise the cooperative offices, a cooperative shop, a roofed edifice to house fiestas and community assemblies, and four school buildings. The church, a large building with a mud floor, wooden stick half-walls, and a zinc roof, and the health center are located at the outskirts of the "urban center." Most peasant houses are made of wooden sticks or rustic planks and are thatch-roofed. The same materials are used in the community buildings, although some of them have zinc roofs. This gives the community a certain flavor of precariousness compared to the more established communities in the region, where the public buildings are typically made of adobe or cement and painted.

The peasant homesteads are spread throughout the community. Each family has a small piece of land in one of the neighborhoods, where they normally have two houses, one where they sleep and store clothes and valuables, the other with a fireplace, tables, and chairs, where they cook and eat. Cooking is done on an open fire and there are no chimneys or similar installations to absorb the smoke. Domestic animals (mostly chickens, turkeys, and pigs) move freely in the courtyard during the day and are locked up in a coop during the night. The houses are surrounded by fruit trees (banana, orange, lime, and mango) giving shade and protecting against the heat, which may be very intense during the dry season. The farming land is located outside the village.

Some of the public buildings have electricity for a couple of hours every night, supplied by a generator. The peasant houses have no electricity. They are normally illuminated by homemade kerosene lamps, which do not give much light. There is no potable water in the community; all drinking water has to be boiled. Those who live close to the river collect water there. The others collect water in the *lavadero,* an outdoor laundry installed in each neighborhood, where women go to wash their clothes. The laundries receive water from the river through a pipe system, which is operated mechanically. Two of the neighborhoods also have a *molino* (corn mill), where the women grind the corn for the tortillas, by far the most important staple food of the community.

La Quetzal is a peasant community, where livelihood first and foremost is based on what can be extracted from the land. However, it is different in many respects from traditional peasant communities in Guatemala, because of its high level of community organization and its location within the Maya Biosphere Reserve (MBR), which is a protected area.[10] The community occupies 5,924 hectares of land, 80 percent of it within the core of the reserve area, which puts heavy constraints on the potential for production. The cooperative Unión Maya Itzá is the owner of the land, but because of its location within the MBR, the use of most of the land must be approved by CONAP (Consejo Nacional de Areas Protegidas), the national entity in charge of the protected areas in Guatemala.

The Fieldwork

The first direct contact I had with people from La Quetzal was in 1997 when I met with their representative in the refugee organization CCPP (Comisiones Permanentes de Refugiados) in the county capital of the Petén. This representative was their official link to the outside world, and I was advised not to approach the community without his approval. I went to the meeting with a colleague from the University of San Carlos. After we explained the general intentions of the project, the CCPP representative asked what we had to offer to them. At that point the UNHCR and several NGOs were supporting the returnee community technically and financially in a number of areas, and I was afraid that a research project with little or no material support to offer would be rejected. I did not pretend to be assessing development needs or collecting aid requests, but simply told him about the research project and what I intended to do. The representative grew very interested, especially regarding my aim to reconstruct their experience of violence and exile. He wanted their history to become "known to the world" in order to prevent similar atrocities from happening again. He also wanted to transmit knowledge of their recent history to their children and grandchildren who themselves had not experienced the violence. The representative promised to present the project to the general assembly in the community, without whose approval there would be no fieldwork. The project was approved.

One condition for living in the community was that we organized our own housing. The housing conditions were still very precarious and there was no guest house available. The cooperative board offered a piece of land in the center of the village where we could build a project house, something we accepted, and we engaged local carpenters for the job. This house, made of wooden planks with a corrugated iron roof, was quite rudimentary but much bigger than we had planned, because it was to be taken over by the community once the fieldwork was over.

Acceptance in the community was easier than I had expected. From the refugee camps people were used to dealing with foreigners and, because of the role foreign relief and solidarity workers had played there, they had an open and positive attitude. They were also used to national as well as international visitors in their new community, and when I first arrived there were still foreign *acompañantes* (accompaniers) living there. It was not always easy for the returnees to distinguish between the escort and the anthropologist, and maybe I was not always understood when I tried to explain what my research was all about, but most people were willing to share their experiences with me. I think that the fact that I lived in the community for weeks at a time, interacting with informants on a daily basis, was important for the openness and confidence I was met with.

My fieldwork was carried out over a period of three years (1998–2001), when I spent one or two months three times a year. The timing was motivated by a desire to follow the community over a certain period of time to better understand the dynamics of the reconstruction process. During the first field trips, I partly overlapped with my colleague from the University of San Carlos, who was collecting data for his Ph.D. thesis, and a Norwegian anthropology student collecting data for her master's thesis. During the final field trips, I partly overlapped with a Norwegian Ph.D. candidate doing botanical fieldwork in the jungle.[11] The rest of the time I was alone.

The fieldwork consisted of a combination of participant observation and other data-collecting techniques, ranging from informal conversations to more formal and focused interviews on specific topics. I talked to women, men, and children individually or in groups, in their homes, in the fields, at the laundry, washing clothes, walking along the roads or paths in the jungle, or in the "house of the anthropologists." Since our house was located in the center of the community, people often dropped by when they finished their errands. Depending on the time of day, this was often a quiet space for conversation.

I also attended a number of public events, ranging from crowded religious sermons and general assemblies to more selective gatherings such as cooperative board or committee meetings and training sessions for midwives or goat-keepers. Twice during my fieldwork I was present during the annual fiesta, which in this case is not in honor of the patron saint but in memory of the day of their arrival in La Quetzal (April 8). I was also invited to a number of private celebrations such as weddings, baptisms, birthday parties, wakes, and funerals. In general, people in the community were extremely friendly and welcoming.

My conversations and interviews with people in La Quetzal were conducted in Spanish. Most people in La Quetzal speak Spanish although the degree of fluency varies; generally the elderly are less fluent. Elderly women, especially the Q'eqchi'-speaking, had difficulty expressing themselves in Spanish, and sometimes communication with them was mediated by a younger relative. In some of the chapters I have let my informants talk, using extracts based on taped conversations. The reader will notice that the narratives depict certain common sequences that are the results of a combination of the life history approach elaborated by me, the similarities of experiences of my informants, and the way they construct their narratives. When narrating their life histories, for example, I asked my informants to start with the beginning—their childhood. I let them talk quite freely, drawing attention to what they considered worth recounting, but at the same time ensuring that certain elements of the stories were consistent, such as how and why they migrated from the Highlands to the Ixcán and the Petén, and how they experienced the arrival and the escalation of violence, the flight to Mexico, exile, and the return process. Among my informants I identified people whose role in the armed conflict had been different from the majority, such as combatants, prisoners of war, and members of communities of people in resistance. Their narratives are in the main constructed by themselves. I have related the narratives as closely as possible to the way they were related to me, even though some editing was required in terms of style, content, and coherence. The real names of my informants do not appear in the text.

I also visited the neighbor communities (all Spanish-speaking), where I spoke with a more limited number of men and women to assess the situation of those who had remained in the region during the armed conflict and their view of the returnees. Finally, I spoke with key persons in the government agencies and NGOs who, in one way or another, had been assisting the returnees before and after their arrival in La Quetzal.

Organization and Structure of the Book

The book is divided into two parts. Part I, The Dynamics of Violence, is a reconstruction of the past experiences of migration, armed conflict, and flight as tied into the wider processes of the development of the armed conflict in Guatemala. First, it brings us back to the 1960s and the process of colonization that motivated my informants to move from extreme poverty in different parts of the Highlands to build prosperous cooperatives in the tropical rain forest in Ixcán and the Petén. It then examines the role of the guerrilla and the army in the gradual escalation of violence that converted these "lands of hope" into nightmarish killing fields, obliging most of the inhabitants to leave their communities in order to save their lives. It reveals how the local peasants were gradually drawn toward the guerrilla, even though most of them initially had little or no sympathy with the guerrilla movement. This part is based on a combination of secondary material, including research undertaken by other scholars, reports, biographical and testimonial material published by observers or participants of this history, and most important, the returnees' own narratives about the past.

Part II, Reconstruction of Livelihoods and Identities, starts with a description of life in exile and the preparation for return to Guatemala, demonstrating how the encounters in the camps between people from different ethnic groups, and between the refugees and the international aid community, inspired the refugees to new ways of thinking and acting, something that became especially salient in the negotiations and preparations for their collective return. The following section about the settlement and the construction of a new community in the Lacandon jungle is based on a variety of sources, along with information collected during my fieldwork in the area. First, it situates the returnees in a national and regional sociopolitical context still characterized by insecurity and threats almost two years after the signing of the final peace agreement. This is followed by a presentation of the returnee community during my fieldwork, characterized by a new, complex, and rather bureaucratic social organization of public life, while little had changed in their domestic lives.

The subsequent sections deal with continuity and change regarding ethnicity and gender. The returnee community presents new ways of being indigenous. Interethnic relations are examined, as is the meaning of ethnicity in a context of return and resettlement, where shared experience of violence and exile are strongly emphasized, and unity and equality are promoted as fundamental values. The returnees stress organizational capacity as a crucial characteristic of themselves and participation as an important requirement for democracy. The process of participation is, however, highly gendered. Women, who played a fundamental role in the preparation for return and during the emergency phase in the new community, face new challenges as life returns to "normal."

Finally, I focus on the relationship between the returnees and the Guatemalan state. This relationship is characterized not only by antagonism and mistrust but also by a striving to become included, to become a community of citizens through the extension of state institutions and new administrative techniques of community organization.

The reader may find that that the two parts of the book are quite different in terms of writing styles, the first part being more affective, the second more straightforward. This contrast is deliberate, as it reflects my informants' relation to past and present. The way they talk about their "extraordinary" past is intense and emotional and contrasts quite markedly with how they live and talk about their "normal" present.

Part I
The Dynamics of Violence

Chapter 2

Migrating in Search of Land and a Better Future

The return to Guatemala and the settlement in La Quetzal were the end of a long sequence of movements that started years before the wave of violence in the late 1970s and early 1980s that was the immediate cause of the massive exodus of refugees from Guatemala to neighboring countries, particularly Mexico. The majority of the returnees in La Quetzal fled to Mexico from two areas in Guatemala: from Ixcán in the northern part of El Quiché and from the western part of the Petén. However, only those who were minors when they left Guatemala had been born in these areas. The rest had arrived there some years earlier, attracted by the colonization projects initiated in the 1960s by the Catholic Church with the support of state institutions (see Maps 2, 3, and 6).

Colonization of Marginal Lands

During the 1960s the question of colonization took on special importance in Guatemala, the most populated and second most densely populated country in Central America.[1] The population was mainly concentrated in the central Highlands, where the scarcity of land and job opportunities for the Indian majority was acute, due to the extremely unequal distribution of land. The land reform implemented by the democratic government of Jacobo Arbenz (1951–54) was abolished after the CIA-supported military coup in 1954, and the land was returned to the previous owners. Because of the boom in the agricultural export sector on the southern coast between 1954 and 1963, large landlords had encroached into fertile land once held by the peasantry, and gradually many peasants lost their land. The growth of the rural population during the same period aggravated the land crisis. Between 1952 and 1973, the rural population increased from 1.7 to 3.3 million, constituting 60 percent of the total population during the whole period (Berger 1992: 130; Hough 1982). As a result, highland peasants were increasingly forced to work seasonally on the large plantations, initiating a flow of temporary migration from the poor peasant areas of the Highlands toward the plantations on the southern coast (see Map 2). In spite of extremely exploitative working conditions offered by the plantation owners, hundreds of thousands of peasants migrated between the Highlands and the coast every year. However, labor migration represented no solution to the poverty problem, only a prolongation of the misery experienced in the Highlands.[2]

The colonization of new lands was a bleak substitute for land reform. It was widely recognized that land concentration was a major problem in Guatemalan agriculture and that it produced underutilization of lands and underemployment of the rural population. However, since there was no political will to change the distribution of land, efforts to improve the situation of the rural poor and thereby alleviate pressures for land reform were concentrated on the incorporation of marginal lands into agricultural production.[3] The colonization projects were strongly criticized for distracting people's attention from the need for a genuine redistribution of land. That is to say, the projects led to a focus on the colonization of unproductive land rather than the redistribution of the productive land (Morrisey 1978: 158).

The land crisis not only represented a problem of subsistence for the peasantry, it also created a national shortage of basic grains for domestic consumption. At times during the 1954 to 1966 period, the Guatemalan government had to import large quantities of basic grains (Berger 1992:130). The vast tropical lowland in the northern part of the country was selected to be an outlet for the excess population in the Highlands. The colonization projects were also designed with the intention of meeting the domestic demand for basic grains, especially in the case of the Petén (Dennis et al. 1988; Manz 1988: 127–30; Berger 1992).

The Catholic Church as Development Agent

One of the most important colonization agents was the Catholic Church. After the Second Vatican Council (1962–65), where, among other things, the role of the Church in the modern world was redefined, the Church could no longer turn a blind eye to political abuses in return for a guarantee of its privileges and rights. It was expected to be at the forefront of protests against the infringement of people's freedoms and rights. Similarly, what was once a fortress Church should now seriously engage in dialogue with non-Christian religions as well as other Christian bodies, and the vernacular should be introduced into the mass and the other sacraments and replace a wholly Latin rite (Ker 2002).

The Second Vatican Council produced a theological atmosphere characterized by great freedom and creativity. This gave Latin American theologians the courage to think for themselves about pastoral problems affecting their countries and led to intensified reflection on the relationship between faith and poverty, the gospel and social justice, preparing the ground for what is known as liberation theology (Boff and Boff 1986). Liberation theology begins with the premise that all theology is biased—that it reflects the economic and social classes of those who developed it. Accordingly, the traditional theology predominant in Europe and North America is said to support and legitimate a political and economic system—democratic capitalism—which is responsible for exploiting and impoverishing the Third World. Liberation theologians claimed that theology must start with a "view from below"—that is, with the sufferings of the oppressed. Gustavo Gutiérrez, the author of *A Theology of Liberation*, emphasized that theology should be done, not just learned. This implies revolutionary action on behalf of the poor and oppressed—and out of this, theological perceptions will continually emerge. Consequently, the theologian should be immersed in the struggle for transforming society and proclaim his message from that point (Gutiérrez 1988).

In Guatemala the theology of liberation implied a radical change in the Church's attitudes toward its parishioners. As in the rest of Latin America, the Catholic Church had up to that point been allied with the power elites. Relations with the poor, indigenous population were marked by continuous attempts to eliminate Mayan religious practices, encouraging peasants to abandon them or practice them underground. After the Second Vatican Council, the Church was expected to look for true faith and collaborate with traditional leaders and practitioners, and at the same time be concerned about the conditions of people's temporal life, not only their spiritual one.

James Morrisey's (1978) study of this process of change in the diocese of Huehuetenango reveals that many priests in this diocese felt that their parishioners were resisting them; they felt rather unsuccessful and started to develop strategies to prove their usefulness. Young priests (in Morrisey's case American, in other dioceses European), who often had lived in cities all their lives, became instant agricultural experts and used their skills to be allowed entrance into resistant indigenous communities. They began to prescribe medicines, pull out aching teeth, and provide fertilizer and transport. In this way, they became important and appreciated members of their communities. Local people learned that the priests had access to power beyond the spiritual. If money was needed, the Father could always make a trip to the capital, or to his country of origin, to raise funds. If the community needed transport, the priest could always find a jeep and even a small plane if the village was not accessible by road. This represented enormous power at the local level. The change in work methods also coincided with a change in the lifestyle of many priests. They started to interact more with local people, to participate in the popular fiestas, where they would dance and even drink with their parishioners (Morrisey

1978: 140–60). It was in this context that the colonization projects of Ixcán and the Petén were conceived and developed (see Map 5).

Colonization in Ixcán

Ixcán was one of the two major colonization areas in Guatemala, located in the northern lowland portion of the county of El Quiché. Until the late 1960s this was an almost uninhabited rainforest. With the exception of a few *fincas* (estates), most of the land in this region was owned by the state. The majority of the returnees in La Quetzal came from two areas in Ixcán, the cooperatives of Ixcán Grande between the Ixcán and the Xalbal Rivers and the cooperatives and *parcelamientos* (small-holdings) in Ixcán Chiquito, also called Zona Reina, between the rivers of Xalbal and Tzejá Rivers.

IXCÁN GRANDE

A process of massive migration to Ixcán was initiated in 1966 when the Maryknoll father Edward Doheny, appointed by the American bishop in the diocese of Huehuetenango, arrived with the first group of people to settle along the bank of the Ixcán River. Padre Eduardo, as he was called by his parishioners, was very dedicated to improving the conditions of the poor and, according to Morrisey (1978), one of the few who were well prepared for this kind of endeavor. Not only did he have a solid technological knowledge, he also had deep respect for the knowledge of Mayan peasants and great confidence in their capacity to manage their own affairs. Moreover, he prepared himself thoroughly for the job. He read what he could find of literature on development, consulted persons with experience from colonization projects, and studied carefully the agrarian reform laws of Guatemala.

Padre Eduardo selected 140 men from 16 municipalities and four language groups to participate in what was defined as the experimental phase of the project. They were recommended by his colleagues throughout the diocese, on the basis of personal capacities and needs. They were outstanding young married men with an interest in improving their lives and willing to move. Padre Eduardo organized courses in agriculture and health to prepare the recruits for the project. They learned about local conditions, about new crops such as cardamom, vanilla, and black pepper that brought high prices in relation to their weight, important in an area without roads, and new production techniques such as composting. They also learned about cooperative organization. Padre Eduardo made a detailed project plan covering social, economic, agricultural, technological, and political aspects. The settlers would gain ownership of the land but also have a social responsibility toward the community; the land would be large enough to provide subsistence for the family and surplus for sale. The set-up was inspired by the Moshavim settlements in Israel— agricultural cooperatives based on family units of production. The plans were elaborated in close collaboration with INTA (the National Institute of Agrarian Transformation), the Ministry of Education, and the Department of Cooperatives.

Most of these first settlers were indigenous people from Huehuetenango (Mam, Q'anjob'al, Popti', and Chuj) but also some Ladinos. They were grouped in centers of 24 families, preferably from the same language group. The center was granted a high level of autonomy in internal affairs as long as they followed certain preestablished rules, most of them in accordance with the Law of Agrarian Reform, such as the prohibition to fell big trees, burn the forest (except in certain defined areas), sell alcohol, or be absent for long periods of time, and the obligation to boil all drinking water. There were also rules against troublemaking, especially adultery (Morrisey 1978: 152–56).

These centers gradually organized into cooperatives. The first cooperative established was Mayalán (from Maya Land), along the Ixcán River. The next was Xalbal, in the extreme east, close to the Xalbal River. Gradually more people arrived and populated the dense jungle of Ixcán. The number of cooperative centers increased and by the end of 1969, three more cooperatives, Pueblo Nuevo, Los Angeles, and Cuarto Pueblo, had been created (Falla 1994: 19–20) (see Map 5). In 1970 the Ixcán Grande Cooperative was established, comprising these five cooperatives founded by Padre Eduardo.

According to Morrisey, the project developed very successfully under Padre Eduardo's leadership. People were highly motivated and well prepared for the harsh conditions. Once they were settled, he trained local people for specific functions within as well as between centers. In this way the centers were provided with health promoters, malaria officers, education promoters, shopkeepers, and people responsible for communal work. Each center had a primary school giving classes three days a week in addition to adult literacy classes. Catechists were trained to provide religious instruction for adults and children and *animadores de la fe* (animators of faith) were prepared to give religious services such as the "celebration of the Word."

Morrisey suggests that Padre Eduardo was so concerned about the perfection of his professional work that he paid little attention to conformity to the missionary subculture and public relations for the project. He preferred, for example, to transport local people and material goods for the project instead of filling the plane with colleagues or other visitors who wanted to see what was going on in the jungles of Ixcán. This

made him rather unpopular among his colleagues, especially his succes-
sor, who, in an effort to take over the direction of the project, discredited
him on several occasions (Morrisey 1978: 685). This may have been the
main reason Padre Eduardo decided to quit as project leader in 1969; he
was replaced by William Woods, known as Padre Guillermo, also from the
Maryknoll congregation. Dissatisfied with the legalistic, participative, and
slow expansion advocated by Padre Eduardo, Woods changed the direction of the project. Without involving local leaders or government agencies, he issued an open invitation to landless peasants in the Highlands to
join the project. Large numbers of people without previous knowledge of
the area arrived and were lodged on old settlers' lands until they were
allocated their own lot. The idea was that the old settlers should instruct
the new ones, something that was easily accommodated if the newcomers
were relatives or acquaintances, but less easily when they were strangers.
Padre Guillermo also insisted on collective ownership of the land, without
consulting the old settlers who had been promised private ownership.

In 1974 the Ixcán Grande cooperative obtained formal rights to the
land. Members were given a document stating their usufruct right, but
the deed covering the totality of the land was in the name of the cooperative, implying that the members could not sell or transfer the land to
their heirs without the approval of the cooperative board.

ZONA REINA

Colonization in Zona Reina was initiated in 1970 under the leadership
of the Spanish priest Luis Gurriarán (known as Padre Luís) from the
Sagrado Corazón de Jesús order, working in the diocese of El Quiché.
Soon after his arrival from Spain in the early 1960s he was approached
about assisting local communities in establishing their own cooperatives. In preparation he spent two years in Canada studying methods and
approaches to cooperative development. The complex colonization process under his leadership began in Santa Cruz del Quiché with the creation of cooperatives. Although these cooperatives were successful, they
had limited reach because of the scarcity of land and of prospects for
accessing more land in the area. Their only way to expand appeared to
be the colonization of unclaimed national land in the inhospitable jungles of Ixcán. The first settlers, assisted by Padre Luís and others in the
diocese, prepared their move for months, expanding their knowledge of
cooperative organization and receiving instruction in health and tropical agriculture.

A group of men spent almost a year, using only machetes and axes,
preparing the site of settlement for the first hundred families in Santa
María Tzejá on the banks of the Tzejá River. In two years, these families

had produced enough food to meet their needs, and, when this target was reached, the cooperative started to produce cash crops, such as coffee and cardamom. Organizing as a cooperative enabled the settlers to buy and sell products more efficiently and to gain a measure of independent power, first through their own organization and later through the confederation of cooperatives (Manz 1988: 130; AVANCSO 1992: 35). Gradually, new communities were established in Zona Reina with the assistance of the Catholic Church, other churches, and INTA.

Making a life in this dense jungle was extremely difficult, but when the first corn started to grow the settlers brightened up, because they realized that this virgin land produced more corn than they could ever imagine. The same happened with the new crops they started to plant. Most of the first settlers in this area were of K'iche' or Q'eqchi' origin who had lived under extremely difficult conditions as tenants or temporary workers on the *fincas* of absentee landlords in the Highlands of El Quiché. As rumors spread to other parts of the country about the wonder of this area, poor people from other parts of the country, and especially from Huehuetenango, started to arrive. In this way, the area gradually became populated by new settlers (AVANCSO 1992: 35–36).

Beginning in 1970 the government also started to distribute land in the eastern and southern areas of Ixcán through INTA. This was part of the so-called Northern Transversal Strip Project, where Ixcán was part of a countrywide belt of low-lying virgin jungle to be colonized (Falla 1992: 19; Fledderjohn 1982).[4] Through this scheme, the government projected an influx of 5,000 people through organized as well as spontaneous settlement (Garst 1993: 17).

COMMUNITY ORGANIZATION

The common feature for most new communities in Ixcán was that they were organized in cooperatives. Even though cooperatives had existed in Guatemala since the government of Juan José Arévalo in the 1940s, they did not gain momentum until the 1960s and '70s, when they were strongly promoted by the government and USAID (AVANCSO 1992: 36). Cooperatives were also promoted by the Catholic Church as well as state agencies like INTA. Many sponsors believed this was a way to create the spirit of community necessary to survive and prosper in the hostile environment of the tropical rainforest. The Ixcán Grande cooperative was the most advanced and best organized in Ixcán. The geographic isolation was soon overcome by air transport and by radio communication between the communities.

In Ixcán Grande as well as in Zona Reina, the centers of the cooperatives were inhabited by people belonging to the same ethnic group and often related by kinship. This was particularly the case during the first years of colonization, when large groups arrived in an organized way and settled together. Later, as will be seen in the narratives of my informants, people arrived in smaller, unorganized groups or individually. This was because they had relatives or friends in one of the cooperatives or simply had heard rumors of land being distributed to the poor.

The settlers spent their everyday life working in and around their house and in the *milpa* (cornfield), interacting only with family members or with neighbors speaking their own language. Most of the settlers were illiterate and could not speak Spanish. As cooperative members, however, the men soon became involved in activities that required interaction with people from other ethnic groups. The clearing of the forest for the construction of public buildings and other infrastructure was required in order to establish the cooperative center, for example. Gradually these centers became meeting places with schools, churches, health centers, shops, markets, and even airstrips. Men were also drawn into Church activities. They were trained as catechists and *animadores de la fe*, gradually taking over the everyday running of the pastoral work. Some were also trained as education and health promoters attending to patients in the emerging health centers. Through their involvement in the cooperatives, the settlers, particularly the men, acquired not only land but also new skills and knowledge and a sense of dignity. They no longer had to accept exploitation and humiliation in order to survive.

The lives of women, on the other hand, continued largely unchanged. They continued to spend most of their time at home. Even though the priests tried to motivate women to participate more in community activities, such as adult literacy classes, few women actually did, except those who were school age at the time and had parents who permitted them to go to school. This was more common in the cooperatives in Ixcán Grande, where some members had been to school for short periods, than it was in the cooperatives in Zona Reina, where most members were illiterate. However, as will be seen in the narratives below, not only economic improvements but also the social rules and regulations associated with cooperative membership, such as the prohibition on the sale of alcohol and the exclusion of men who committed adultery, contributed to the improvement of the lives of the women.

Colonization in the Petén

The Petén is the other major colonization area in northern Guatemala. Its vast territory, comprising 36,000 square kilometers, was until the 1970s mostly covered by dense rainforest. Together with the Northern Transversal Strip, it constitutes one-third of Guatemala's national territory. Like

Ixcán, much of the Petén was sparsely populated before the 1960s. As late as 1964, there were scarcely 25,000 people in this county with about 45 percent of them residing in twelve small towns and the rest in still smaller villages. In the early 1990s the population increased to more than 300,000 people. This increase was partly a result of organized colonization in the 1960s and 1970s, spontaneous migration in the 1980s and '90s provoked by scarcity of land and employment opportunities, and the excess of violence in other parts of the country (Schwartz 1990: 10–11).

My informants arrived in the Petén in the 1970s as participants in the colonization of the jungle areas along the Pasión and Usumacinta Rivers, the latter marking the border between Guatemala and Mexico (see Maps 2 and 6). This process of colonization started with the creation of FYDEP (National Enterprise for the Promotion of Economic Development of the Petén) in 1959.[5] Colonization of uncultivated Petén lands was only one of the many goals of FYDEP. It also promoted agrarian export activities, scientific exploitation, and preservation of its forests and natural resources, and industrialization. During the first decade of its existence, few projects were realized. It lacked the funds to provide needed infrastructure, services, and technology. Moreover, its director, Colonel Oliverio Casasola, was against peasant colonization, maintaining that the Petén was not suited for agriculture. To believe that the Petén should be the site of agrarian reform constituted a national crime, he argued. He wanted to attract Ladino businessmen and not Indian peasants to the area.[6] Casasola did, however, support government-controlled peasant migration to one area of the Petén—the lower basin of the Usumacinta River. In the late 1960s Mexico was planning to construct a hydroelectric power plant in Chiapas, involving the construction of a huge dam on the Usumacinta and the flooding of western Petén. This motivated the Guatemalan government to accelerate settlement in the areas along the river. Between 1969 and 1973, approximately 600 peasant families settled in 16 cooperatives along the Usumacinta and its tributary (Berger1992: 148–50; Egan 2002).

The first settlements were rapidly established. Don Luis, one of my informants in a neighboring village, who settled in Bethel, told me that those who arrived with him were Ladinos from the south coast, where most of them had been landless plantation workers. From the village of Sayaxché, they were transported by boat to the shore of Bethel, which at that point was nothing more than dense jungle. No preparation whatsoever had been made to facilitate their settlement. After the migrants unloaded their limited belongings from the boat, the boatman returned to Sayaxché, leaving them to their own devices. Don Luis told how their fear of the jungle, during those days still inhabited by jaguars and other dangerous animals, swarms of insects, and torrential rain made the first nights almost unbearable. With the help of their machetes, however, they were able to clear a plot in the forest to raise some temporary shelters in order to start working. Their hunger for land was so strong that they were able to endure terrible hardship and suffering. These first settlers received little or no assistance from FYDEP.

My informants in La Quetzal were among the last to take part in government-organized settlements in the Petén. Most of them were members of Centro Campesino, a cooperative located on the bank of the Usumacinta in the far northwestern corner of the Petén. This cooperative was first established in what people refer to as El Oriente, more specifically in Camotán, the county of Chiquimula, in the mid-1960s, under the guidance of the Belgian Catholic priest Hugo Bruyère. However, the poor soil as well as the general lack of natural resources in this area made development very difficult, not to say impossible. Aware of the colonization efforts in the Petén, Padre Hugo (as he is called by my informants) started his search for new land for those parishioners willing to move. He identified a suitable area for settlement, and after some difficulty he obtained permission from FYDEP. This settlement was established in close collaboration with the government through FYDEP and with the assistance of the army. Returnees who were among these settlers speak of such a friendly relationship between the priest and the army that, when they first arrived in the Petén in 1971, they were transported by a Guatemalan air force plane. When they fled the country in 1982, crossing the river to Mexico by boat, they were pursued by the same air force, this time trying to kill them.

With organizational and material support from the Catholic Church, these settlers engaged in a process of development that they could only dream of in El Oriente. Transport was cheap, and there was a demand for their agricultural products on the Mexican side, with better prices than in Guatemala. Similarly with consumer goods, the variety was better and the prices lower than in Guatemala. In five years the cooperative managed to pay for the land and obtain legal property documents.[7]

The majority of those who settled in the Petén arrived from El Oriente or from the south coast. They were poor peasants or landless plantation workers and Spanish-speakers. In Ixcán the picture was more complex. This region attracted mostly indigenous people, but also some Ladinos, from different parts of the western Highlands, primarily from the counties of El Quiché, Alta Verapáz, Huehuetenango, and San Marcos (see Map 2). A number of ethnic groups were represented, most of the people illiterate and with little or no knowledge of Spanish.

Narratives About the Transformation of Peasant Life

In what follows I let some of my informants tell about their lives in the Highlands and what the move to Ixcán and the Petén meant to them. I have selected narratives that reveal different aspects of the complexity of being poor peasants in the Highlands of Guatemala during the period ranging from the late 1930s to the late 1960s, when the colonization projects started. Most voices are indigenous, representing a number of ethnic groups and places of origin, while some are Castellanos. What all of them share is the experience of poverty, scarcity of land, and lack of other resources to make a decent living in the Highlands, something that made them easy prey for exploitation, humiliation, and suffering. But they also share the memory of having participated in a great project that they believe could have changed their lives had it not been destroyed by the armed conflict.

FREEDOM FROM FORCED LABOR

Don Lucas is one of my oldest informants, born in the early 1920s in San Sebastian Coatán, Huehuetenango. He is a Chuj, as is his wife Navidad.

I come from a family with many children and almost no land. Because we had no land we were obliged to participate in the system of "jornadas," which meant compulsory work 150 days a year.[8] The mayor, always Ladino in those days, called upon us once a year and gave us a piece of paper. Since I could not read and did not understand one single word of Castilla (local label for Spanish), I had to go with somebody who could help me fill out this paper. Each time we finished a job the patron wrote down the number of days at his service and signed the paper. We had to continue like this until we had reached the obligatory 150 days. If they caught us without the papers that showed we had complied with our obligations, we were punished. Only those who owned more than 4 manzanas or 64 cuerdas of land were not obliged to participate in this system.[9] The "jornada" system continued until the government of Arévalo (1945–51). Not until then was I free. Arévalo also increased the salaries. Then I could travel to the south coast to work on the coffee plantations and I could stay as long as I needed.

The working conditions at the plantations were also very hard, but much less so than on the fincas in Huehuetenago. That I was free also felt very good. When I found out about the distribution of land in Ixcán I was renting land in Nentón.[10] I found out because Padre Guillermo sent a letter to the catechist in my community informing him that he was distributing land to poor and landless peasants. I went to Ixcán with my wife to find out what was going on. We liked it there and decided to move. One year we stayed there until we finally got our parcela of land. We had to prove that we were honest and hardworking. Many people tried to cheat. They said that they had no land, when they had land in other places or things like that. This was in the Mayalán cooperative. For fifteen years I stayed in Ixcán; I had a very nice parcel, where I could grow

everything I wanted. I had coffee, cardamom; I had my oranges, my pome-
granates and my animalitos (small animals). The soldiers destroyed everything.
They burned everything, my house, my blankets, everything, everything; we
became poor again without anything.

For Don Lucas, who had been involved in the "jornada system," being
able to migrate to the coast was to experience being a free man. This was
a kind of freedom that younger people would see as inhumane due to the
hard and exploitive labor conditions that some could not abide. This was
the case for Nicolás.

Violence, Impunity, and Unconventional Survival Strategies

"I was a smuggler," Nicolás (49) told me when I asked him what he did
before he settled in Ixcán. Nicolás is Q'anjob'al, born in a village near
Ixtahuacán, in the municipality of Santa Eulalia, Huehuetenago. He is
now a teacher appointed by the Ministry of Education, and a highly respected community leader, something that he could not even imagine
becoming in his childhood and youth in the Cuchumatanes Mountains.

I grew up in a small hamlet where we only had the lot the house was built on.
We had only a small piece of land, therefore my father used to work on the
fincas or wherever he could earn some centavitos (small change). When I was
ten I went to school. My parents did not want me to go before that age,
because I had to walk one hour and a half to get to the hamlet where the
school was. I attended school only for two years, but enough to learn to read
and write. Then my father died; he was killed. This happened in another municipality where he had gone to find work. My father was fond of the bottle. One
night he went to a cantina to have his tragos (drinks). This was what they
told us. Some men started to quarrel and one of them was killed. My father
got very upset and said that he would report what he had seen to the authorities. This was probably why he was killed. After three days they found his body
on a slope by the river, with his throat slit. They had apparently tried to throw
him into the river, but the bushes had obstructed his fall. His assassins were
never caught even though everybody knew who they were.
    When my father died, I had to leave school to help my mother. We lived in
tierra fría[11] and the milpa my father used to till did not yield much; we barely
had enough to feed the family. I think I was fifteen when I first went to the
coast to work on the coffee plantations, weeding. I was not accustomed to
such work; it was very hard. Five times, I went to work on the coffee plantations. It was very hard, and we earned nothing. In order to avoid returning
to the coast, I decided to start smuggling. I crossed the border to Mexico to
buy medicines, biscuits, sweets, and other things that I could sell in my village

and elsewhere. It was very dangerous, you could be robbed and killed or imprisoned, which was not much better, but I was still single and I earned my centavitos. I had an uncle in Ixcán. I wanted to join him to have a more normal life, but my mother refused to leave her home, and I had to take care of her.

When I was twenty-one (1973) my grandfather told me that it was time to find a wife. "How can I maintain a wife?" I asked. But thinking about it, I changed my mind. "If I have a wife I can go to Ixcán," I thought. I decided to propose to my now wife. Her mother, as well as mine, was against our plans to go to Ixcán. We decided to go anyway. We arrived in the Xalbal cooperative where my uncle had his land. I had to work with him for six months in order to prove that I was a decent person. Not until you had proved that, would they give you land. Mine was one of the last parcels left in Xalbal. Once I had received my land I went to talk with my mother, to tell her that I had decided to stay in Ixcán. "Now that I have my own land I cannot visit you very often. If you want you can come with me. I will get you a piece of land for you and my brothers." She decided to come and have a look; first she came for 15 days, then, for three months, and finally she decided to apply for land. At that point there was no more land available in Xalbal. We had to go to Cuarto Pueblo. I decided to change to Cuarto Pueblo to be close to my mother. Once again I had to start felling trees and clearing the land to plant milpa and cardamom. My cardamom did not start producing well until 1981. Then the violence came and everything was destroyed.

Nicolás's story draws attention to the level of daily violence and impunity that was, and still is, common in the poor, indigenous areas of Guatemala and the vulnerability of poor families. Nicolás lost his father at the age of twelve and had to quit school to help his mother feed the family. Few labor opportunities, other than the exploitative and humiliating work on the coastal plantations for *centavitos* were open to uneducated, indigenous youth. Therefore, he chose the risky life of a smuggler. Nicolás was lucky because he grew up in a harmonious and healthy family with parents who got along very well. Conflictive family relations, characterized by alcoholism, adultery and violence were also recurrent themes in many stories. Doña Julia, a Jakalteca in her late fifties, has experienced it all. When you meet this gentle and talkative woman today, it is difficult to imagine her in the situations of the past which she describes.

Illness, Alcohol, and Family Violence

Doña Julia was born in a small village in Jacaltengango, Huehuetenango, where she grew up in a family with 13 children. She is one of the eight local midwives who were trained in exile to serve in the returnee community.

My poor father had no land, he worked as a casual worker when work was available and he was sober, but most of his earnings were spent on "tragos." My mother suffered a lot; she was the one who fed us. She used to get up at three o'clock in the morning to fetch firewood and tortear (make tortillas). At about five she left to collect chipilín (an herb)—far away she had to walk to find it, beyond the milpas, like the distance from here to Retalteco (14 km), only there was she allowed to collect and she knew it. My God! If she were caught collecting in places where she had no permission. . . . When she had her load of chipilín, she returned home, classified and bundled it, and walked to Jacaltenago to sell it. What she earned in this way was spent on food for the family. My father did not contribute. When he found some work he spent everything on his tragos.

We were thirteen altogether, three girls and ten boys. Two of my brothers died from illness; one died from scarlet fever when he was eight, the other from whooping cough when he was three. One of my sisters died too—a very beautiful little girl, her face very pure. So beautiful she was that when my father saw her for the first time he started to quarrel. "Why is she so beautiful," he screamed, "she is not mine, she is from another man." Barely three months did my little sister live and she cried a lot. When I woke up one morning my sister was dead. I told my mother that I had heard her cry, that I had tried to wake her up and that my father had treated me badly. "You killed her," my mother said to my father and they started to fight. My mother screamed until our neighbors came to help. They came to help in the funeral wake, too. In those days people used to bring centavitos or frijolitos (beans). Nowadays they barely bring anything. "Maybe your father killed her," my mother used to repeat from time to time. . . .

My brother Miguel also died, at the age of thirteen. One day, he and his friend Angel helped an acquaintance to slaughter stolen cattle. They were discovered and in the exchange of fire one of the men was killed. The boys witnessed the killing. They were put in jail with some others. Afterward they told us that Miguel was shot when he tried to escape with his friend Angel. Angel ran away, my little brother died. This was very sad, because my mother commended him to me just before dying. I think she had the presentiment that something terrible was going to happen to him. She did not say anything about my other small brothers.

Doña Julia also told about her turbulent life with her husband, who used to be a heavy drinker, violent, and a womanizer, something that changed when they moved to Ixcán.

I knew my husband through a neighbor. After having met him a couple of times he persuaded me to run away with him. Later I understood that this was very silly of me. A man, who is not willing to spend money to obtain a wife, will not respect her.[12] After only two months together, we were living with his parents then, he beat me with a cudgel. I returned to my mother's, but the very same day he came to pick me up. I did not dare tell my mother, because I was afraid that he would hurt her if she confronted him. Life became worse when he took another woman. When he returned after several months working in the south coast without bringing any money to us, I denounced him to the mayor who sent the police to find him. But since he had some money left he bribed the policeman and he let him go. After that I was obliged to feed myself and my children. I used to carry water for other people and help shell corn, things like that, qué vergüenza! (What a disgrace!). This I had to do in order to eat. The problem was that we had no good clothes; at the end we had only rags.

When my husband got tired of the other woman he returned to us. By then he had heard about the possibilities of getting land in Ixcán and he wanted to move there. I was afraid of going with him. "What will happen to me if I live far away from my family," I thought. My neighbors tried to convince me. "If you go to Ixcán your husband will change," they said. "He will get enough land, plenty of work and there are no cantinas where he can go to drink. Your life will be much better there," they said. My brother-in-law also decided to go and together we made the long trip to Ixcán. When we arrived in Pueblo Nuevo we found shelter with a family from our hamlet who had already received a parcel of land.

One day I was talking about my marital problems with the wife of the house. I did not realize that my nephew was outside listening to us and he told my husband. When my husband returned home that night I was lying on a mat on the floor in the middle of my four sleeping children, the smallest at my breast. He had a cudgel in one hand and a whip in the other. What scared me the most was that he was not drunk. I tried to remain completely still pretending to be asleep but, as always when I felt threatened by him, I started to tremble. I hoped that he would not beat me since I was with the children, but I was wrong. He grabbed my hair, lifted me up from the floor, and started to beat. I thought he was going to kill me. I screamed, and so did my children. The neighbors arrived and grabbed my husband and made him stop.

After this incident the owner of the land had a serious talk with my husband. He told him that he, being a cooperative member, would have problems with Padre Guillermo if it was known that he permitted wife-beating in his parcel. Moreover, he said that if it was known that my husband beat me up he would not obtain land in the cooperative. This is how my husband changed and my life changed. We got our parcel of land and stayed ten years in Ixcán. The first two years were very, very hard; lots of work and scarcity of everything, but my husband stopped drinking and beating. He worked hard; he wanted to improve our lot. When we started to enjoy the fruits of our hard work, the violence came and we lost everything.

A Past as a Hacienda Serf

Don Gregorio, a sixty-five-year-old Q'eqchi', was among the settlers in Zona Reina in the southern part of Ixcán, brought there by Father Luis Gurriarán in the early 1970s. In contrast to Lucas, Nicolás, and Julia, who grew up in land-poor or landless peasant families in Huehuetenango, Gregorio was born into a family that had been hacienda serfs for several generations. The Q'eqchi's, who constitute the largest ethnic group in La Quetzal with approximately 40 percent of the population, are considered by the others to be the most traditional, trying to preserve customs related to the agricultural cycle as well as to the religious calendar. The concern with traditional practices is reflected in Don Gregorio's narrative, as are also the changes in these practices during the different stages of migration.

I was born in the finca Tesoro in Uspantán, El Quiché where I, like my father and my grandfather, worked as a mozo (serf) until I left for Ixcán in the 1970s. All the land belonged to the patron; he had several fincas, plenty of land. We were allowed to plant our milpas as long as we complied with our duties to the patron. Some 260 families I think lived on this finca. All of us Q'eqchi's, we were not revueltos (mixed) then, like we are now. In other fincas there were people speaking different languages but in our finca it was not like that.[13]

When we planted our own milpa we practiced our costumbres (customs).[14] The day before planting we went to the milpa and planted 12 seeds in a circle in the middle of the field. Inside the circle we planted a cross made of branches. This cross could be made of any tree growing in the area. Then the owner of the milpa burned candles and pom (incense)—katuluntú we call it in Q'eqchi', which means the one who burns candles—and he said some prayers. The owner used to bring four or five people with him to the field to celebrate the custom. In the prayer we asked for permission from the holy land to plant corn, beans, and pepitoria. This is what we do when we say our prayers in the field. We also ask God to protect our fields, from insects, animals, and other things that may destroy our plants. The same evening we put the seeds on an altar in the house, burning candles and incense. The owner had to watch over the candles and keep them burning all night. Some of those who were going to participate in the planting spent the night with him, drinking, talking, and playing games of dice. The owner could not play. He had to watch the altar, take care of the candles, and say the prayers.

The next morning, before going to plant, those who were going to help came to have breakfast at the owner's house—tortillas, beans, and boj (homemade fermented corn brew). We did not bring food to the field, only boj. The wife of the owner also got help from other women, relatives, comadres (godmothers), or simply neighbors to prepare the food—chicken or a piglet—

for the men when they returned from the field. The customs of the planting was like a fiesta, with lots of joy, eating and drinking.

We continued with our customs in Ixcán, but during exile we rarely practiced them. There we also planted our beans and corn, we got land from COMAR (the Mexican refugee agency), but we were so sad that we did not practice our custom. Only after we had returned here did we start to practice it again.

When we lived in the finca in Uspantán, we also had our cofradías.[15] We had our patron saint, the Virgin of Dolores, placed on the altar of the chapel. We had a huge chapel; we needed a huge one, because we were many workers. It was not made of concrete, only of wood covered with a thatched roof. We constructed it ourselves. The patron of course also had one. The Father came to celebrate mass every three to four months; sometimes he did not appear for six months. He did not speak Q'eqchi' so he celebrated mass in Castilla. Most people did not understand a word. But we had catechists who could speak both languages. They translated what the Father had said and in this manner we received the mass.

We continued with the cofradías when we arrived in Ixcán. We constructed a chapel and had our catechists. In exile we stopped. Some of us (referring to the Q'eqchi's) have tried to start again here in La Quetzal, but the others did not support us. You know, having cofradía means expenses, billetes (paper money); they like to look, but not to spend.

The patron saint fiesta was the most important event of the year. First, we celebrated the mass early in the morning. Then we passed on to the guaro (hard liquor), it was served by liters, and the marimba. The mass started between six and seven in the morning. By eight o'clock it was over and the food was served. The Father ate with us, then his duties ended and he left, and we continued with our fiesta—marimba and dancing. We used to dance the whole day and we continued until the next morning.

When I was young, the Fathers did not bother about our drinking. In Ixcán everything changed, we got a new Father, and he did not like our drinking. He removed the guaro from the chapel, we had to raise a house at some distance where we placed the marimba, and there we had the guaro too. In the finca all this that I told you took place in the chapel. Father Luis ordered us to remove the marimba and the guaro from the chapel, far away from the virgin, he said. Father Luis came to celebrate mass, to baptize the children, a lot of work he did. He traveled on horseback, very bad roads around there. I don't think he was Guatemalan. He did not try to forbid our fiestas. Have your fiestas he said, but not in front of the virgin. Imagine a bunch of drinking and drunk people there in front of the virgin. The Father was right. We continued to organize fiestas in exile, but it was not the same, friends and neighbors were dispersed. We lost our virgin. Some told me that another group who fled from our village saved her, I don't know.

I used to be a catechist in Tesoro, but the problem I have is that I cannot read or write. Only in my head can I store some of the things I learn. I learned the commandments and helped to prepare the children for the first communion. This I learned from other catechists, those who had the gospel and could read the books. Some but not all the catechists could read and write. This was when I lived in Tesoro. When I arrived in Ixcán I stopped.

In Ixcán our lives changed. We had our own, very nice parcel. We had a lot of space, we could keep chickens, turkeys, and pigs, the animalitos could walk around freely, they grow very nicely that way, not like here (referring to the returnee community) where you have to tether your pigs. We settled close to Rosario de Canijá, a little hamlet where we organized a cooperative. The cooperative leadership told us to till the land we liked and that is what we did, as much as we had strength to cultivate. The land was not measured. We just took the parcels we liked the most. I found a nice place where I put up a house and settled with my family.

I joined the cooperative because this was a way to gather more people to claim the land. I think we numbered between 80 and 90 members, because the finca was very big. I don't know how many caballerías,[16] but it was very big. I had no leadership position in the cooperative, I was a simple member, but I had to participate in the communal work, as we had to build the community, construct buildings—a shop, a school, a church. . . . The cooperative had only existed for one or two years when the guerrilla appeared and the army started to kill people.

On the finca Tesoro everything was very controlled, but they did not kill people. But we were very poor, lots of work and lots of other obligations, that's why I decided to leave for Ixcán. I had several sons by then, I felt sorry for them. At the finca, they would only work and work and still be poor. I thought that maybe our lives would be better in Ixcán and I wanted to try. I had heard that there was plenty of land where we could plant coffee and cardamom. That would give us income and a better future.

Life was very hard in Ixcán. No roads, only dense jungle that needed to be cleared in order to plant and lots of rain. But the land was good; bananas, sugar cane, whatever you planted grew; beans; everything; it was very nice. It is a pity that we could not stay. I did not want to return to Ixcán. A group of people who tried to return to a neighbor community was chased away by those who live there now. These people were brought there by the soldiers after we left. Now we are returnees here, we cannot return to Ixcán; I am content here.

The practice of *costumbres* described by Don Gregorio had largely been abandoned by the other groups even before they joined the cooperatives in Ixcán Grande. As we have seen in the first section of this chapter, the traditional Catholic Church had been quite successful in its fight against Mayan religious practices. Only a few of the old people spoke of how they practiced certain Mayan rituals while still living in the Highlands, but had stopped after moving to Ixcán.

Those who used to live in the cooperatives in the Petén before going into exile in Mexico define themselves and are defined by their indigenous neighbors as Castellanos, even though some of them claim to be of Ch'orti' origin. This is because they do not speak a Mayan language. However, as we will see in the following stories, there were many similarities in their life conditions and sometimes, as in the case of Isabel, there were also close biological links.

GROWING UP WITH A LADINO FATHER AND AN INDIGENOUS MOTHER

Isabel lived in the Centro Campesino cooperative in the Petén before fleeing to Mexico. She was born in Jocotán, in the county of Chiquimula, approximately fifty years ago. She is a midwife and an open and articulate woman.

My mother was Ch'orti', my father Castellano. He did not allow my mother to speak her language. My grandparents and my uncles and aunts on my mother's side did not speak Castilla. My mother learned Castilla after she married my father. We were nine sisters and brothers, but only four of us survived to become adults, three females and one male. The others died, one when he was born, the others of various illnesses.

I never went to school. There was a school in my community but my father did not permit me to go. My father was very jealous, not only with my mother, but also with his daughters. He did not allow us to leave the house alone, he had to accompany us. My mother did not dare greet people when she met somebody on the road. If she did and my father saw it, he beat her badly. That is also why she did not speak her language. "I don't want you to speak Ch'orti' to my children," my father said, "I don't want my children to speak like chumpipes" (locally bred turkeys). My mother never dared to speak Ch'orti' to us, she was afraid of him. My father died before my mother. He went to the river and drowned himself. I was fourteen by then and pregnant with my first child.

I had no say in my marriage. My father made the deal with my husband and his parents. When I tried to object, he brushed me off. "I am the one who decides here, neither you, nor your mother," he said. I knew who my husband-to-be was and I did not dislike him, but I had never talked to him. I was afraid that he was like my father, nice when dealing with strangers and terrible with his family. My husband lived with his parents and I went to live with them as well. My parents-in-law were rather well off and they treated me very well; like a daughter. We lived with them for one year; then we made our own house and moved.

My first child died. Elena was the next. When she was nine, the nuns came to offer her a place in a boarding school in town. They had a project offering education to one child per family. It was very hard to let her go, but this was an opportunity that we could not deny her. When she finished she got a job with a doctor; she helped her with her practice. The doctor offered to support her further education if she stayed with her, but my husband did not allow her to stay behind when we went to the Petén.

My husband got to know Father Hugo (Bruyère), who prepared him to become a catechist. The nuns who worked with the Father asked the catechists to bring their wives to the church, they wanted the women to become involved as well. In contrast to my father—and the husbands of my daughters—my husband was never jealous. He always encouraged me to participate in community activities. When we were younger we even used to go to fiestas to dance. We danced with each other and also with other partners. My husband was always generous with me; imagine what a difference from my father who did not allow my mother to greet her male neighbors!

It was because of the nuns that I started with family planning. The nuns informed us and encouraged us to use it. We were poor and the nuns said that it was better to take good care of a few children than care badly for many. We agreed to that, because we had seen so many children die from illnesses caused by malnutrition and lack of medicine. After the birth of Jorge (her third child) I got a birth control device, copper T. We did not dare to tell anybody, to avoid gossip, because I was active in the social work of the nuns and moved around with them. If people knew, they would start saying that I was sleeping with the gringos and things like that. I kept the copper T until we had settled in Centro Campesino. Jorge was seven by then. There our situation changed, everything was abundant. In addition to the milpa, we had lots of fruits and vegetables and all kinds of small animals. We had much more food than our small family could eat. Then I went to the doctor to remove it and after that I had my three youngest.

It was Father Hugo who obtained the land for us in the Petén. He was a good friend of President Kjell [17] and convinced him to give out land in the Petén to landless peasants. Father Hugo went with a delegation to the Petén to identify land. He established a colonization project with money from Belgium, I think. The cooperative had a long strip of land along the riverbank, a very nice place. Sixteen cooperatives were founded in Western Petén in those days. The majority of the people in these cooperatives came from El Oriente or the south coast.

ETHNICITY AND POVERTY

In Guatemala Ladinos are associated with being well off and exploitative, while the Indians are the poor and exploited. One tends to forget that most Ladinos and Indians have the same class position. This is something that I was constantly reminded of in La Quetzal, because people were minimizing their ethnic differences and emphasizing their common condition as poor returnees. The story of Josefa is quite illustrative of this commonality.

Josefa and her husband Luís used to live in the Petén before they went into exile. They are both in their early eighties, Spanish-speaking, and locally defined as Castellanos. Josefa related the following about her background:

My father had some land, but he lost it and died landless. He was very poor, my mother, too. I had some luck, because I grew up with an aunt and she had some money. She used to make and sell cigars. I came to her when I was three. My mother was pregnant and I was often ill and cried a lot. Therefore, my aunt had to take care of me for a while. When my parents came to pick me up, I did not want to return with them and they let me stay. Thanks to my aunt I learned to read and write. I finished sixth grade and my aunt encouraged me to continue studying; she would pay for my studies, but I was ignorant and did not want to. When I finished school I returned to my parents and worked with my father. I helped to cultivate tomatoes, yucca and rice. I continued with this work until I married at nineteen, voluntarily and in love.[18] With my husband, I went to Escuintla, Tiquisate, and eventually to Nueva Concepción, to work on the cotton plantations.

Life was difficult on the plantations. Hard work and low pay, we barely had enough to feed the family. I was always very thin, maybe that was why my children died; I didn't have enough milk. Four of my first five children died, the first three, all girls, died when they were around three; they fell ill with high temperatures and just died. There were no doctors in those days and the local healers could not save them. The fourth was a boy, who grew to be an adult, but the fifth—also a boy—died. For nine years we lived in Nueva Concepción. There we got to know about the land in the Petén from a speech made by President Kjell. In the Petén there is land for all the poor, landless peasants, I remember that's what President Kjell said. Thus, we came to the Petén. We first settled in the Ixmucané cooperative. We stayed there for three years. Then my two married daughters arrived, but there was not enough land for them in this cooperative. They traveled around the area trying to find land for all of us somewhere. In Armenia they found land, good land. This was not a cooperative, only smallholdings. It was also a small hamlet, only 65 persons I think we were. We had a very good time there. Plenty of food, and it was good food too! We grew corn, beans, fruits, and I had my animals. When the violence came we had to leave everything.

Poverty, exploitation, and humiliation have been recurrent themes in the stories we have seen thus far, the product of an unequal distribution of land, power, and other resources between Ladinos and Indians, rich and poor Ladinos, but also between men and women. The following story draws attention to the fact that the Indian population did not live in homogeneous harmony either. Discrimination and exploitation also occurred between rich and poor Indians or, as in the case of Gregorio, between Indians belonging to majority and minority groups in a certain area.

Leona and Gregorio are two of the very few people in La Quetzal who have not been cooperative members in Ixcán or the Petén. They used to live in the Ixil triangle, one of the other areas of Guatemala which was very hard hit by the armed conflict (Stoll 1993). Gregorio's father, who was an orphan, grew up in a Spanish-speaking family and did not learn to speak Mam, his mother's language. Gregorio's mother was a native-speaking Mam, but since her husband did not master this language, Gregorio also grew up speaking Spanish.

When my father was about to marry, he tried to get back the land that my grandfather had in Chiantla, in the county of Huehuetenango. When he found out that the land had been taken over by his cousins who did not want him there, he and my mother started to roam around (rumbear) in search for land. They found land for rent in Salquíl Grande in the municipality of Nebaj and settled there. That's where I grew up and on the south coast. The Ixils discriminated against us. Since we were not Ixils, they sometimes told us to return to the place where we came from, that's what they said to us. They had communal lands—parcialidades I think they called them. On the communal lands they could take a piece to cultivate. Finally, they were willing to give us a parcel. Sometimes we paid rent in money, sometime in products. Poor land it was. They gave us the worst, the steepest, and the rockiest piece of land, while they cultivated the nicest and flattest parcels. It was very hard and we were so poor that we had to go to the south coast all the time. My father was away most of the time; he went from one finca to another depending on the seasons for coffee, sugar, and cotton. When I was around twelve years old, I started to go with my father. It was a miserable life, not enough food. We only received six tortillas for breakfast, four for lunch, and six for dinner. Once a week they gave us some beans to cook but the rations were so small that after a couple of days there was nothing left. We were lodged in galeras (precarious shelters) where we slept on straw mats on the dirt floor. When it rained we were soaked because the water entered under the walls. A miserable life! Only for 15–20 days we stayed at home between each trip to the fincas. They paid very badly too.

Leona is the only Ixil in La Quetzal, born in a hamlet close to the municipal capital of Nebaj, El Quiché.

My father had some land close to the pueblo of Nebaj, so we lived in the pueblo. My father died when I was rather small. He fell from a horse, injuring his ribs and back, and was never really well again after that. Nevertheless, in order to survive, he had to work on the fincas in the south coast. He died there. I remember it very well; we were all there in the shack, my father was ill, resting on his petate (straw mat) and some of the people of the patron came to pick him up. They were going to take him to the hospital, they said. We don't know what happened to him, we never saw him again. They came to tell my mother that he had died. We did not see him; they did not give us his body. Who knows what happened to him? When we returned to Nebaj my paternal grandparents wanted to raise my brother to take over the land of my father. When my mother refused, we were obliged to leave our home. We returned to my mother's hamlet.

In contrast to those who lived in Ixcán and the Petén, more or less close to the Mexican border, Gregorio and Leona had no chance to leave the country. Not only was the distance to the border very far. They simply did not know that the border existed, "that there were other countries in the world than Guatemala," to quote Gregorio. They hid in the mountains not far from their village, where they spent almost ten years in the CPR-Sierra (Communities of People in Resistance), and another couple of years on foot before they eventually managed to leave the country and become refugees in Quintana Roo. I will return to Gregorio's narrative of this overwhelming experience in Chapter 4.

Toward a Prosperous Future

With few exceptions, the narratives about life in the Highlands and the south coast are colored by suffering, hard work, exploitative labor conditions, illness, alcoholism, violence, and death. Very few mention the good moments that also must have existed before they moved to the cooperatives. This makes the contrast with the life in the new communities very striking. Even though people referred to the hardships they had to endure, especially during the first years, the focus is on the positive aspects. Access to land, abundant and fertile land, is a common theme. Most people associate their previous misery with the scarcity of land. This was what obliged them to accept the dreadful labor and living conditions in the coastal plantations or on the haciendas in the Highlands, conditions shared by Indians and non-Indians alike. However, the fact that most Indians were illiterate and did not speak the dominant language made them even more vulnerable than the poor Ladinos.

The settlement projects in Ixcán and the Petén offered a unique opportunity for these landless and exploited peasants to start a new life. Most of my informants were rather young people, often newly married with small children, people in their twenties and thirties. What motivated them was a dream of obtaining their own piece of land, big enough not only to produce for their own consumption, but also to produce a surplus for sale that permitted them to build a safer and more prosperous future. Land was abundant and available to those who could prove that they were landless, hard working and well behaved. However, it was covered with dense tropical vegetation and very hard work was required to make it productive.

After a few years of hard work and many sacrifices, the settlers experienced a relative prosperity that they had never experienced before. The cooperative members in Ixcán could, for example, sell their products directly to Guatemala City, thus eliminating exploitive middlemen. They started to earn money that was invested in animals, improved housing, agricultural and household equipment, and radios. Moreover, their cooperatives also prospered and became quite dynamic. By the mid-1970s most cooperative centers had schools, health centers, shops, cardamom wringers, and rice threshing machines (AVANCSO 1992: 38).

The encounter with the jungle was challenging. My informants remember the suffocation of the humid heat, the torrential rains, the mud, the impenetrable vegetation, the fight against insects, especially *sancudos* (gnats), and the fear of lethal snakes. They also recall the difficulties associated with the lack of roads and the long distance to commercial centers. However, what seems to occupy a privileged place in their memory is the image of the abundance and fertility of this virgin land that enabled them to grow crops that they had barely heard about before, and to raise animals. The dramatic circumstances that led to the destruction and loss of the land and all the work and dreams they had devoted to it, also certainly contributed to anchoring this image in their memory.

When they arrived at the jungle areas, most people aspired to a sustainable peasant life through the work of their family and what their land produced. They had no revolutionary interests, perhaps because the move from the Highlands to the rich rainforests had already produced a revolution in their lives in many ways. The cooperative system offered a new space for organizational learning and increased awareness. The same was true for the Church. The Catholic Church played a crucial role in introducing into these settlement communities not only a new religious ethic, but also a new economic ethic, that of justice and development. The equal distribution of land and the participation of the peasants in the church and community institutions and activities demonstrate an impetus toward egalitarian democracy, where there was no distinction based on language, religion, or color. Hard work, conscientiousness, and will power to comply with the rules and regulations of the cooperative were what counted. It should be noted at this point that this participative democracy was mainly for men, while women continued in their traditional roles. However, certain changes in male practices and values had positive effects on the lives of many women. Their husbands no longer had to spend months at a time away from home to make ends meet, and the ban on alcohol led to fewer family conflicts and violence. Many women remember the years in Ixcán and the Petén as "muy buenos y tranquilos" (very good and quiet).

Le Bot suggests that the network of pioneer communities in Ixcán, characterized by ethnic diversity and great social cohesion, a strong religious expressivity, a rejection of a racist society, and a desire for integration, may be analyzed as the contemporary version of the search for the "land without evil" reached by pacific means. This utopia clashed with another one that followed along the road of armed struggle, bringing the war and destroying both the hope for the future and fifteen years of hard work in the settlement areas (Le Bot 1995: 128–29).

A number of my informants remember that they were so dazed by their new life, especially the fact that they had become cooperative owners in what they imagined as some of the "best land in the country," that they sometimes found it hard to believe that it could last. As we have seen from their narratives, it did not last: "the violence arrived and everything was destroyed." In the next chapter, I will discuss the process that led to this destruction and the displacement of most people from these promising lands.

Chapter 3

The Escalation of Violence in Ixcán and the Petén

Violence and killing of civilian populations is one of the characteristics of what Kaldor and Vashee (1997) call the "new wars," that is, wars not between national states with technically well-equipped armies, but wars taking place within the borders of a national state where civilians are the victims of armed conflicts between military, paramilitary groups, and guerrillas, or liberation armies. Only 10 percent of the casualties in the wars of the last three decades have been soldiers, with more children than soldiers having been killed (Sivard 1996; Nordstrom 1997). Another consequence of the "new wars" is the dramatic increase in the number of refugees and internally displaced people throughout the world (Malkki 1995). In Ixcán and the Petén this type of warfare was carried out in the most gruesome way. No other region in Guatemala has experienced the degree of destruction and dislocation as has Ixcán, giving it the grim distinction of having produced more refugees than any other single region of the country. In terms of the number of refugees, Ixcán is followed by the western section of the Petén (Manz 1988: 127).

Insurgency and Counterinsurgency

The violence against civilians in these areas is primarily associated with the counterinsurgency campaigns of the Guatemalan army, initiated in 1960 after an abortive rebellion carried out by young liberal officers who attempted to take power to "institute social justice" and "fight American imperialism." This rebellion was defeated, but some of the officers managed to escape and, in 1961, they created the first guerrilla movement in the country's history. Despite a commitment to the armed struggle, this guerrilla lacked a clear vision of how to relate to the majority of Indians and Ladinos. Inspired by Ché Guevara's *foco* theory, postulating that it is not necessary to wait until revolutionary conditions have developed, since a dedicated small group can ignite a revolution, they reproduced some of the weaknesses of earlier Guatemalan movements for change. Reformers such as Juan José Arévalo and Jacobo Arbenz envisaged a small minority of educated Ladino reformers, not the Guatemalan masses, as the driving force for social change. Just as Arbenz was unable to defend his government in 1954, the FAR (Fuerzas Armadas Rebeldes), similarly without a structure capable of mobilizing mass support, suffered military defeat when the government launched a counteroffensive with strong U.S. support in the mid-1960s. By 1968, reportedly eight thousand villagers had been killed in the "pacification" campaigns during which villages were napalmed and sympathizers murdered (Fried et al. 1983: 258–59).

In the 1970s, two other guerrilla groups were established, EGP (Ejército Guerrillero de los Pobres, Guerrilla Army of the Poor) and ORPA (Organización Revolucionaria de Pueblos en Armas, Revolutionary Organization of People in Arms). This led to an escalation in the counterinsurgency strategy of the different military regimes in power from 1966 on, and it culminated in the military offensives during the period from 1978 to 1982. During this period, the type of counterinsurgency tactics used were "scorched-earth" policies of burning crops and forests, bombings, massacres, destruction of villages, formation of "strategic hamlets," and civic action programs designed to win the hearts and minds of surviving villagers. The resemblance to U.S. actions in Vietnam in the 1970s is striking.

In her study of the Guatemalan military, Jennifer Schirmer (1998) shows that violence and killing of civilians were an integral part of a military strategy that her informants reveal in detail.[1] General Gramajo, who coordinated part of this military campaign, tells Schirmer in detail about how they divided the country into different zones. Within each zone the villages were marked with red, pink, or green pins indicating their destiny. The red villages were defined as subversive villages where all inhabitants should be killed. In the pink villages only a number of identified villagers defined as subversives were doomed to be killed; the green villages should be spared. Ixcán was defined as a red zone or *matazona* (killing zone), where an *operación limpieza* ("cleansing operation") was carried out. Most communities in western Petén were defined as pink areas, to be subjected to a more selective and targeted destruction of civilians and their belongings. Few areas of the country were spared such destruction (Falla 1992; Schirmer 1998; Stoll 1993).

In this chapter I will attempt to reveal the local dynamics of the armed conflicts in Ixcán and the Petén, as documented by other scholars, guerrilla leaders who have written about their participation, and, above all, my informants in La Quetzal, who were among the survivors. The narratives of my informants reveal the gradual transformation of the relationship between the peasants and the army from the early 1970s, when the army presence was conceived as normal and, in some cases even helpful, to the early 1980s, when the army had become a feared and dangerous enemy and the primary cause of their flight to Mexico. The narratives also reveal how this transformation was related to the movement and actions of the guerrilla, on the one hand, and the army's desperate need to show results in its counterinsurgency campaign, on the other.

My findings largely confirm what has been argued by David Stoll (1993), based on his study in the Ixil towns: that the peasants in these areas got involved in the armed conflict mostly against their will. They were driven into participating by the army as well as by the guerrilla. My study also confirms the findings of a number of scholars and is further supported by the report published by the Guatemalan Truth Commission (Falla 1992; CEH 1999). The military forces were the party responsible for most massacres as well as most individual assassinations. According to the Truth Commission, 93 percent of the total number of assassinations were committed by the army and 7 percent by the guerrilla. In contrast to the torture, killing, and massacres by the army, in some areas directed indiscriminately against the civilian population, the killing of civilians by the guerrilla was generally selective and directed at those accused of collaborating with the military and thereby defined as traitors. A number of internal executions within the guerrilla ranks have also been reported (Payeras 1983; Ramírez 2001; Macías 1999). In spite of the fact that the violence committed by the guerrilla against civilians was numerically much more limited than that of the army, several of my informants maintain that the guerrilla responsibility for the massive annihilation is more far-reaching than the numbers indicate. This is because the guerrilla, or at least the leaders, knew about the devastating consequences of their actions for the civilians, even though they hardly imagined that the army would be able to reach the level of violence executed in the scorched-earth campaign. The examples from Ixcán and the Petén demonstrate that violence and the killing of defenseless civilians was part of a military strategy planned outside the context where the violence was executed. This was the case not only for the military forces, but also for the guerrilla. In what follows, I will return to Ixcán and the Petén and the concrete context of my informants.

EGP Brings the War of the Poor to the Jungle of Ixcán

The promising life in the cooperatives did not last long. After a few years the settlers were drawn into the armed conflict taking place in these parts of the country. The military had limited presence in the newly settled areas until the mid-1970s, when the guerrilla movement started its "armed propaganda actions."[2] Falla (1992: 9) reports that scattered units of the FAR guerrilla had been in the area in 1969, but they found no support among the local population and the army had written them off. In 1972 a new group of insurgents had reorganized and formed what would become EGP and entered Ixcán from Mexico in January 1972. This experience has been described in detail by one of the participants, Mario Payeras, alias comandante Benedicto, covering the period from 1972 to 1976. What Payeras in quite lyrical terms refers to as a "beautiful adventure" contributed to triggering a nightmare of death, destruction, and displacement for my informants.[3]

According to Payeras's account, the group of 15 armed men, several of them survivors from the old Edgar Ibarra guerrilla of the 1960s, had decided to return to the struggle after having learned the lessons of defeat. The *foco* theory, which had proven so inadequate during the first guerrilla actions in the Sierra de Minas in the early 1960s, was now replaced by a theory of the war of the poor. These men, together with the commanders who were directing the war from abroad, among them Rolando Morán, the long-standing leader of EGP, no longer believed that a brave elite with limited or no contact with the people could carry out an insurrection on their behalf. The war of the poor was considered to be a prolonged one based on mass organization. This implied that the guerrilla had to fight in such a way as to incorporate the masses into their organization as well as allying with existing social groups. The first step in this strategy of war was the "implantation phase," which aimed at gaining and securing an organizational base among the people, village by village, plantation by plantation, factory by factory. Not until the masses were organized for popular rule would there be an attempt to take power from the Guatemalan government and institute a new society based on popular rule. One leading idea was that the revolutionary society must be built before the revolution and not afterward, when the disorganized people have unrealistic and often contradictory demands (Fried et al. 1983). It was part of this newly formed group that entered the jungles of Ixcán to build a network of peasant support where the local structures of the state were the most vulnerable. This marked the beginning of the planned prolonged armed conflict in Ixcán. Eleven of the men in the group were Ladinos of urban extraction, four of them were indigenous, but none were from the same region, nor were their languages of the same groups as those of the settlers in Ixcán (Le Bot 1995: 114).

During the first two years, the group roamed around in a nightmarish jungle environment, occupied as much with fighting off hunger, diarrhea, and leeches as with forging a people's army from what they, in their romantic ignorance about local conditions, defined as "desperately poor slash and burn settlers." In spite of their stress on the importance of popular support, they had not identified one single contact person in the region when they started their first march and after two years they had succeeded in recruiting only one Ladino peasant who joined them in their second march towards the mountains (Payeras 1983: 51).

Most of Payeras's book deals with the hardship faced by the group simply struggling to survive in the dense jungle, where it rains torrentially eight months a year. In what follows, I will focus on his descriptions of the group's interaction with the local peasants, confirming what my informants have told me. In short, they did not understand and were not interested in what the guerrilla told them about the war of the poor. For the first time in their life they had access to land and hopes for a better future. They did not identify with the image of the desperately poor and exploited peasants that dominated the minds of the guerrilla leaders.

The following quote from Payeras's book refers to the first encounter with the peasants of Ixcán few months after the group of fifteen had crossed the border between Mexico and Guatemala. Payeras reveals both the enormous distance to be covered and the will power that was required in order to approach the indigenous peasants:

Our sense of hope and danger was mixed with apprehension about the villagers' response to us. Alejandro, when he reflected on what a tiny group we were, sometimes predicted that there would soon be a long column of recruits marching with us. This demonstrated his limitless faith in the people. But more often he talked about the terror he had witnessed in the villages near Zacapa during the army's anti-guerrilla attacks in 1966 and 1967. He had seen huts burned down and peasants who had collaborated with the guerrilla suddenly fleeing from them. Thus, as we came upon more and more signs of habitation we all experienced a growing tension. At the same time, we realized that we were living the most beautiful adventure of our lives. . . . For a long time we waited, listening to our hearts beat. Then a rooster crowed in the direction of the village. It was the first time in months that we had heard that pleasing call. We exchanged looks that were a mixture of anxiety and joy. There they were at last, our country's poor, but we had no idea how they would respond to us. (Payeras 1983: 32–33)

Payeras continues with his narrative relating how they were well received by the people of this first hamlet, which was composed of six families, and he concludes: "That night we met with the men of the village. We explained the purpose of our struggle, and solemnly announced that we would triumph" (33).

Encouraged by this first encounter, the group continued their march toward the mountains. After a long and very difficult march they eventually arrived in the Zona Reina. Their next encounter with the "country's poor," the Q'eqchi' peasants of Dolores de Tzejá, was much less encouraging. At that point the insurgents were desperately in need of provisions.

On learning about our presence, the inhabitants either locked themselves into their houses or fled to the hills. Suddenly the situation became dramatic. Some of us were forced to chase after the runaways and warn them to return. Those were moments we will never forget. Suddenly we found ourselves walking in deserted streets. The few remaining inhabitants who might have talked to us barricaded themselves behind the dialect and it was impossible to get any information from them, or even purchase food. . . . There, for the first time, we heard the word macá—a terrible word which for us at the time meant something far worse than "there isn't any" because it was a rejection that had its roots in the past. We could see in the granaries of the very people who told us that they had no corn, mounds of what we needed so badly in order to survive. (35)

From Dolores the group continued to Santa María Tzejá, which at this point had become a more established community with street merchants and even shops. Now the insurgents were so desperate that they had to change strategy in order to obtain food. They pretended to be an anti-guerrilla patrol and also pretended to demand that the merchants sell to them, even though this was not the case. At last they obtained food, having to spend almost all their money in the village stores.

The next village on their march was one along the Chixoy River, where the Q'eqchi' inhabitants were squatters who had settled there long before. They occupied considerable areas of land, won from the endless jungle with their machetes. Not much is said about the place but the following observation is quite telling: "The villagers watched us with a mixture of astonishment and pity, taking in the rags, skeletal thinness, shaggy beards and hair, the hungry stares of a group of castaways spewed out of the jungle" (39).

Rubelolóm, the last village they came to during this first march, was almost empty, with the exception of an old man who was too sick to move and a couple of others, who eventually were willing to sell them a bunch of bananas at a very high price. The insurgents were struck by the particular silence prevailing in the village and the indifference of the few people who were around. They did not speak Spanish and claimed not to understand one of the insurgents who talked to them in Achí. Payeras claims that they would neither tell them where the road led nor the location of other villages. The group remained three days in this village before they realized that the army was present in the area. One of their scouts who had gone to pick some sweet potatoes from a field discovered the soldiers and managed to shoot one before he retreated safely into the jungle.

Our experience in Rubelolóm should have taught us that the problem of survival required more complex solutions than we had imagined, and that we could not simply station ourselves in populated areas. However, for a while we completely lost our perspective. We even discussed issuing our first war bulletin—at a time when we had no communication with the outside world. The urge to engage in combat was a kind of mirage on our horizon. In our desperation we almost believed that the indifference of the people was the result of fear and lack of confidence in our military project. This explanation was by no means illogical. To believe in the possible victory of an army in tatters was almost impossible for men who had grown accustomed to trusting in concrete realities. But reality itself dissuaded us from deciding on battle as an immediate possibility. We could not shoot our way to the truth when the protagonists themselves did not even under-stand the phenomenon of gunpowder. The use of firearms would have to wait for more opportune moments. Much would have to happen before the inhabitants of that world would be willing to make our cause theirs. (42–43)

Following this experience, the group decided to go back to their previous stopping places and, eventually, to the first and only village where luck had smiled on them. Again they were well received by these villagers, who generously offered them a variety of food. They stayed in the area for seven months. During this period the group was reduced by two persons. Efraín returned to his job as a store clerk in Guatemala City after having deserted when he was given permission to go to the city for treatment of a sore foot. The other, Minche, was executed by his *compañeros*. Minche was accused of demoralizing the group: "When hunger was a crucial issue for all of us, he (Minche) openly proclaimed his skepticism about the chances for improving our lot. He doubted our ability to win the people's support, and belittled the peasants' first modest contribution to our wel-fare" (48).

What is said to have sealed Minche's fate was that he announced that he was a victim of a general conspiracy to isolate him, something that his *compañeros* saw as a proof of never having understood revolutionary life. About the execution itself Payeras reports:

We shot him one April morning when many birds were singing. . . . We had told him of our decision at a general meeting of our unit. He seemed bewildered, as if he could not believe what he had heard. He then made desperate efforts to save his life. In his desire to live he promised loyalties and many other virtues. . . . As he walked towards the execution place he asked for a bit of sugar loaf he car-ried in his backpack. As he faced the firing squad, he seemed to regain his pride and stood upright during those final moments. A few seconds before the order to fire was given, he attempted a confused speech in which he seemed to call for a rift between Indians and Ladinos. He refused the blindfold; then turned his face away from the firing squad. We returned to our posts. A profound silence reigned. The unit had reached maturity. Perhaps from that moment on, each of us was a better person. (48–49)

The group remained in the jungles of Ixcán until December 1973, when they started their second march toward the Cuchumatanes Mountains. At that point, almost two years after they entered the region, very few set-tlers were sympathetic toward the war of the poor, and the only guerrilla recruit they had obtained was a Ladino named Saturino, who joined them in their further endeavors. About him we can read: "He imagined that in the mountains he would find an army as vast as in our conversation" (51).

Payeras confirms what I have been told by my informants in La Quet-zal, that what the EGP defined as the "implantation phase of people's revolutionary war" was not very successful so far as the settler areas of

Ixcán were concerned. Their lack of knowledge of local conditions prevented Payeras and his *compañeros* from understanding that the interests of the settlers did not align with what the EGP had to offer. After years of poverty and exploitation in the Highlands, as well as in the plantations on the south coast, the settlers had gained access to enough land to create a better life for themselves and their families. Moreover, as members of a cooperative they were engaged in common efforts to create dynamic communities in the jungle together. Their hope to create a future for themselves, their families, and their new communities was destroyed rather than furthered by the insurgent movement.

Beatriz Manz, who visited the cooperatives in Ixcán Grande as well as Santa Maria de Tzejá in Zona Reina in 1973, tells about how impressed she was by the courageous Highland people she met, who, under the most arduous circumstances, had carved out a life over which they had gained some control. She observed that these Indian colonizers had not only survived but prospered, providing food for themselves and cash crops for the market, which she emphasized, demonstrated the development of highly successful cooperatives.

I was deeply moved by the early experience of these rainforest colonizers. Not only was their courage and resourcefulness impressive, but their optimism was infectious. They had few illusions about conditions becoming easier, but they had enormous pride in what they had accomplished and this pride generated confidence and hope for the future. (Manz, 1994: 193)

What happened in Ixcán that made some people support or even join the rebel forces? It is a fact that EGP gradually gained support and increased its ranks in the late 1970s and the early 1980s. The support in this area was certainly not in reaction to worsening economic and social conditions, as is often argued by members and sympathizers of the insurgent movement. I will argue, based on the accounts and testimonies by people who in one way or another were connected to the insurgents, that this was not because EGP gained popular support for "the war of the poor." It was rather a reaction to increased military repression following the guerrilla incursions and actions in the region. In what follows I will discuss the process that led to this change in attitude.

"Armed Propaganda" and Reprisals Against the Peasants

By the end of 1974, EGP had established a base and begun to carry out open military-political actions, a phase known as "armed propaganda." This consisted among other things, of occupying villages, agitating for the war of the poor, distributing flyers, and executing army spies or others defined as "enemies of the people." The first important military action in the region, a kind of declaration of war, took place in June 1975 when they killed the owner of the large estate La Perla, Luis Arenas, alias "The Tiger of Ixcán." He was known as an exploitive and cruel employer. Regarding this action one can read in Payeras's book:

> The first shots in the people's war had sounded in this part of the mountains. The next morning the sky thundered with military planes and helicopters and during the following months the enemy army carried through the largest military operation that had taken place in Guatemala so far. . . . Hundreds of soldiers were parachuted from old C47s into the Ixcán settlements and columns penetrated by land from different military bases, occupying key points in the jungle. . . . They established permanent detachments in the main pueblos, and from there, troops trained for jungle combat combed the mountains. For three months they took over the roads and searched the villages, arresting anyone who seemed suspicious or who was listed in their intelligence files. . . . After the action at La Perla, our patrol withdrew without problems to a more distant area. . . . Through scattered radio transmissions and the distant sound of helicopters we understood what was going on in the jungle. (Payeras 1982: 132, my translation)[4]

In the above quote Payeras reveals what was to become a constant factor in the armed conflict in Ixcán, the high price paid by the local population compared to the one paid by the guerrilla. The military operation that was launched after this incident was certainly not organized during the three days that passed between the killing of Arenas and the military intervention. It was the result of months of preparations. Alarmed by the guerrilla presence in Ixcán, the army had collected information through their local spies (*orejas*, ears), who identified people defined as supporters or potential supporters of the insurgents. Such accusations were often motivated by personal resentments, conflicts, or simply by the fear of the *orejas*, of being accused for not complying with their mission. Even though church and cooperative leaders were the most exposed to such accusations, many people without such positions were also affected, as we shall see below.

The killing of Arenas, like the killing of an *oreja* in the Xalbal cooperative a few weeks earlier, was typical of the way EGP operated in Ixcán in the late 1970s. A major objective was to gain publicity and subsequent support from the country's poor. Therefore, a frequent way of operating was to appear at people's homes or at the cooperative centers where, as a group, they tried to gather the settlers to preach the message of the war of the poor or to distribute flyers on the paths around the hamlets. They would also sometimes paint their initials on tree trunks or poles close to the peasants' homes. These actions in themselves were apparently not very effective in mobilizing people. Indirectly however, they had a strong mobilizing effect. Following the guerrilla actions, the insurgents returned safely to their camps in the jungle, and left the communities defenseless and vulnerable.[5] The army's counterattacks were therefore directed at the civilian populations. When this happened, The Guerrilla Army of the Poor was no longer around to defend them. Nevertheless, the army's reprisals against civilians contributed to the recruitment to the guerrilla ranks as stated in the following quote from Payeras:

> The barking of dogs would announce some midnight capture in a hamlet. Pointing their guns at the women and children, the soldiers would make the adult males come out of the huts. They were never seen again. Terror began to spread. . . . In less than a week we tripled our membership, augmented by the peasants who sought our protection. (Payeras 1983: 79)

The killing of the Tiger of Ixcán initiated the first phase of the military counterinsurgency thirty people were kidnapped and killed by the army. During the same period the persecution of church leaders started and a number of catechists were also killed (AVANCSO 1992: 40).

The army had a deep mistrust toward the priests in the settler areas: they talked about the liberation of the poor, a language that the military automatically associated with the insurgency. Therefore, the Church and its servants were defined as actual or potential supporters of the guerrilla. Moreover, since the Church was involved in development projects among the settlers through funds raised abroad, it appeared as competing with the army at a point when the army was applying a strategy that consisted of a combination of repression and provision of services. Finally, the priests also had contacts and means of communications with the outside world.

In November 1976 William Woods (Padre Guillermo), the coordinator of the cooperatives in the Ixcán Grande, died in an air crash. There are contradictory opinions as to whether this was a real or an arranged accident (Morrisey 1978: 761–66 ; Falla 1992: 17–20). The last foreign priest, Karl Stetter, a diocesan from Stuttgart (Germany), was captured by the army and deported from Guatemala in December 1978. He was particularly disliked by the armed forces, not only because he observed how the army conducted itself in Ixcán, but because, being an amateur radio enthusiast, he communicated his observations to the outside world. In June 1980, the Spanish priest José Maria Gran and his sexton from the diocese of El Quiché were assassinated by the army on their way back from a community in Zona Reina. Through these assasinations the settlers lost their most important contacts with the outside world (Falla 1992: 17–24).

From 1979 to 1981 the elimination of local cooperative and community leaders accelerated. According to Falla, approximately 100 persons were assassinated or disappeared in Ixcán during this period, most of them as reprisals for guerrilla appearances in the villages, or in some cases guerrilla attacks on military personnel or equipment. Even though the army reprisals initially were selective and targeted at local leaders, such as those who participated actively in the Church and cooperatives, they created an atmosphere of terror. People lived in constant fear and insecurity. They never knew why or when they could be accused of insurgent activity.

In early 1982 the violence in the Ixcán escalated. The scorched-earth offensive launched in Chimaltenango in November 1981 reached Ixcán in February 1982, moving geographically from east to west and north (Falla 1992: 51–187). By destroying the civilian population, in their minds the support base of the guerrilla, the army attempted to force the insurgents out of the country. The army was trying to "remove the water from the fish," the water being the civilian population, the fish the insurgents.

"The Violence Destroyed Everything for Us"

The above statement was a very common conclusion when my informants talked about their life in the settler areas, a life full of hardship and difficulties, but also of opportunities and hopes for the future. In what follows I will let my informants speak of their experiences with the escalating violence in Ixcán. The narratives from this period are so overwhelming that they alone could fill a monograph. Therefore I have made a careful selection, trying to cover a variety of voices of people who used to live in different villages or cooperatives in the Zona Reina, as well as people coming from different cooperatives in Ixcán Grande. Women and men of different ages and ethnic groups are represented, some more articulate than others.

THE KILLING OF THE TIGER OF IXCÁN

Diego, a Jakalteco in his late forties, used to live in Xalbal, the first cooperative to be affected by the repression of the army after the assassination of the Tiger of Ixcán. He associates the origin of the military presence in his cooperative with the incident in La Perla. Diego is a contemplative and articulate man. When he arrived in Ixcán he was, like most of the new settlers, a poor, landless peasant. However, he was soon drawn into the activities of the cooperative, where he held leadership positions. In the camps in Mexico he was elected to become an education promoter. He received teacher training and at present works as a teacher at the local school. He is a cooperative member, but has limited ability to do physical work due to back problems. This is how Diego remembers the development of the armed conflict in his community:

The problems in our cooperative started after the guerrilla killed Luis Arenas, the owner of La Perla. They said that he treated his workers very badly, almost like slaves. That is why the guerrilla killed him. One morning planes arrived in the center of Xalbal dropping paratroopers. People were standing around observing this; we were not afraid of the military then, because before that they had not done harm to anybody. A group of peasants were building a hammock bridge over the Xalbal River. The soldiers approached them. They had a list of names of people living in our cooperative. They started to read the names. Three of the people present had their names on the list. The soldiers captured them but they did not kill them. They used them as guides to find the houses of the other people on the list. Some of them were at home and they were also captured, others were not and they escaped.

A few days later the soldiers returned to the center of Xalbal with some hooded prisoners. All the men were ordered to line up. Then the prisoners were asked to point out the guerrilleros. The two persons who were pointed out were captured, killed, and thrown into the river. After that, the situation calmed down again, but the military established a unit in all the cooperatives. They also requested the appointment of a military commissioner who would observe what was going on in the cooperative and report strange behavior to the army. Our commissioner was appointed by the people. We appointed a cooperative member, and he did not denounce anybody. We heard that in other cooperatives the commissioners denounced people because of gossip, personal envy, and things like that. This was not the case in our cooperative.

The relatively harsh reaction by the army in this incident was an attempt to get rid of the "rotten oranges"—a metaphor often used by the military about guerrilla supporters—once and for all, giving a warning that would prevent the peasants from having any relation with the insurgents in the future. However, the establishment of detachments and the appointment of military commissioners led to a qualitative change in military presence in the region. This is reflected in the continuation of Diego's narrative.

RAPES, ROBBERIES, AND ABDUCTIONS

Between 1975 and 1980 many things happened. The soldiers raped several women, they captured them on the paths around the hamlets, to frighten people, I think. In 1978 the cooperative shop was robbed twice. The military accused the guerrilla, but we knew that the soldiers had done it and the second time the military recognized our claims. This was when the soldiers one night entered the shop and stole, among other things, 1,500 quetzales, a tape recorder, and a wristwatch. Next to the shop there was a room used by Padre Guillermo when he visited our cooperative. It was very dusty because it had not been used after his death (in 1976). The soldiers had entered through the window of this room. One could see their footprints in the dust at the table placed in front of the window. That's how we knew that it was the soldiers who had been there. I was a member of the cooperative board responsible for the running of the shop at that time. Therefore, I went to the detachment with the military commissioner to register a complaint. A corporal received us. We told him about the robbery and the footprints. He did not believe us; he said that the footprints must be of the guerrilleros, who also used military boots. "You have to register this complaint with the air force," he said, "they are the ones to investigate such cases." We did this and the officer promised to come the next day. In the meantime we found out that somebody had come across some of the stolen goods in the bushes beside the airstrip. We found the stolen things and also some other things that confirmed that soldiers had been involved. The next day the air force people came to investigate the case. They asked thousands of questions. Finally, they recognized that the soldiers had robbed our store. "What shall we do now?" the colonel asked. "Do you go for civil law or military law?" I realized that we had no other option than use what he called military law. That implied that they return what had been stolen and they punish those who had to be punished. Three military police accompanied the soldiers. "We want our things back—you can do whatever you want with the soldiers," I said. "I congratulate you, that we can solve it this way," the colonel said. "Others would go to the press. I will draw up the minutes and you recover the tape recorder, the wristwatch, the cigarettes, and the biscuits. God forgive us for the burglars among us! I will take care of our own."

I don't know what he did in the end. I told the people how we had solved the case; that I did not want to tell the press what had happened. People were satisfied and relieved with this solution. . . .

In 1979 two members of the cooperative board disappeared. They were kidnapped from their houses. I don't know what happened to them, but I suppose they were killed, because they never turned up again. I was constantly afraid that something like that would happen to me, but it did not. Compared to other places, I think there were few kidnappings in Xalbal. I think the reason was that our commissioner was a cooperative member who did not report people. From 1979 the guerrilla appeared more frequently in the village distributing flyers about the war of the poor or they appeared in people's houses trying to convince them to support the guerrilla. A few were willing to collaborate, but most people were afraid of them. They did not understand what was going on. The guerrilla said that they wanted to change the nation, but most people did not know about the nation, they were not prepared, they had no ideology. Moreover, the guerrilla disarmed the peasants. Some people had firearms that they used for hunting in the jungle. The guerrilla demanded they give up their arms. The guerrilla could maybe have gained some support if they had distributed arms to people to defend themselves. What they did was to take the few arms that were around and leave people totally defenseless.

On April 30, 1981, the EGP attacked the military detachment in Cuarto Pueblo in an attempt to seize the barracks and distribute the weapons to form another military unit. The combatants stationed themselves in three different places in the center of the cooperative surrounding the military post. The combat started at 5 A.M. and lasted for two hours, until the air force arrived, bringing additional forces and bombing the area. No civilians died in the air attack or in the combat crossfire. However, the army carried out a massacre in the village after the guerrillas had withdrawn (Falla 1992: 41). This combat initiated a new stage of counterinsurgency in Ixcán. It demonstrated that the civic actions introduced in 1975 to capture the hearts and minds of the settlers had not succeeded in putting an end to "subversion." Everyday life in the settler areas became increasingly more difficult and terrifying as illustrated in the continuation of Diego's story.

TERRORIZATION OF EVERYDAY LIFE

After the guerrilla attack on the detachment in Cuarto Pueblo in 1981, things became much more difficult. People had to report to the detachment when they traveled, neither catechists nor cooperative members were allowed to meet without the presence of military people and, we had to be very careful what we talked about, not to be misunderstood. The guerrilla blew up bridges, airstrips, and roads and for a year we were almost completely isolated. We lived in constant fear of what would happen next.

With the guerrilla and the military permanently present in the area, people who were not involved in leadership positions either in the cooperative or in the church were also affected. Each cooperative had established a center where the communal buildings such as the cooperative shop, the market, the school, and the church were located. The military detachments were normally placed in these centers. Most peasants, however, used to live scattered on their parcels throughout the larger area of the cooperative. In order to move from their homes to the fields or to the center of the cooperative they often had to walk long distances on the narrow jungle paths, the same paths that were used by the army and the guerrilla. With the escalation of military repression this became increasingly dangerous, something that is reflected in Doña Dominga's narrative. She is a fifty-eight-year-old Mam who lived in the Cuarto Pueblo cooperative.

The problems started before the massacre. (She refers to the massacre in Cuarto Pueblo in March 1982.) One day I went to the market with my oldest son Raúl to sell some cardamom. He was twelve by then. On the path we met some soldiers from the army. They grabbed my son, held him, and asked his name. He got so scared that he forgot his name. Instead of saying Raúl

Sanchez Vasquez, he said Raúl Sanchez Pérez. The problems started when he showed them his identity card and they realized that the second surname was different from what he had told. None of us spoke Castilla then, and we could barely talk with the soldiers. They accused him of being a liar, they beat him and kicked him and wanted to take him with them to the detachment. I cried and begged for him, explaining that he was my boy and that we were on our way to the market to sell cardamom. "If he is your son, take him with you, the leader of the group said, "but you go home, not to the market." That is what we did. How scared we were! We did not have peace in our minds after that.

An equally terrifying incident happened to Don Lorenzo, who survived almost by accident. He used to live in a parcel of land that was part of the Xalbal cooperative. One day his son fell ill and he had to go to the center to buy medicine.

I was walking on the path to the center when I was surprised by a battalion of soldiers. It was midday, around one o'clock, I think. I got very scared when they stopped me on the path and I realized that I was surrounded by soldiers. Some three hundred, I think. The major stopped in front of me and asked where I came from and where I was going. I told him about my son who was ill. I begged him to let me continue to the pueblo, but nothing happened. He said nothing; they only stayed around watching me. After a long while I took courage and begged him once more to let me continue. No way. The same thing happened. They stayed around, watched me without talking or doing anything to me. When it started to get dark and I lost hope that they would leave me alive, I eventually asked the major for permission to return to my home, now that they would not let me go to the village to buy the remedies. The hours passed. At about one o'clock in the morning the major gave the marching order, he wanted to bring the battalion to my house to find out whether the things I told were true or a lie. It was very dark, difficult to find the path. Two soldiers went in front of me the rest behind. I had no chance to escape. After having walked for a couple of hours we approached a cliff with a waterfall. I was very thirsty and thought that the soldiers must be as well. I asked the major: "Are your soldiers thirsty?" "Is there water here?" the major asked. "Yes," I said, "just here." "Show me," he said. I did, and he gave his soldiers permission to fetch water. Ten at a time, they could go to the waterfall and fill their canteens. I was also allowed to drink. When everybody had served themselves, the major called on two officers, a lieutenant and a sergeant I think they were. Like the story in the Bible he said: "You can decide what to do with this man. Should we let him go or should we eliminate him here? "You first, the major said and pointed at one of them. "He did not lie about the water, maybe we should let him go," the officer answered. The other said he agreed with him. "Then we will let you go," the major said, but I was not at all sure that this is what should happen.

"Go straight forward, don't look back," the major said. "If you do we shoot you." I walked very slowly some twenty steps; then I started to run. When I arrived home I aroused my family and we went into the jungle.

Other informants could speak about similar episodes with less fortunate outcomes, of what happened to their kin or neighbors. For example, Theresa's husband and two neighbors were killed when they returned from their *milpas*; the same happened to Nicolás's father and a number of others. Nobody actually witnessed what happened to them. However, their destroyed bodies, found by neighbors or relatives showed traces of a tortured end.

Not only did it become increasingly dangerous to move about in the jungle, life at home, whether in isolated parcels or in hamlets, also became more insecure. Direct military presence, as well as indirect presence through the system of local commissioners and spies, also affected people's lives, as illustrated in Doña Candelaria's narrative. She is a Q'anjob'al woman in her fifties, mother of seven, who used to live in the Mayalán cooperative.

During the first years in Ixcán we did not have enough money to buy what we needed. Therefore, my husband used to go back to Barillas (Huehuetenango) to chambeár (work temporarily). Once he returned with some money, I went to the market to shop. I remember that among other things I bought four blankets and a whole parcel of meat broth portions (people would normally buy only one or two portion packages at a time). I did not understand anything when the commissioner suddenly came to interrogate me at home. He wanted to know why I had bought so much of this and so much of that. I told him like it was; that my husband had been working in Barillas and that I finally had some money to spend on the needs of my family. Afterward I realized that people who bought certain quantities of goods were reported to the commissioner, who, in turn, reported such people to the military detachment. That is why the guerrilla later killed this commissioner. One day they (the guerrillas) came to my house and told us that nobody should leave the house at two o'clock, because they were going to kill a dog. At about two we heard gunshots. It turned out that they had killed the commissioner, precisely because he used to denounce innocent people, who in some cases were killed by the army.

This kind of action was always followed by reprisals against the villagers.

One day my husband attended a cooperative meeting. At one point he left the meeting to relieve himself in the bushes. When he was about to pull down his pants he discovered the dead bodies of two of his fellow cooperative members.

They lay beheaded on the ground with their heads placed on their bellies. My husband got so scared that he lost his urge and ran away. The military said that the guerrilla had killed them, but that was a lie, they had killed them themselves. This does not mean that the guerrilla did not provoke, as well. I remember once, it was at the celebration of the closure of the school year and the teacher had brought bread to give to the children. When we arrived at the school we realized that the guerrilla had put up a banner denouncing the military repression. We got so scared that we did not dare attend the ceremony; we only picked up the bread and returned directly to our homes. The guerrilla actions were always reported to the military detachment and the soldiers came to punish the people, because they could not punish the guerrilla who had hidden in the jungle. It was terrible, because you never knew who would be the next.

Doña Candelaria was lucky; she was not punished for her purchases. Rosalía, a Jakalteca in her early thirties, told another story where purchases of goods became an important element in the tragic killing of her father. It should be noted, however, that the incident Rosalía refers to happened some months later, when the level of violence had escalated even further.

We lived in Mayalán cooperative, where my uncle was the president. Our problems started one day when my uncle was about to take the plane to Guatemala City to do some paperwork for the cooperative. Several neighbors had asked him to buy commodities for them. They needed things such as sugar and coffee—things that were not available in the cooperative. I was with my uncle at the airstrip when some military people arrived, a colonel with a group of soldiers. They asked him what he was going to do in Guatemala and he told them calmly. When the colonel found out that he was going to buy commodities for his neighbors he got annoyed and said: "If you return here with commodities you will be a dead man." My uncle answered that the people who ordered the commodities paid his ticket, and that he felt obliged to comply with the deal he had made with them. I did not understand much of what was going on, but what the colonel said about the dead man called my attention. When I returned home I asked my father what it meant. Nothing, my daughter, he said, don't worry, these are not things for girls.

My uncle returned from Guatemala on the 29th of November 1980, I remember the date because it was my birthday. We went to meet him at the airstrip when the plane arrived. I was eager to pick up my birthday present that my father had ordered from Guatemala—a pair of shoes. My uncle arrived in the afternoon and we made a nice birthday party in his house. Everybody was happy, eating and dancing. We returned home at around nine o'clock. I had enjoyed the party, but I felt very uneasy. I had a feeling that something bad was going to happen and I could not sleep. My father realized that I was sleepless and asked me why. "I feel that something bad is about to happen," I answered, "that there is a poisonous snake in here or something like that." "No my daughter, nothing will happen, sleep now," my father said.

In my grandmother's house located close by, my father's little brother had the same problem as I, he was anxious and could not sleep. He used to sleep in my grandmother's bed but had started to sleep in a separate bed a few days earlier because he was growing up. When my grandmother found out that he could not sleep, she thought that it was because he was still not accustomed to sleeping alone. "Come here to sleep with me," she said to him. Just when he was passing from one bed to the other the soldiers entered the room. They grabbed him by the neck and dragged him outside. "Mama, Mama!" he screamed. We heard him and thought that something had happened to my grandmother. "Maybe my mother fell ill from too much dancing," my father said. He got up to see what was going on. "Don't leave, papa," I begged," I am afraid." "Don't worry," he said and walked toward the door. When he opened the door the soldiers were outside. They shot him with machine guns and he fell down dead. I think they killed him because they thought he was my uncle, the president of the cooperative. That same night my uncle disappeared and I never saw him again.[6]

My life turned upside down with the death of my father. He was a very special man. After his death we felt very unsafe and in March or April 1981 we decided to go to Mexico. This was before masses of refugees started to arrive. We settled at the farm of Señor Sanchez in Puerto Rico (Chiapas). I had to work with a machete, a man's work; I had to be mother and father for my younger sisters and brothers, because my mother was pregnant.

SMALL ACTIONS, BIG CONSEQUENCES

Leonardo is a Mam in his fifties born in Todos Santos, Huehuetenango. He was a member in the Pueblo Nuevo cooperative, the last one established in Ixcán Grande. He and his family lived on their parcel some three hours from the center of the cooperative, when their lives were turned upside down due to army reprisals after guerrilla actions in their neighborhood.

I was one of the latecomers in Pueblo Nuevo. When we arrived the detachment was already there, there were some five hundred people in this detachment. In the beginning our relationship with the army was calm. They were just around, greeted us, and talked to us in a friendly way. The soldiers even helped me to prepare the site for building the house at my parcel, I asked the colonel to do me the favor, and he agreed. When the violence arrived I had just bought the iron sheets and the nails to make a casa de cuatro esquinas (a proper house). I had everything to start building.

First, they started to kidnap people, usually cooperative and church leaders. They kidnapped the president of our cooperative. He simply disappeared. They kidnapped other cooperative leaders too, but they appeared again, dead. Then they started to control ordinary people. For example, the soldiers suddenly appeared when we were on our way to the milpa. They controlled the content of our morrales (colorful handknitted bags used to carry food or other smaller belongings). If we had more than four or five tortillas each they obliged us to return home. "Why do you bring so much food," they said, "are you going to feed the guerrilla?"

Then they started to burn hamlets. They burned two on the other side of the river. They belonged to the INTA cooperatives. We found out because we saw the helicopters and the smoke and heard shooting and the screaming of people. Since we lived so far away from the cooperative center of Pueblo Nuevo we felt rather safe.

One day the soldiers arrived at my neighbor's house. They lived at a distance of some 300 meters. They had a convivencia (family party). The old parents were there, and their five sons with their wives and children. The soldiers tortured and killed all of them except the old father. They hanged him, but the rope was put in such a way that he survived. Poor old man, he could not continue living with his grief. A week later he died too.

After the massacre in my neighbor's house the military returned to the camp in Playa Grande. We got so scared that we hid in the jungle. During the following three weeks everything was calm again and we started to relax a little bit. Then they returned. This happened one afternoon when I was at home with another neighbor. We came there to fetch some fruits and vegetables. At one point my neighbor went outside to pee. I followed behind and saw that he started to run. When I turned around to see what was going on I discovered that a soldier stood close by pointing at me with his machine gun. I realized that I had no chance to escape because there were soldiers all over the place. They had surrounded my house. The colonel approached me and asked who had escaped. "He is my neighbor," I said. "Why did he run?" the colonel asked. "I don't know," I answered, "maybe he got scared." "Where is your family?" "My family is at the riverbank taking care of our milpa. We have to protect our corn now, because lately thieves have been around stealing corn. We don't want to loose our food," I said. That was not true. My family hid in the jungle, my wife with my four children. "If you want we can go and find them," I said. I thought that if we reached the riverbank I could throw myself into the river and in this way escape, alive or dead. I was convinced that they were going to kill me. They believed that I was a guerrilla; therefore they did not kill me immediately.

Sons of a bitch the guerrillas!! They had nailed a placard on a tree close to the entrance of my house where they had written "Viva EGP!" (Long live EGP!) I had not seen this placard; if I had seen it I would have taken it down immediately. Obviously the soldiers thought that I was a guerrilla when they saw that placard and they had come to punish me. They could not punish the real guerrillas because they had hidden safely in the jungle. These people (referring to the guerrillas) are really cabrones (sons of a bitch).[7] I think that the guerrilla showed great irresponsibility. When they realized what the army was doing to the people without being able to defend us, they should have withdrawn. They are cabrones! Those who suffered were the innocent people; the majority of the guerrillas saved themselves. . . .

The soldiers, sons of a bitch, destroyed everything on my site. They punctured my iron sheets. They destroyed the fruit trees, the plants, they killed my animals and burned the house; nothing was left. Finally, they took me to the military base in Playa Grande. On our way, they captured other people too; we were five in the end. For more than two months I was a prisoner in the military camp, but that is a long story that I will tell you another day. My wife managed to get safely to my brother's who lived in Flor de Todos Santos, one of the INTA cooperatives.

Caught in the Crossfire

With the escalation of violence people could not feel safe anywhere. They had to be prepared to leave their homes to hide in the jungle any time the army turned up. That is how they saved their lives. Gradually, the settlers developed a warning system, passing information from one neighbor to the other about the movement of the army. In some cases the guerrillas also contributed in keeping them informed. To be discovered while hiding in the jungle was, however, extremely dangerous, and many of my informants lost family members in such situations. Those who did not manage to escape were usually killed without mercy. In the following section Candelaria, the Q'anjob'al woman from Mayalán, gives us a glimpse of what it meant to live with the permanent threat of armed persecution.

Our farmland was located about one hour's walk from the center of the cooperative. We had a site in the center, too, but we preferred to live on our land. When the violence came we were well prepared. We knew the surroundings and where to hide. I am a clever woman. By the time the violence came I had already hidden two quintals of totoposte. Totoposte is made of sun-dried tortillas ground into fine flour—if you mix it with water you can make porridge or a soup. The advantage of totoposte compared to tortillas is that is can be stored for a long time without spoiling. When the violence arrived, I had six children. My firstborn Juan was ten years old. Catarina, the youngest, was only one year and six months. Several times we had to hide in the jungle. When we heard that the enemy was in the area, we took no chances, we hid until we were sure that they had left the area again.

On the day that I will tell you about, my husband was not at home. A neighbor came to inform us that some 300 soldiers were less than two kilometers away, heading toward where we lived. We had to leave immediately without bringing anything. This happened at eleven o'clock in the morning, I was preparing lunch. I knew that we could not get very far because Juan had to carry his small brother of two and a half years, since I had to carry the baby, some "nailon," and a couple of "cortes" to protect ourselves against the rain.[8] When the fights between the soldiers and the guerrilla started, we took shelter under a big tree. Fortunately they did not strike the place where we were hiding, nor did they see us. When the shooting finally stopped we hurried away down a small path in the jungle. I had not seen it before and did not know where it would take us. In the late afternoon we arrived at an opening in the jungle where they had planted milpa. Close by there was a house under construction, they had raised the walls, but there was no roof. It was getting dark and I decided to stay in that house for the night. I was terribly worried about my children. They had not eaten during the whole day and I had no food to give them. I was so afraid that they would start crying or otherwise make noise. Juan helped me to make a roof with the "nailon"; I put the "cortes" on the ground where the children lay down. They were so exhausted—the poor things—that they fell asleep immediately. I could not sleep for a single moment.

At dawn I heard the crowing of a rooster and dogs barking not very far away. I got up carefully not to wake up my children. I wanted to see if I could find people and something to eat. The path ascended a hill. From there I could look down on an opening in the jungle. I saw a woman who was cooking on an open fire. I called to her, but when she saw me she ran into the jungle. I suppose that she was afraid of the enemy, too. After a little while I heard men's voices, they asked what I wanted and I told them. Then I returned to pick up my children. They were awake and terribly scared when they realized that I was not there, but they were not crying.

We were well received by the people; they gave us food and water to drink. They were also hiding from the enemy. I was terribly worried about my husband. I did not know whether he was dead or alive and I wanted to return to my home to try to find out. I left the children with the refugees and returned home. There I was met by a very sad view. My house was burned down, so was the milpa, the fruit trees, and all the rest—there was nothing left. When I returned to where my children were, my husband had turned up. He was very happy to find the children, but worried about me when he heard that I had returned home. He knew that the soldiers had burned our home and that they were still in that area. Therefore, he was relieved when I returned safely.

Like many of the other settlers Candelaria and her family hid in the jungle of Ixcán for about a year after their home had been burnt down, reluctant to give up their hardwon parcel.

Violence and Terror in Zona Reina

The repression in Zona Reina was perhaps even worse than in the cooperatives in Ixcán Grande. The area was very isolated due to difficult access. The majority of inhabitants were Q'eqchi's, many of whom came from extremely exploitative conditions on the *fincas* in Uspantán, and had very limited or no knowledge of Spanish. In addition, church activities and cooperative development were just getting started, making people more vulnerable to the circumstances. Domingo, forty-two, a Q'eqchi' who used to live on a smallholding on national land close to Santa Maria Dolores, was one of the migrants from the *fincas* in Uspantán, El Quiché. He relates his experience with the escalation of violence in his area:

When the violence started none of us could speak Castilla, nor could we read or write. At first we did not understand what happened. Some of the people who went to the pueblo (Santa Maria) to sell and buy did not return. There was a bridge over the Copón River people had to pass to go to the pueblo. There was a military detachment close by. It was at that bridge that people disappeared. We also had a military commissioner. One day, I had to go to the pueblo to sell a piglet. When I approached the bridge the lieutenant asked for my ID card. He took it and went to check in a book. He did not find my name. "Anda a la chingada!" he screamed at me. "Go to hell!" I got so scared that I decided to return home with my piglet.

A woman, whose husband was violent and used to beat her up, registered a complaint against him to the detachment after such an incident. The soldiers came to the man's house, dragged him outside, and killed him. We also had cases where people, out of resentment, jealousy, or envy, reported others for being guerrilleros. During the night the soldiers arrived, took them out of their beds, killed them, and left them on the road. They dropped the dead bodies away from the houses where the victims used to live, giving the impression that they had been out during the night. After that we got afraid of walking along the roads.

One Friday, it was market day; the soldiers arrived and captured seven people. There was a local de baile (a kind of closed dancing hall) in the hamlet where the prisoners were shut up. One of them managed to escape during the night, the other six stayed until daybreak when the soldiers took them, with their hands tied behind their backs, to a hill outside the hamlet, where they cut off their heads. An old man happened to pass by. The soldiers grabbed him and put him face down on the ground, telling him not to move. He could only hear what was going on (Solo su oído sabe lo que está pasando). He waited a long while before he dared to lift his head to figure out what had happened. Then the soldiers were gone, only the dead prisoners were there, their heads and bodies spread around. The old man hurried to the village to tell what he had witnessed and some people went to see if it was true. They found the six persons as the old man had told them. Suddenly, the guerrilleros came out from the bushes. "We will defend you," they said, "we don't kill you, the soldiers kill you. We will be in a certain place," they mentioned the name of the place, "and if you let us know we will come and defend you when the army arrives." But the guerrillas were not able to defend us, we were many people and they were very few without the means to defend us. When we realized that we could not stand it any longer, we hid in the jungle. For some time we stayed in a camp in the jungle. The soldiers found us and killed between 60 and 70 persons, the majority women and children. They could not escape. But we were many, some 800 persons, so most of us survived. But we had to move, people were on the move all the time; the army behind us. The second time we were surprised by the army more people were killed, and we decided to start walking toward the Mexican border. It was quite far and we took almost a year to reach the border. We had no food, only fruit and other things that we collected in the jungle. We were scared of the Mexicans as well; the guerrillas told us that they were going to kill us. The guerrilleros were around all the time. They wanted to recruit young people, but they did not have weapons. Finally 80 young men decided to join them. We went to the EGP and requested arms. "Give us arms and we will defend ourselves," we said. But they did not have arms. Finally, we were so desperate that we decided to cross the border (mid-1982).

Abelardo, thirty-five, also a Q'eqchi,' was a young boy when the violence obliged him and his family to leave Guatemala. He lived at a *finca* near San Antonio Tzejá, Zona Reina, where his grandfather was a foreman.

The owner gave us a piece of land and we had to pay rent in labor. There was no school in this finca. The landowner rejected the offer from the government to pay a teacher for the children of his workers to attend. We were between 60 and 70 families so you can imagine that there were lots of children. My father died of illness when I was three or four years old. Then my mother became a widow with two children, my brother Pablo and I. We also had a sister but she died from measles. We lived with my grandparents when the problems started. I was thirteen by then. The military raised a detachment in the finca and after that the killings started. Accidental killings it seemed to us. Some were killed when they returned from their milpas; others were taken out of their houses at night and killed. The guerrilla passed through the area and appeared at the finca from time to time. They wanted us to organize, but we were afraid of them, because they always brought problems. That is why the army started to kill innocent people, I think.

One day we went to make molasses in my uncle's house. Following Q'eqchi' customs many people were around to help. Around three o'clock, when we were resting outside the house, the soldiers took us by surprise. They shot my grandfather in his head and chest and he died immediately. My uncles, my brother, and I managed to escape, while all the women, who were inside the house, were kidnapped. My grandmother was killed later; my aunt and her two daughters were released after having been captives for several months in one of the detachments in the area. We were told that they had been raped many times, by different men. I have heard that they now live with Amelia's father in Ixcán. Many years passed before we heard what had happened to them. Now my uncle is married to another woman.

After my grandfather was killed we hid in the jungle. EGP supported us. They kept guard and informed us about the movement of the army. We moved from one place to another in the jungle, it was terrible. Sometimes we had no food and lots of people, especially women and children, died from illness and malnutrition. In the beginning, EGP tried to prevent people from leaving the area, they threatened those who wanted to leave. Afterward the situation was so unbearable that they helped people find the border. The guerrilleros were armed, but they had no good arms, only old rifles. When we crossed the Mexican border in Boca de Chajúl at the start of 1983, the organizations were there to receive us.

The Massacre in Cuarto Pueblo

The massacre in Cuarto Pueblo holds a special place in the history of violence in Ixcán, perhaps due to the large number of people killed, the level of cruelty that characterizes this massacre and, the relatively detailed documentation available (Falla 1992: 62–103). This massacre started on March 14, 1982, when the army surrounded the village preventing people from escaping. During three days, 324 people were killed. This massacre was part of the scorched-earth campaign in Ixcán, which had been initiated a month earlier in Zona Reina. (Parts of Domingo's and Abelardo's narratives above refer to the massacres in Zona Reina.)

When the scorched-earth campaign was launched in Chimaltenango in November 1981, the army withdrew from all the detachments in Ixcán. This was partly because the armed forces were needed in other parts of the country, partly as a preparatory maneuver for the next phase in the counterinsurgency war. The peasants in the Ixcán Grande cooperatives were much relieved by this, and many of them believed that they would finally be left in peace. During the absence of the army, the insurgents sabotaged several military outposts and airstrips, including the ones in Cuatro Pueblo, in some cases with the participation of settlers who were tired of controls, abductions, and killings of innocent people.

Nicolás, forty-nine, a Q'anjob'al from Santa Eulalia (Huehuetenango), used to live in Cuarto Pueblo, where he had become an active member of the cooperative. He had also received some courses in health care and when the health promoter was killed by the army he helped in the health post. According to Nicolás it was not by accident that Cuarto Pueblo was so hard hit by the army. The guerrilla presence was strong in this area and the EGP had attacked the military base and the reprisals were very hard on the villagers.

As a member of the auditing committee of the cooperative, I had to spend a couple of days at the end of each month to keep the accounts. By the end of April that year (1981) I had to go and do my monthly duty at the cooperative. This was exactly the time when EGP attacked the military detachment. Fortunately, God saved me. My obligation was to go and keep the accounts in the cooperative, and up to that point I had always been faithful to my duties. This time a thought struck me that I should not go, I was convinced that I should not go, and I did not. I woke up the last day of the month and I decided to weed my cardamom, instead of going to the center. Tomorrow at five o'clock in the morning I will be there, I thought, today I remain here. In this way I escaped my certain death. That same night, at five o'clock in the morning the guerrilla attacked. The attack lasted for two and a half hours. Then, two helicopters and two planes arrived with more forces. The members of the auditing committee stayed in the cooperative offices. They did not worry because the military commissioner had told them that if they had their ID cards with them there was nothing to worry about. At nine o'clock in the morning the army started to capture people. Marco, one of the local catechists, was accused of being a guerrilla. They killed him. Eighteen persons were captured. The soldiers dressed them in guerrilla uniforms, put them in line, and shot them. My fellow committee members were among them. Thanks to my thoughts, I was saved. I got to know about this event when I returned from my cardamom field in the afternoon and met the military commissioner of my group, who was my closest neighbor. He had just returned from the center. He told me what had happened. The army remained between two and three months in the area, and then it withdrew. The military said nothing about what was going to happen. Once the army had withdrawn the guerrilla appeared trying to recruit people. They distributed flyers and visited the farms. This led to a new wave of kidnappings and executions, but it was not until 1982 that they started to massacre people. . . .

The massacre in Cuarto Pueblo started on March 14, 1982. It was a Sunday, the day when most cooperative members would go to the market. I had become a health promoter at that point—I had started to learn about medicine in 1977. I had agreed to replace the previous promoter, who had been killed by the army. This morning I was there with my friend Juan. "Why don't we take separate turns?" he said, "because I would like to attend mass in the evangelical church." I agreed, he left, and I stayed attending patients. I had brought a small load of cardamom to sell in the marketplace. At one point when there were no patients around, I closed the clinic to go and sell my cardamom. On my way I met a friend who told me that he had heard rumors that somebody had seen the army crossing the Xalbal River. "Why don't you go and find out," I said. He went to talk to a man who stood close by and returned quickly. "He says that the army will surround the village," he said. "Let's go, soon they will be here." "No," I said, "first I will sell my cardamom." I went to the marketplace. I was not afraid. At one point I realized that people were starting to scatter, like when a wolf enters a flock of sheep. "What is happening to these people," I asked. I was not afraid at all. All of a sudden somebody in the market started to scream. "SOLDADOS!!"

When I turned around I saw files of soldiers entering the airstrip. "Let's run," I said to my friend. When we reached the last house at the market they started to shoot. Not only from the center did they shoot, but also from the hills around the village. "Why run," I thought, "they will kill me." Then I thought, it is better that they kill me with bullets than that they capture me alive, who knows how they will kill me then, it is better to run; and we ran. In this way we saved ourselves, we ran among bullets, but we survived.

We ran some fifteen minutes before we dared to stop. We were then in the jungle and sat down to talk about what would happen to those who did not manage to escape. "They will kill them, I am sure," my friend said. "My brothers," I said, "they came with me to the center, I am sure they remained behind." We decided to go to our homes and meet again at five o'clock in the afternoon. When I returned home we gathered some blankets and other things that I had hidden for situations of urgency. Then we met with several neighbor families and decided to hide in the jungle until we knew more about what was going to happen.

The army remained in Cuarto Pueblo for a number of days, killing all the people that they had surrounded. We decided to stay in the jungle until we knew what the army was going to do next. We started to organize in order to determine what to do if the army started to search for us in the jungle. After two weeks, when the army had withdrawn, we went to the center to see what they had done.

They had burned everything, only the school building that was under construction had been saved. Not one single house remained. There used to be many buildings in Cuarto Pueblo, those at the market, the cooperative and the churches. . . . There were two churches, the Centroamericana and the Catholic that was still under construction. The Catholic church was located on a hilltop. When I passed by I heard somebody call me. I could not answer, I ran so fast. The Catholics had recently been renewed to become charismatic. [9] Those who had converted had a strong belief in the power of God. I think they were convinced that he would protect and save them. That's why they remained in the church in spite of having the opportunity to escape. Since the church building was somewhat withdrawn from the center, the congregation could have fled before the soldiers reached them. This was not the case of the evangelicals. The soldiers surrounded their church immediately and they had no chance to run away. They shut the door and all of them were burned alive. When we arrived their bones were still there—some of them with flesh. . . . Lots of people were burned alive in the cooperative shop as well. There at least they had tried to bury the bodies in some pits dug in the patio, but the pits were so shallow that the animals had managed to reach them. . . . Lots of people were burned there too!

We also went to Nueva Resurrección; this is a hamlet close to Cuarto Pueblo where Don Diego's father used to live. His relatives were also burned alive, eighteen people in the house, only one boy survived. We only found bones in the ruins of his house. In one of the other houses we found a woman whose body had not burned completely. We could see that her throat had been slit. We only went to have a look, we did not dare to bury the bones or anything; we were too scared.

The army also killed my grandfather on its way to the Xalbal cooperative. He was caught on the path returning from his milpa. They dragged him some two or three hundred meters. Then they killed him and left the body on the path. When my grandmother found out what had happened to my grandfather she decided to hide in the jungle. She escaped with my aunt, her husband, and their children. One day they were taken by surprise by the army. My uncle managed to escape with two children. The others were kidnapped. We don't know what happened to them. I heard that my aunt was taken to the military base at Playa Grande. I also heard that her son went to the base and found her there. Then she was the woman of every officer who passed through. Her son was also a refugee in Mexico, but when I tried to find him to verify this incident he had already joined the CPR (Communities of People in Resistance), and it was impossible. Of my grandmother and the others who were captured with her, we know nothing.

After the massacre the guerrilla tried to support us, but there was not much they could do, only inform us about the movements of the army. They had no weapons—or at least very few—to defend us. They always pretended that they were much stronger then they actually were. When we realized that the army continued their campaign of the scorched earth in the jungle, we decided to leave Guatemala; that was in October 1982.

Due to the unrest in the region during the weeks before the massacre in Cuarto Pueblo, many women had remained at home this particular Sunday, together with their children. Normally the whole family would go to the center to attend mass, make purchases in the market, or simply meet relatives, friends, or neighbors. Dominga, a Mam woman of fifty-eight was one of those who remained home the Sunday of the massacre.

The day of the massacre was a Sunday and a market day. Normally all of us used to go to the market, but that Sunday my husband insisted on going alone. He said he felt that something bad was going to happen. I remained at home. We lived so close to the center that we could hear the shooting and the screaming of people and we could see the smoke from the burning houses. They will kill everybody, I thought. I was scared. Without eating I went to the mountains with my five children. Raúl, the oldest one, was twelve, Elisa six, and the others four, two, and my youngest was only 20 days old, you can imagine the situation. . . . My husband did not turn up until the next evening. I had been convinced he was dead. My husband told me that he had been at the marketplace when the army surrounded the center and started killing people. He managed to escape, running and crawling among the dead bodies until he was safe. I don't know exactly what happened to him until he found us, but when he arrived he was in very bad shape. He fell ill after that, he almost died from fear. His face swelled, he had harsh pains in his eyes and ears. I cured him with hierbaespanta, an herb that is used to cure susto.[10] The swelling disappeared but he lost an eye.

We stayed in Guatemala for more or less one year after the massacre, hiding in the jungle. We did not want to leave because we were afraid of losing our land. At the end, we could not abide the suffering any longer. We had little or no food, the army was after us all of the time, and we were too scared to sleep at night. Then we decided to cross the border and we arrived in Chajúl in Chiapas.

The Armed Conflict in the Petén

The cooperatives of the Petén suffered much the same type of repression as described for Ixcán. The Petén was the area of influence of the FAR guerrilla, and there was strong repression against those suspected of supporting them. However, the scorched-earth campaign was not implemented systematically in the Petén, even though the army exterminated several communities.[11] Persecution was generally more selective, directed at villages and persons accused of supporting the guerrilla movement. Because the cooperatives were located on the Usumacinta riverbank marking the Mexican/Guatemalan border, people could more easily leave the country. They were quite familiar with places and people on the other side, because most commercial relations were with Mexico. Unlike what happened in Ixcán, where the villages were emptied completely, we commonly find a selective abandonment in the Petén. Only those accused of supporting the guerrilla abandoned their communities; the others chose to remain and often became the objects of vigilance and harassment by the army. This often created antagonistic attitudes toward those who left; the refugees were seen as a major cause of many of the hardships endured during the 1980s and early 1990s.

Juan, fifty-four, is one of those who fled from the Petén. He was born in Camotán Chiquimula, in the eastern part of the country. He arrived in the Petén in the mid-1970s and settled in the Centro Campesino cooperative.

We were around 60 families who came together. The plan was to recruit 200 families, to have one caballería (111.36 acres) per family. The land was handed over to us little by little until we reached our caballería. Padre Hugo (Bruyère) obtained financial support from abroad. This was used to buy equipment. We had a caterpillar, a tractor, and even a sawmill. We lost all of it during the violence. The army took most of it. The things they did not take, they destroyed.

The problems in our cooperative started in 1982. By then there had been problems in several other cooperatives. The army had been present in the area for some time and they showed up in the village from time to time, but before 1982 they did not do much harm. In 1982 they turned up in the middle of the night and ordered everybody to gather immediately at the football field. There they told us that they were not going to punish us this time, but if they found something out about any of us, they would kill everybody. This happened twice, and we became very frightened. Our fear was also fomented by the stories we heard from other communities. For example, we had been told that on various occasions the army brought hooded men to such gatherings. The men pointed out persons who supposedly collaborated with the guerrilla, and these poor people were separated and shot in front of everybody. On February 13, 1983, a man from a neighboring community came to tell us that the army would arrive the following morning. We organized a meeting to discuss what to do, whether we should leave or stay. The majority wanted to remain. Since we had nothing to do with the guerrilla they believed that the army would not do them any harm. Some of us did not agree. We argued that the army does not behave like that; they may kill anybody. The others did not believe us. Therefore, only seventeen families decided to leave, among them Alfredo, Ramón, and myself.

The army tried to kill Padre Hugo too. That happened on the day of the massacre in Los Arbolitos.[12] He was approaching the village with another person in a speedboat, when he realized that there were soldiers at the riverbank. He turned around and managed to escape the burst of the machinegun fire. He fled to Mexico.

The day we left, the army turned up in the community. When they found out that we were gone they started to interrogate people, trying to find out if we were guerrilleros, why we had left and not they, and things like that. My brother who had decided to remain was obliged to accompany the soldiers for three days searching for people in the jungle. They believed that he knew about people hiding there. Finally they let him go. Those who remained in Guatemala suffered more than us, I think. After we left they were removed to a camp in Bethel (a neighboring village with an army detachment), where they were locked up for one month. After that they were resettled in a place close to San Andrés (central part of the Petén). Like us, they were not able to bring many of their belongings; the army did not allow them to. Therefore, they had a rough time and they blame us. They believe that we caused their suffering, if we had decided to stay, the army would have left us in peace, they said. I don't think so, just look at what happened in some of the other cooperatives!

Informants who had fled from other cooperatives in Petén told similar stories. Only a few families had left, fearing accusations of being associated with the guerrilla. The majority decided to stay, suffering military reprisals.

Remaining Under Fire

Don Raúl, who lives in the neighbor community of Retalteco, is one of those who decided to remain in Guatemala. He is very explicit about the impossibility of being neutral when living under crossfire, as well as why he and his neighbors actively opted for an alliance with the army.

Our problems started when somebody denounced us for being supporters (base), not guerrilla supporters, but supporters of the people who left the country. The troops came one night at one o'clock in the morning; everybody was sleeping, because, you know, the one who has nothing to hide has nothing to fear. At daybreak we were besieged by 400 soldiers, during the month of February I think it was—or maybe March. What we did was to gather by the ditch that we had dug ourselves, to ask the military people if we could offer them some help. Instead of assaulting us, the captain started to talk with the people. He realized that the people did not hide. The first detachment was installed at our request. We wanted to protect ourselves against the guerrilla. The guerrilla killed eight people in our village, accusing them of being spies. They came for me, too, a couple of times, but fortunately I was not at home. I was the "alcalde auxiliar." We had serious problems. We did not agree with any of the two bands, we wanted to live in peace, but it was impossible because both bands had spies in the village. When the army arrived, we requested a detachment. The detachment remained for two years. During this period the guerrilla destroyed, among other things, the machines to make and repair the roads. We had to walk some twenty kilometers to Palestina (a village located by the main road) to reach the means of transport to get out of here. We were caught between the two bands and we had to choose. You should see them! (the guerrilla.) Sometimes they arrived in quantities (en cantidad)—some one hundred people altogether, men, women, and children, dressed in camouflage, what a shame! Women and youth, you can imagine, dirty, smelling bad and their faces full of pimples! How could they fancy that we were going to support them! And now, you see, the returnees receive a lot of support; we get nothing. Everything that you see around here we have made with our own efforts.

Don Raúl takes for granted that those who left the country were guerrilla supporters; according to him, they had something to hide.

Subversives Against Their Will

From what the informants relate, there is no doubt that the blood shed by the army was disproportionate to that shed by the rebel forces. Nor is there any doubt that the peasants were captured and killed without sufficient proof of their "subversion," or without a warrant of arrest of any kind. The settlers certainly had contact with the guerrilla; it was inevitable, the insurgents operated in their area. They turned up at their fields and at their homes, in their villages, and along the paths that connected their homes with the fields and the cooperative centers, agitating for the war of the poor. And my informants confirmed what has been documented by Payeras and others, that the message of the war of the poor did not awake much enthusiasm (Payeras 1983; Colom 1998). We have seen that after two years in Ixcán the EGP had only recruited one new member. This is not surprising for people who knew the settler areas. The settlers, who for the first time in their lives had access to land, and a generous portion of land it was, were more concerned with creating a decent life for themselves, their families, and their communities, than with struggling for access to land for all the poor, overthrowing the government, and instituting a new society based on popular rule, which was the agenda of the guerrilla movement.

A number of my informants who used to live in Ixcán associate the beginning of the violence with the assassination of the "Tiger of Ixcán" in 1975. This was the first important EGP action after its change of military strategy, the passage from "implantation" to "armed propaganda." From now on the army presence became more permanent and the persecution and repression of the civilian population more visible. Even though this created an atmosphere of terror and fear, most people did not believe it could happen to them, since they had not been involved in anything that they considered subversive. They liked to think that those who were abducted or killed had been involved in "something."

The increase of guerrilla actions in the late 1970s created a need in the army to demonstrate results of its counterinsurgency strategies. Since the army had not much success in preventing guerrilla actions or detaining the guerrillas who, after their actions, retired in the dense jungle, re-prisals were directed arbitrarily at the local peasants accused of being subversives. Gradually the peasants realized the arbitrariness of the use of violence. The mere fact that they were living in an area of operation of EGP was enough to be treated as a subversive. As we have seen from the narratives, meeting a group of soldiers on the way to the pueblo or back from the *milpa* could be enough to be killed or not, depending ap-parently on very accidental circumstances. Before the massacre in Cuarto Pueblo, in spite of the high level of violence, people did not foresee or imagine that the army was able to kill people and destroy villages and fields the way they did. Many people still believed that having "nothing to hide," having their identification documents in order, and behaving with caution would keep them safe. After this massacre they knew that they had to escape army soldiers at any price; the army had become their most dangerous enemy.

The escalation of violence in Ixcán favored recruitment to the EGP ranks, as noted by Payeras (1983: 79). However, as we shall see in more detail in the next chapter, those joining the insurgents were not motivated by the ideological program professed by the guerrilla, which in most cases had no relevance to those who joined. They were, rather, motivated by an urge to defend themselves or revenge their dead or abducted kin. With hindsight, some EGP leaders also recognize what Colom (1998) refers to as "an underestimation of the range and intensity of the repression against the civil population." Some of my informants would say that the guerrillas were well informed about the consequences of the armed propaganda for the civilians, and were willing to sacrifice them. In their view it was a calculated part of the guerrilla's military strategy.

From the narratives of my informants who used to live in cooperatives in Western Petén, defined by the army as "pink" areas, where only a num-ber of identified villagers were defined as subversives to be exterminated, we see that repression was more targeted and selective. The majority of those who fled Petén were lucky to live on the shores of the Usumacinta River, forming the border with Mexico, because they could easily cross the river and be safe. However, by leaving the country they were defined as subversives by the army as well as by their neighbors, even though most of them maintained that they had nothing to do with the FAR. Those who stayed suffered severe military control and even deportation away from their homes in the border area, and developed a strong resentment towards those who left and thus had "caused their misery." This made it impossible for the refugees to return to their old communities.

Chapter 4

Witnesses, Victims, and Perpetrators of Violence

When the information about the massacre in Cuarto Pueblo spread to the other villages of Ixcán, people started to abandon their homes. Some immediately fled the country, crossing the border to Mexico. The majority, however, stayed in the region for shorter or longer periods, hiding in the jungle. There were several reasons for this. First and foremost, people were reluctant to leave the land they had struggled so much to obtain and make productive. They hoped that once the army had "passed through" the populated areas, it would withdraw. This hope was fomented by the guerrilla, who told them that they were winning the war in other parts of the country and that they would soon put an end to the violence. A number of informants also related that the guerrilla actively tried to prevent them from leaving the country by telling them that the Mexican migration authorities were deporting people, handing them over to the Guatemalan army, who, in turn, would kill them, something that certainly happened in some cases during the earlier phases of the refugee exodus (Aguayo 1985: 91–94; Fagan 1983: 179, Kauffer 1997: 95). Finally, those who lived far from the border did not know how to reach the border and were afraid of crossing the jungle. This was particularly the case for the Q'eqchi' settlers, who used to live in Zona Reina at the foothills of the Cuchumatanes Mountains.

Lost in the Jungle

There was, however, no quick end to the violence. Once the villages were destroyed and emptied, the army started to search the jungle. People managed to group and reestablish a certain form of organization in order to subsist in their hiding places and to prevent the military from attacking. But in spite of having established their system of vigilance, many people were surprised and killed by ground troops or by bombs dropped by the air force. In these cases, the army killed without mercy and in the most gruesome way. Women, children, and old people were the hardest hit in these ambushes. They often remained in the provisional camps while the men went out to search for food and keep watch and did not manage to escape. People speak of the guerrilla approaching them regularly during this period; they would inform them about the movement of the army and try to recruit people to join their ranks. Mostly young unmarried men accepted, as we shall see in more detail later.[1] However, several of those who were married with families at the time describe how they approached the insurgents with the idea of becoming guerrillas to be able to defend themselves and their families, but when they realized how few and badly equipped they were, they changed their minds.

The army was not the only menace faced by the fugitives. Due to the extreme living conditions, scarcity of food, clean water, appropriate shelter, and medicines, and living under intense psychological stress, many people fell ill and died. In what follows, some of my informants describe what happened to them and their neighbors during the period of internal refuge.

Mario, sixty, and his family lived in the jungle some six months before crossing the border to Mexico. They were among the lucky ones; all of them survived the hardships and arrived safely.

Even though the army had destroyed everything—burned our houses, our milpas, killed our animals—we did not want to leave. We hoped that the army sooner or later would go away and that we could return to our land. At first we had some corn; we found some abandoned milpas that had not been destroyed. The women could not sleep at night; they had to tortear (make tortillas) because we did not dare to make fire during the day. When we had corn they made tortillas and dried them so we could have food for a while. We also gathered roots and fruits in the jungle, pacayas for example—there were lots of them. We ate them with salt and chili. At the end we could not endure it any longer, the army was everywhere and we had almost no food. We could not rest, we could not sleep, and we were hungry all of the time. People started to fall ill and die, especially children and old people; many would remain forever in those mountains. We realized that we had to reach the border if we wanted to survive and we decided to leave.

The mother of Faustina—a thirty-year-old Q'eqchi' woman—was one of those who remained forever in Ixcán.

My mother fell ill, "se secó y se murió" (she dried up and died). Things were so terrible that we had no choice but to leave, and we were on our way to Mexico. But we did not arrive in time to save my mom. She died in my father's arms there on the path in the mountains and we had to leave her. We remained on the path alone, while my father carried my mom into the jungle to bury her. "Stay here," he said to me, "take good care of the small ones." I had four sisters and brothers. "I'll return as soon as I can." We stayed there alone, it seemed like an eternity. Finally, my father came back, alone, and we continued our walk toward the border.

Simón, a Mam in his early fifties and one of my close neighbors at La Quetzal, was always hospitable and friendly when we met, but not very talkative regarding the past. One day when we were sitting together outside his house he asked me about my family. I told him, and at the end I asked him if he had sisters and brothers. "We were six," he said, "now we are only two left, my brother Mariano and myself, all the others died." When I asked him what happened he told me the following story:

I came too late to get land in the cooperatives in Ixcán Grande. I got land in Samaritán, not far from the cooperative of Mayalán. This land had been purchased by a gringo reverend—I think he was an evangelical. At least he did not belong to Padre Guillermo's church. I don't remember his name. When the violence came I was married with one child, my daughter who now lives in Mexico. We managed to escape, hiding in the jungle, but the army found us and I lost three sisters and one brother, two of my sisters were killed by the army, one died after we arrived in Mexico. My two sisters were killed when we were hiding in the jungle. The soldiers captured and killed them with machetes; they made mincemeat of their heads and bodies. At that point they did not find my brother, who was hiding close by. He was captured later when he returned to his house to pick up the chicken he had left behind when he had run off in a hurry. When he arrived home the soldiers were waiting for him. He was taken by surprise, and had no chance to escape. They killed him. Afterward they took off his clothes and hung him naked upside down in a tree with his legs spread, so the vultures could eat him. One of his neighbors told me that when he passed by the house a few days later only his skeleton was left. Now only my brother Mariano and I are left in this world. Mariano returned to Ixcán to recover his land in Pueblo Nuevo. Other people had occupied mine. I did not want to return to Ixcán anyway—I was afraid.

A few days later Simón's nephew Miguel told me more details about the family, among other things, what happened to Simón's brother Mariano who survived the violence and later returned to his land in Pueblo Nuevo.

My uncle Mariano and his family were attacked while hiding in the jungle. Those who kept guard discovered that the military was approaching and informed the people in the camp. People started to gather their things to run away. My uncle had climbed a hill to watch the movements of the soldiers. The guards had not realized how close they were. All of a sudden the soldiers entered the camp from three sides. Some people managed to escape, others did not. Among them were my aunt and her four small children, one of them she carried on her back. The others screamed to her that she must run, but she stayed, petrified with her children around her—she did not move at all. One soldier approached her and with his machete he cut off her face, including her nose, a bloody pulp hanging down on her chest. Before they killed her, they shot the baby on her back, a bullet though his head blowing his scalp off. My other aunt was also shot in her head. All this happened while the other children were clinging to their mother. Afterward the children were killed. We don't know how they were killed, because when this happened, those who survived had left. The children had no visible marks on their bodies. That was what we were told by those who found them the next morning. These people had been hiding in the jungle until the soldiers withdrew and when they returned to the camp they found my aunts and the children lying in a row on the ground covered by a nailon (plastic sheet).

My uncle survived, but he lost his whole family, wife and four children. He came to Mexico and stayed with us for a while, but he was very sad and could not forget what had happened to his family. After a few months he decided to join EGP to get revenge. This was by mid-1983. He felt that he had nothing to live for any longer. My uncle stayed three and a half years in EGP before he deserted and settled in a camp in Quintana. During these years he killed and injured all the military he could get, at least that is what he told us. Now he lives in Pueblo Nuevo (Ixcán Grande) with his new wife and two children.

Benancio, fifty-two, is a Q'eqchi' who used to live close to Rosario Canijá (Zona Reina). In early 1982 when *la violencia* arrived, he was the father of ten, and his wife was pregnant with their eleventh child. When they realized that the army was bombing their neighbor village, they decided to leave their home and hide in the jungle. For several months they moved around trying to escape the ground troops and waiting for the army to withdraw so they could return to their land. Benancio, who is a man of few words, gave the following description about what happened to his family:

The army treated us very well, maybe because the guerrilla never appeared in the area where we lived. We had occupied land on a finca, the land had an owner; it was not a cooperative or anything. We were about 60 families. The army came to see us, Colonel Castillo and his troops. "This land has an owner," the colonel said, "but he lives close to Guatemala City and never comes here," and he let us stay. We had heard that the army was burning villages and killing people, but not until they bombed Santa Maria Dolores (a neighboring village), burned everything, and killed lots of people, did we decide to abandon our homes and hide in the mountains. One day we were surprised by the army.

They killed forty-five persons, among them my oldest children Lionza (20), Isabel (18), and Angela (17) they had no chance to escape. Pablo, David, Domingo, Nazaria, and Maria died afterward, I think they died of susto (fright), but we had very little food too. My wife gave birth to a little girl. The delivery went well, but the poor girl died after a few days because my wife had no milk in her, I think she died of hunger, the poor thing.

When Benancio arrived in Mexico, the aid organizations were already there to receive them.

My poor wife died after only one week in Mexico. Her body was so swollen that she could not walk, la pobre (poor thing). I was also very ill, but I recovered gradually. Only my son Diego and my daughter Delia remained with me. They were taken care of by the nuns, they gave them food and medicine, and little by little my children recovered as well.

People like Benancio who used to live in Zona Reina suffered the greatest losses. Like the settlers in other parts of the region, they were reluctant to leave the land that they had acquired with great sacrifice. Add to that the distance and difficult access to the border and the insecurity due to lack of reliable information about what was going on the Mexican side. In contrast to those who lived in Ixcán Grande, closer to the border and with contacts on the other side, their only source of information was the guerrillas, who tried to dissuade people from leaving the country, as a means to expand their ranks and also to increase civilian resistance to military repression.

Nearly all my informants from Zona Reina who survived the first phase of the scorched-earth campaign in their villages suffered army ambushes and subsequent massacres when hiding in the jungle. The number of people who died from *susto* and illnesses during this internal flight and long march toward the border is also much higher among them than among those who lived closer to the border.

By the end of 1983, when a group of old cooperative members organized what later became known as the CPR-Ixcán (one of the Communities of People in Resistance), most people from this region had crossed the Mexican border and become refugees. The CPRs remained clandestine in Ixcán until 1991–92, when the situation started to change (CIDH 1993; Sosa 2001).

Surviving in the Community of People in Resistance

Gregorio is one of the few residents in La Quetzal who did not live in Ixcán or the Petén before going into exile. He and his family used to live in a hamlet in the municipality of Nebaj. They managed to flee to the nearby mountains when the army entered and burned their village. Most of their close kin were killed. Gregorio and his family spent almost ten years in the CPR de la Sierra, located in the Ixil area of El Quiché. Before flying to Mexico they spent some time in the CPR-Ixcán. That is why he compares the conditions of the CPR-Sierra with the one in Ixcán.

The first eight years we stayed in the mountains of Salquíl Grande. The guerrilla maintained a kind of big fence around us; we were closed up there. We moved in families. It was not like in Ixcán (referring to the CPRs) where people moved in bigger groups, some forty families, I think. In the Sierra it was not like that, we were spread out. We had no collective production; everything was individual. We could live for some time in one place. We built a hut to protect ourselves against the rain. Then the army discovered our hiding place, they burned it and we had to move to another place. That's how it was. We always used to locate our milpas a good distance from the places where we lived. If the army found our milpas when they patrolled the area with helicopters, they threw bombs and sprinkled the surrounding areas with machine guns. This did not affect our milpas too much. When they arrived by land, though, they destroyed everything. In addition to the corn we planted potatoes, beans, chilecayote, herbs, and chili. Ay, Doña Kristiana, during almost ten years we had no salt. We used chili to give the food some taste. I remember very well a couple of times when we obtained an ounce of salt. The food was so tasty, almost like eating meat.

   My daughter Basilia was born in the mountains. We were attacked by the army on precisely the day she was born. We had to leave our hut where we had been for some time and hide in the mountains. We found a hiding place under a huge rock. We had to crawl in because the cavity was quite low. In the evening my wife's labor started. "What do we do now?" I asked myself. I could not leave her and the children to find a midwife because I did not know the hiding places of other people. I had to help her give birth. I remembered something my mother had told me, when she was still alive. "If you need to help a woman to give birth some day, remember that the umbilical cord should be cut at a distance of three fingers from the navel if it is a girl and four if it is a boy. Once you have measured the distance, you tie a knot and you cut." That is what I did. The problem was, Doña Kristiana, that we had no light. Only by touching my little girl in the dark I managed to measure and cut the cord. (When telling me this he imitated the movements with his hands). Fortunately, the labor did not last very long and the girl came out well. She started to cry and I managed to cut the cord. Afterward I had to wash her. I had only cold water in a clay mug; very cold it was, because the nights can be very cold in these mountains. I poured water in my hand passing it over her little body. In this way I tried to remove the blood from her body the best I could. This was at the end of our stay in the mountains. We had almost no clothes left.

Therefore, we had collected dry leaves to protect her against the cold. I put her on my wife's belly and covered both of them with leaves. In this manner my little girl survived. By dawn I brought the bloodstained clothes of my wife to a river to wash them. Fortunately the day was sunny. I found a place in the forest where the sun entered so that the clothes could dry. The only piece of clothing we had to cover the baby was a piece of a worn-out shirt of mine.

For two days we stayed there under the rock. Then we decided to return to our hut. The military had already been there and burned everything. We had to move to a new place. Fortunately, I had hidden some planks of wood in the forest. I used these planks to construct a roof to protect my family. Following this experience, life became gradually unbearable. Almost every day helicopters passed over the area, calling on the people hiding in the forest. "Señores de Salquíl Grande, surrender! Don't suffer any longer in the mountains! Your parents and siblings are with us, we will give you land to cultivate, iron sheets to construct your house, and food while you wait for the harvest."

A lot of people surrendered during these days. They left during the night; they simply disappeared. We do not know what happened to them. My brother, for example, surrendered and returned to our village. When he arrived there, he discovered that somebody had taken his land. He went to the authorities to claim his land and he was killed. The PAC killed him.[2]

What happened to my brother happened to a number of other villagers too, I was told. They were accused of being guerrilleros and this was a good enough reason to kill them. On many occasions, such accusations were made because of envy or personal resentment. We did not surrender; we were too frightened. The guerrilla distributed pamphlets with information, telling us what would happen to those who surrendered. The guerrilla were our only source of information during our years in the mountains. They continued telling us that they were about to win the war. "The whole country is at war," they said, "and we will soon take the power." At first we believed them, but with the passing of the years we lost our hopes, in spite of their continual assurances that they were winning. They also repeated that if we surrendered, the army would kill us. Since we had no information about what happened to those who surrendered at that point, we thought that this was the case. We were also afraid of the guerrilla, because they threatened those who wanted to leave the area. This was understandable because we knew where people were hiding and where they had their milpas. We had also seen that some of our previous neighbors who disappeared had joined the PACs and returned to kill people in the mountains. I saw it myself. One day I observed a patrol—the members of the patrol always walking first, the soldiers behind. They found a family with five children. All of them were killed and left on the ground to be eaten by animals. Some people were more afraid of the PACs than of the soldiers, because these people had to prove that they did not sympathize with the guerrilla, they committed the cruelest acts, out of fear, maybe?

The army was after us all the time. It was impossible to rest due to the fear. They captured many people. Those who were captured were killed. They used a special method—a bit of nylon rope with a piece of wood at each end. They put the rope around the neck of the prisoner and tightened it little by little turning around the pieces of wood until the person was strangled. They also hung people or killed them with machetes, cutting off their limbs and head while still alive. The worst I think were the rapes of pregnant women, sometimes up to 40 soldiers raped one woman. Lots of people became desperate and surrendered, according to what we heard, most of them were killed. That was what the guerrilla told us. We became more and more desperate, too, but we did not surrender; we decided to leave the area. With two other families we managed to arrive in Villa Amajchél, still in the Sierra, where we stayed for almost two years. There our lives improved a little. We lived in a hamlet and we were able to keep poultry. It was in this hamlet that we sometimes were able to get some salt.

In Villa Amajchél we found out about the existence of the CPR in Ixcán. Here I also found out about the existence of other countries, that there was another country called Mexico and that one had to cross a border to arrive there. Before that I did not know of the existence of other countries; it never occurred to me. Nor did I know much about Guatemala, for example, that there were other languages than those spoken in my region. I remember that I thought about the border, what a border looks like. Is it like a wire fence, is it like a brick wall or maybe it is like a road. I thought like that, I had no idea. Since people had told me that there were guards watching the border I imagined that it must be like a kind of road, because I imagined the guards marching. Afterward when I moved to Ixcán and arrived at the border I realized that there was only a passageway in the jungle where they had cut the trees, Guatemala on one side, Mexico on the other. When we crossed the passageway I realized that there were no differences between Guatemala and Mexico. This first time I crossed the border I only saw Guatemalan refugees. We went to fetch provisions. What about the Mexicans, I thought, how are they, güeros (fair-haired), black, fat or slim, how do they look, I thought to myself. Later, when I moved to Mexico I realized that they were like us, at least the people in Chiapas, they looked like us. There, I also learned that there were a lot of other countries in the world than Guatemala and Mexico. I knew nothing about these things when I lived in Salquíl Grande.

After two years in Amajchél, the army launched a very aggressive offensive. That was what eventually forced us to move to Ixcán. For five days we walked in the jungle guided by people who knew the paths. When we arrived in Ixcán we were well received by the CPR people. The evening we arrived they sent us to different houses. You eat here, you there, and so on. When we had eaten, they gave each family a piece of nylon to make our roof for the night. We slept very well that night—on the ground—we were terribly tired. Moreover, we felt protected there in the middle of these people who had survived in the jungle for a long time. I remember very well when I woke up the next morning and realized that we were surrounded by unknown people speaking languages that I had never heard before. It was strange, but they received us very well. That same day they gave us some clothes. I received pants and a shirt, my wife received a dress, and my children also received clothes. We had no clothes left ourselves, only rags. In Ixcán we started to eat salt regularly. How delicious the food tasted! Moreover, we ate primarily meat. Wild animals abounded in the area and the men used to go hunting. They had hunting rifles. Since everything there was collective, I had to work with them. We felt safer in Ixcán than in La Sierra even though the army was present there as well. Almost daily we saw or heard helicopters and planes. One day when we were working in a corn field at some distance from the camp, we heard the bombs. "We have to return immediately," we said to each other. "Maybe they have found our camp." When we approached the camp we saw that the army was there. What a shock! We were very glad when we realized that our people had left before the army arrived; none had been killed. They had, however, burned everything and killed all the animals. They had left the animals there on the ground, without eating them. For two days the soldiers remained in the camp; then they withdrew.

In Ixcán the food situation was much better than in La Sierra. We had a number of depots of food. If they found one, we had another, and so on. Therefore, we were never short of food after arriving in Ixcán. It was not until we arrived in Ixcán that we realized that there were lots of Guatemalan refugees in Mexico, and that some of them had been there for more than ten years. I wanted to go to Mexico; I was tired of the suffering in the CPR. I desired to give my children some joy—but at the same time I was afraid.

In Ixcán my children learned to read and write. The children had their notebooks—one each—Spanish in the front, mathematics in the back. These were the only subjects taught. The teaching material we received from abroad. In La Sierra teaching was not possible.

As I told you before, I wanted to go to Mexico. One day I decided to talk with the representative of our group. Why do you want to leave, he asked? The leaders were against people leaving the area. I knew that and I said that my wife was very ill, that I wanted to take her to Mexico to be cured. When she is well we return here, I said. That was all I said, because my wife was in good health. They finally agreed to let us leave and we crossed the border to Mexico and settled in Los Lirios camp in Quintana Roo.

Gregorio's story gives a glimpse of what it meant to live in the CPR-Sierra, in the Ixil country known for its unusual level of resistance and its unusual level of militarization. For the revolutionary movement, the displaced villagers became CPR. Gregorio, like many of the Nebajeños interviewed by Stoll, simply fled to the mountains to save his life (1993: 131–32). He had seen what the army had done to his family and neighbors, and there was no reason to believe that the same would not happen to him if he remained in his village. Once he was in the CPR he was defined as a subversive and a priority target by the army, and for this reason he did not dare to leave. Even though Gregorio was never a supporter of the guerrilla, the insurgents, at least during the early years, represented his only hope to survive; first because they gave the impression that they were winning the war, and second because their description of the situation outside the CPR was even more terrifying than the situation they endured inside. For many years Gregorio believed that there was no way out. He was told that the whole country was at war and the possibility to go into exile simply did not occur to him because he did not know that "there were other countries in the world than Guatemala."

In contrast to the people who lived in the CPR in Ixcán, relatively close to the Mexican border and thus with a certain contact with the outside world, the displaced people in the Ixil area were completely isolated. The insurgents were their only source of information about the development of the conflict. The guerrilla told the refugees time and again that they were about to win the war and that those who surrendered would be killed by the army or, if they were saved, they would be obliged to join the Self-Defense Patrols and kill those hiding in the mountains. Several years passed before Gregorio actually found out whether people were killed or not. What he knew was that acquaintances from his years in the mountains who had disappeared had reappeared with the army to kill refugees. For a long time that was an even more terrifying prospect than the suffering he and his family had to endure.

Memories of a Prisoner of War

One of the darkest sides of the armed conflict in Guatemala is related to the prisoners of war or, more precisely, to the lack of prisoners of war. Many people were captured, abducted, and kept in prison for shorter or longer periods of time in one of the many detachments throughout the region, but very few survived. Don Leonardo is one of those who did survive. We met Don Leonardo in Chapter 3, where he spoke of how he experienced the escalation of violence in his cooperative and about the circumstances of his capture; the army had discovered a placard with "Viva EGP!" nailed to a tree close to the entrance of his parcel. According to him, this totally irresponsible act by the insurgents unleashed a "nightmare" he will never forget.

I came to know Leonardo upon my arrival in La Quetzal, but because some of his sons and daughters were very active in community affairs, I often ended up talking with one of them instead of him when I visited Leonardo's house. Not until the end of my last stay in the community did I have the opportunity to talk at length with him about his imprisonment. The day he told me his story, he had to travel outside the community and would not return until after I had left. I commented that it was a pity that he was leaving; I would have liked to have the opportunity to continue talking with him. "Don't worry," he said in a comforting tone, "if I don't have the time to tell you everything today, don't worry, I can tell you whenever you return. I have all of it inscribed in my memory. I still have a lot of scars on my body and I will never forget."

I had noticed that Leonardo talked without moving his upper lip, and I asked him why.

This is also a result of torture. It happened the day they captured me. After having walked for several hours, we arrived at an empty peasant house. Those who used to live there had most likely already escaped. They hung me up from a rafter, hands pinioned, to interrogate me. They thought that I was a guerrilla, and wanted to know the whereabouts of my compañeros. When I told them the truth, that I had no idea, they gave me four kicks in my stomach. (He imitates their movements and points at the part of his body that was hit). I fainted for a moment, but regained consciousness with a penetrating pain in my arms. They had taken a burning log from the fire and burned my arms, first one then the other. (He shows me the scars). Since I did not give more information, simply because I had none, they put a red-hot piece of wood on my upper lip. When I still did not give information they got furious. "I will make you talk, you cabrón (son of a bitch)," screamed a tall fat soldier. He took his bayonet, that's what they call their knives, and stabbed me three times here (he shows his scars), but I think that no vital organs were perforated, because I did not die, but you should have seen the spurts of blood, Doña Kristiana! By then I was more dead than alive. They took me down and threw me on the floor where I remained until the next morning, when we continued our long walk toward Playa Grande. They hung sacks on me, the ones soldiers usually carry. My hands tied behind me, connected to a long rope held tight by a soldier walking behind me. He was a real son of a bitch. Sometimes he pulled the rope and I fell backward. Sometimes he made me run and sometimes he just threw the rope in front of me to make me stumble. They gave me almost nothing to eat or drink. They were drinking all the time; all of them carried a canteen of water. They also brought along nice pineapples that they slurped. Finally, I had the courage to ask for something to drink. Then, the soldier responsible for me did this (he pretends to open his fly and take out his penis). "Open your mouth guerrillero, son of a bitch," he said to me. I had to obey and he pissed in my mouth.

I don't know how, but I endured all of this and we arrived at Playa Grande.

When the catechists and the evangelicals talk about hell, I don't know what they are talking about. What I know is that Playa Grande was a hell. If I am going to describe to you how this hell was we would need five empty cassettes, and a lot of time. We don't have it so I will only tell you a few things. . . .

The first month I spent most of the time with some 30–35 other prisoners. We were locked up in a shack, lying on the earth floor, our hands tied behind our backs and our heads covered with burlap. They gave us very little food, only four tortillas a day and a small bowl of beans mixed with water once a day. Since our hands were pinioned we could not help ourselves, the soldiers had to feed us, which meant that our small rations were reduced even more. Due to their purposeful careless feeding, parts of the food easily fell to the floor and then it was lost, you cannot image how dirty that floor was. The same happened with the water. They passed a pot from mouth to mouth and you had to drink intensely before they took it away from you. They treated us like animals, worse than animals. They beat and kicked us every day, several times a day. Everybody who entered the shack, for whatever reason kicked somebody. At night they started the interrogations. Doña Kristiana, I would need a lot of time to tell you about all the things they did to me. . . .

For example, sometimes they brought a few of us to the river. They tied us up, arms and legs until we looked like a kind of ball. Then the soldiers carried us one by one into the river. The captain stood on the shore with a stopwatch counting: one, two, three in order to start and then he controlled the time of submersion. Every time they brought me to the river I was the last one. I had to watch how they tortured the others before my turn came. When the prisoners were taken out of the water their heads were hanging as if they were dead. Then they were beaten to see if they were alive. If they were, the treatment was repeated, if not, they were thrown into the river. When they submerged me I felt that I was going to die, that was the only thing I wanted, every time I prayed to die, but I did not die. When they took me out of the water I felt that my head was going to explode. Then the beating started—real blows! When I recovered my breath, they submerged me once again. . . . Many people died of this, but I survived.

Another thing they did to us was to electrocute us. They put cables in my fingernails and on my genitals. The captain had an instrument connected to the cable. When the captain pushed this instrument, light (luz) entered my body. It was then that I realized, Doña Kristiana, the number of veins there are in the human body. I felt that the light passed through all of these veins; in my arms, in my trunk, in my legs, I could not remain standing. I crouched on the floor. The next day I suffered terrible pains, my whole body hurt. It took me two to three days to recover. I received this treatment more or less once a week, together with beating and kicking every day. (At that point he showed me a sore on his neck; it looked like an eruption of eczema, red and crusty.) This is a consequence of the kicks. They always preferred to kick in the neck.

More than anything else, it was el hoyo (the pit)[3] which makes me think of Playa Grande as a hell. It was located about one kilometer from the detachment. It was a pit of some three meters in diameter and one or two meters deep. It was located in an open field. Around it were piles of wood, any quantity of firewood. The field was so big that several vehicles could enter at the same time, trucks and pick-ups. . . . There were no fences; it was not necessary, because of the number of soldiers patrolling there. Nobody else was allowed to enter. In this pit they burned people. Dead people were brought there from the detachment, people who were killed on the spot, sometimes people who were alive but tortured. Seven times they brought me to the pit, to threaten me, to make me speak. "We will show you what we are going to do with you if you don't speak, you guerrillero, son of a bitch," they said to me. I saw that people were piled up under the firewood; sometimes the wood moved because people were alive. Then they threw in some gallons of petrol and moved away at some distance. A single match thrown into the pit (he imitates a movement in the air) was enough to burn it all. Seven times they brought me there. "This is what we will do to you if you don't speak," they said, "we will burn you alive." Can you image that I survived all this, Doña Kristiana?

When I asked him to tell about how he succeeded in escaping, something that is considered almost impossible, he continued as follows:

How I succeeded in escaping is also a long story. After I had been in the detachment for some 30 days, the captain called me, by name he called me. All of us had a label with our name, date, and place of capture fixed on the chest. I had been careful in observing the behavior of the captain in relation to the soldiers. When he called on them, they approached him quickly, right hand to the forehead, heals together, and "Presente mi capitán!" (Present, my Captain!) I had also noticed that if he was not satisfied with their salute, he mistreated them. He treated the prisoners worse! When he called on one of the prisoners you never knew what was going to happen. If he called upon one by name he had to approach him immediately. Some got so nervous that they just walked up to him without saying anything. The captain pretended not to see them. He took his binoculars and started to look at the mountains or he took some paper or document and pretended that he was reading. This increased the nervousness of the prisoner who started to tremble in front of him. All of a sudden the captain turned toward the prisoner and pretended that the prisoner frightened him. "Are you here, son of a bitch," he screamed. Then he called on the soldiers. "Crush this son of a bitch" (Hacé mierda a este cabrón), he ordered. The soldiers would then grab the prisoner. This incident could be a sufficient reason for being killed. Some were beaten to death then and there. Others got their limbs broken and continued to live for a few more days.

Fortunately, I had the opportunity to observe the behavior of the captain before suffering this treatment myself. Therefore, when he called upon me I approached him in the same manner as the soldiers. I walked directly toward him, right hand to my forehead, heals together and: "Presente mi capitán!" My knees were trembling, but, fortunately, the trembling did not make noise because I had no shoes on. My behavior seemed to please the officer. He looked at me and said: "Do you know how to make "chirmól?" "More or less, my captain," I answered. "Then, come with me to the kitchen," he said. Fortunately, I had some cooking experience from the time when I was employed by INTA constructing "la tranversal del norte."[4] Once, in the kitchen with the captain, I took the tomatoes and washed them thoroughly before I put them in boiling water for a moment to loosen the skin. Once peeled, I chopped them finely, the same with the onion and I prepared the "chirmól." Before I offered it to the captain I put a spoonful on my hand, tasted it. Then I filled the spoon again and offered him a taste. He seemed to like it. Then, with the same spoon he offered a taste to the others present. Notice the hygiene of those who accuse us of being dirty pigs! "It seems that he knows how to make "chirmól," this son of a bitch," the captain said and he then ordered the soldiers to re-pinion me and put on my hood.

Once back in the shack, life continued as before with interrogations at night and all that. The next time the captain called on me, he gave me the dirty clothes of two officers and ordered me to wash them in the river. "I want them clean, dry and nicely folded," he said. When I finished, I was returned to my normal condition once again. The third time he called he asked me if I could make lemonade. "More or less, my captain," I answered. This I also had learned when I worked for INTA. I had learned to make it really good. Once again he brought me to the kitchen. He screamed to those who were around to make space for me. They did, but stayed around observing. I took the lemons, washed them thoroughly with water and soap, rinsed them, and dried them well. When this was done I cut them and squeezed the juice into a jug. Then I put in the sugar and beat it with a whisk. At the end, I added the water and mixed all of it. When one makes it this way the sugar dissolves and the lemonade tastes very good. I should also tell you that before I added the water I had taken out the lemon seeds. The captain tasted it. He seemed to like it and invited those standing around to taste as well. "I will save your life," he said. You are most probably a pinche guerrillero (a damn guerrilla), but you are intelligent and courageous and you have passed the tests I have made for you. He brought me to the officers" building; a lot of people were there, lieutenants and sub-lieutenants, captains, who knows. . . . "I don't want any of you to touch this prisoner," he told them. "He is intelligent and courageous and he can become a good military man." "You stay with us for a while," he said to me, "I will find a place for you in the Military Academy (or something like that) in Santa Cruz de El Quiché. In two years you will be an officer and receive a good salary." They gave me a pair of pants and a shirt. Find yourself a pair of boots, he said and took me to a place where they had thousands and thousands of boots and shoes. They had belonged to the poor people who had been through this detachment. Once a prisoner entered the camp, his shoes and belt were taken away. He was barely left with pants and a shirt or t-shirt. I got very sad looking at the piles of shoes, but finally I found a pair of boots that fit me.

I was transferred to Cobán, where I was set to work as a gardener. I planted vegetables, transplanted sprouts, fertilized the plants; in short I did everything related to the cultivation of vegetables. At last, I started to recover the strength of my body. We ate very well, a lot of meat, fruits, and vegetables, as much as we wanted. I started to feel strong again. For a few weeks I stayed in this place. Then, I was told that I was to be transferred to Playa Grande again. The officers called on me. They asked me if I was familiar with the area of the Ixcán Grande cooperatives. I said yes—that I knew this area very well because it is where I used to live and work. "That is fine," they said "because we will bring you there to help us find the people who hide in the mountains." Then I started to feel bad again. I strongly disliked the idea of betraying my compañeros of the cooperatives. Moreover, I knew that if the guerrilla got to know this, they would kill me.

Fortunately, I never arrived at Playa Grande. I was sent with a group of soldiers to Santa Maria Tzejá (Zona Reina), where a number of Q'eqchi' families, who had been hiding in the jungle, had decided to surrender to the army. Those people were to be transported to a model village to be resettled, but before that, they were obliged to harvest their milpas in the jungle, thus destroying the food provisions of those who still remained. We used seven days to do this work. I was impressed by the amount of corn brought out of the jungle. We piled it in the center of Santa Maria. When the job was done, we started our transfer on foot to Playa Grande and I heard that the officer in command ordered that the corn should be burned.

Before leaving Santa Maria, one of the officers asked me to carry a very nice axe handle that he had stolen from one of the peasants. "I want to bring this as a gift to my godfather in Jutiapa," he said. "I am afraid it will become dirty," I told him. "Never mind, I know that you will take good care of it," he answered. I knew that he trusted me. I took the axe handle and joined the row of people who had already started to walk. In front of me there was a group of peasants, behind me there was a soldier, the son of a bitch who treated me so badly during my first transfer to Playa Grande the day I was captured. Behind him walked another group of peasants, followed by a group of soldiers. At some point I told the soldier that I wanted to leave the column to shit. "What do you think cabrón, you don't move from this line, cabrón," he said and pushed me with his machine gun. I got so angry that I turned around and beat him with the axe handle, first in the face, then in the head, before I ran into the jungle. Almost immediately I heard the burst of machine guns while I crawled away on the ground as fast as I could. I came to a ravine and fell down and that's what saved me. There was a small hill close to the path. The soldiers certainly thought that I had run up there because that was where they targeted their bullets. In this way I saved my life. I had no idea how to return to the places that I knew. I had no idea where Santa Maria was located. Little by little I found out, asking people I met, and I finally found my family. My wife had managed to arrive safely at my brothers' in Flor de Todos Santos.

We decided to leave the country immediately. We did not know how to get to Mexico, but we knew that we would be safe there. We walked twenty days in the jungle before we arrived at the border. My God! It was hard. We crossed the Mexican border on the 25th of December 1983. Then COMAR and the Church were there helping the refugees, and we were taken directly to the camp in Puerto Rico (Chiapas). An unforgettable experience.

Leonardo's story offers a detailed description of the army's treatment of prisoners, which for most ended with death. He gives a voice to the large number of people who were captured, brought to these detachments, and killed there, and therefore never had the chance to tell what had happened to them. What seemed to have saved Leonardo's life was not only his intelligence, but also his usefulness for the army in searching and capturing his old neighbors who were still fugitives in the jungle. His usefulness would probably have been short-lived and he knew that his chances of being released after having collaborated with the army in this kind of operation were very small. If he had been released, he would have been deemed a traitor and most probably killed by the guerrilla.[5] His story also reveals what happened to fugitives who decided to surrender. If not killed, they were often moved to model villages where they had to live under close military vigilance.[6]

What happened to Leonardo is inscribed in both his mind and his body. His scars and other visible injuries bear witness to the "hell" he cannot forget. But he also has a certain pride, a pride of having survived: survived the submersion in the river, survived the *hoyo*, and survived the brutal beatings. Leonardo does not appear to be a defeated and traumatized person. Like many of his neighbors who have survived the violence, he has turned his devastating experience into something generative and creative, the partaking in the construction of a community and society where he wants to make certain that these kinds of atrocities will not happen again.

Combatant Life: Perspectives from Below

In addition to Payeras's and Colom's descriptions of the internal life of the guerrilla, a number of other books have been published by people who were themselves insurgents or in other ways had the opportunity to observe the movement from the inside (Andersen 1982; Harbury 1997; Macías 1999; Ramírez 2001). They give a rather romantic picture of combatant life. One of them is Andersen (pseudonym), a European philosophy professor who through some Guatemalan students at his university in Copenhagen was able to get in contact with the Guatemalan insurgency movement. He published a book on the basis of visits to EGP camps in Guatemala in 1982, the year of the scorched-earth campaign. It is a kind of testimonial publication by a man who has only superficial knowledge about the context of the events that he is observing. He conveys a fascination for what he observes in the guerrilla camp: mostly young illiterate men and women from different ethnic groups who live in harmony and solidarity deep in the jungle. He describes how they are trained, not only in the use of arms, but also in reading, the principles of Democratic Centralism, criticism and self-criticism, correct revolutionary behavior, and verbal communication, where swearing and coarse language are banned. He also praises the poetic veins of the young combatants, including a chapter of poems in his book. He criticizes his best friend back in Europe for not understanding the guerrillas' executions (*ajusticiamientos*) of "enemies of the people." A similar picture of combatant life is given by Jennifer Harbury, who spent some time in an ORPA camp in 1990, where she met the man of her life, *comandante* Everardo (Harbury 1997). This camp is a mixture of Mayan peasants from different ethnic groups, university students, teachers, unionists, and cooperative workers.

In these descriptions of the internal life of the guerrilla, young combatants associate joining the ranks with the military repression of their community or their family. Some of them had been persecuted themselves; others had lost parents or siblings. Harbury observed that "All left their home on the run, leaving everything they had known behind. Their stories overwhelm me, leaving me sleepless at night. Day after day they tell me of their lost villages, the people massacred and the homes burned to the ground. . . . They tell of lost friends and lovers, of army tortures, and cruelties that I cannot bear to imagine" (36).

Harbury also speaks of her roommate Emma, who joined the insurgents when her father was killed and her family left for exile. Their testimonies give the impression that most ordinary combatants were not recruited on the basis of their support for the revolutionary cause, something that is confirmed by my findings based on interviews with ex combatants in La Quetzal.

A number of people living in La Quetzal fought in the guerrilla ranks, most of them with the EGP, a few with the FAR, one with the ORPA. With two exceptions and for different reasons, all of them abandoned the guerrilla and went into exile in Mexico. They were part of the collective return to La Quetzal. Combatants who stayed in the ranks until the demobilization, after the signing of the Peace Accord on the Definitive Cease-fire in December 1996, do not generally live in returnee communities, even though they may have close kin there, as is the case for some ex-FAR combatants whose parents live in La Quetzal.[7] They were allocated land in a community of ex-combatants in the central part of the Petén.

In what follows, ex-combatants in La Quetzal talk about their experiences in the guerrilla ranks; how and why they became combatants; why they left and how they get along in civilian life in the returnee community. The picture is complex, but what seems quite clear is that most insurgents, at least among my informants, were not revolutionaries representing popular aspirations. Most of them were recruited when they were very young, thirteen to fifteen years old and, after years in the armed ranks, they were not able to account for the cause they were fighting for. There are a few exceptions: those who not only obtained military training but also embarked on political and intellectual training that was later converted into political positions in the returnee community.

Fighting for a Just Cause

Santiago was an outstanding figure in La Quetzal, Q'anjob'al, thirty-eight at the time, referred to as very central in the return process and in the cooperative. I got to know him shortly after arriving in La Quetzal the first time in 1998. Santiago was twenty-two when he joined the insurgents in 1982. At that time his family had not yet left the country. They were hiding in the jungle together with a group of people from the Mayalán cooperative.

One day walking along a path in the jungle, I met some acquaintances who had joined the guerrilla. Before the massacre, when I still lived in the cooperative, these people had left. Some said they had gone to San Francisco to work, others said they had gone to the south coast. When I met them I asked why they had left. That's how we started to talk. They began to explain why they had "gone to the mountains." I told them that I understood very well, because I went to the south coast when I was seven. Therefore, I had experienced the poverty and the exploitation that the peasants are suffering. They went on explaining that they were struggling for a change of life; that they were thinking of changing society. If we are to change society we cannot only talk politics, it is necessary to take up arms in order to negotiate changes, they said. By the use of arms we can create a base so that the government respects us in negotiations. It was after this conversation that I decided to join the guerrilla instead of going to Mexico with my family.

In the beginning, I spent most of my time getting accustomed to living in the mountains. For example, they sent me with messages from one camp to another; in this way I became familiar with the jungle. You receive training according to how you carry out your tasks and also according to your own ideas. They also observe how you react to order and discipline. Since I liked all this, I soon received military training and I was integrated into the military ranks. First I was a simple combatant; then I became a squad leader. Later I started to receive leadership training to be given more responsibility, but that was in 1988 when I became so ill that I had to leave.

We asked him to describe life in the mountains for us.

What I liked the most about life in the mountains was that I got to know new people, friends, people from different places, counties, municipalities, even people from the capital, men and women. Another thing, in the mountains you not only learn how to use a gun or how to do combat, you also learn to study, read, and write. In my case, for example, I never went to school because of the poverty of my parents; I have not passed a single grade at school. I learned to read and write in the mountains. I also liked to learn about the situation in other countries where they had had similar struggles, like Nicaragua, Cuba, and Vietnam. They gave us talks about this. I learned many new things. This is what I can say about the positive aspects. The hard things were the hunger, the thirst, the lack of sleep, the rain, all this was very hard, especially if you were not clear about the reasons why you were fighting. It was different if you were convinced that you were fighting for a just cause.

Not all joined the guerrilla because they understood the cause of the struggle. Many people also joined because of the massacres, because their mother or father, daughter or son had been killed. They joined the guerrilla in order to avenge their lost family members. Many people went to the mountains to avenge this situation. I joined the guerrilla after the massacres in Santo Tomás and Cuarto Pueblo, as well.

There was no difference between Indians and Ladinos—we supported each other. Ladinos generally knew how to read and write, and they shared this knowledge with those who did not know. They organized literacy training. The Indians were used to life in the countryside, the Ladinos who grew up in villages or towns had difficulties getting used to life in the mountains. The strength of the peasants was that they were used to life in the countryside, their major weakness was that they could not speak Spanish and they could not read and write. The weakness of those who came from the pueblos was that they had difficulties in walking long distances, in carrying heavy loads and getting used to the food and preparing the food. The Ladinos did not know how to prepare the corn, the beans and the herbs like we do. In this way the Indians and the Ladinos supported each other. In combat we supported each other too; there you have no differences. If a compañero, for example, was not well prepared physically we would help him. If someone is injured you never leave him, you are obliged to bring him with you. We were not like the army that just left their dead soldiers behind.

Santiago was largely operating in Ixcán, in the region where he had lived during the previous ten years. We asked him about the relationship between the guerrilla and the local population during his period as a combatant.

From 1983 to 1985 the population reacted against us. This is when the military established the PACs. Lots of people did not understand what was going on. They did not know who the guerrillas were, who were "the people of the mountains." The policy of the army was to tell people that the guerrillas were foreigners; that the guerrillas had the intention to invade and take over the country. This is what the military told the population when they established the PACs. Many of the patrollers believed that they had to defend the country. Others were afraid. They did not want to die. If they did not carry out the service in the PACs they were punished and even killed. Therefore, by obligation they had to react.

The guerrillas were conscious about the situation of the peasants, that the population was confused. We were given orders not to undertake combat with the Civil Patrols. If they surprised us we should run, hide or if that was not possible shoot, but in the air, to confuse the patrollers. These were the orders we had. I would say that in 1983–85 the situation was very harsh. When we met peasants they ran away or they returned to their hamlets to get their patrol together to go out and find us. Later we started to work on them. If we met peasants in their fields or on the roads we tried to stop them to explain why we were in the mountains, why we were fighting, that we were not fighting against them, but against the system of poverty and exploitation. That is what we explained to them. Little by little people started to understand. In 1985–86 the patrols no longer hunted us in the mountains. We started to gain acquaintances and friends among the peasants; they realized that we were not foreigners. When we arrived in a Q'anjob'al municipality, for example, we spoke our language, that is, Q'anjob'al. If the people were Mam, we had people with us who spoke Mam, the same with Q'eqchi' and Kaqchikel. We could give our explanation in any language the people were speaking. In 1986–87 we had certain support from the peasants. When we met them in the fields and asked them to sell us a quintal of corn, for example, they did. We never took products from them without paying; in this way we showed them that we understood their situation. We also warned them not to tell about the sales to the army because they would kill them. They sold food to us; I think this was a support. The same happened when we stopped merchant trucks on the roads. They also sold food to us. This was also support. . . .

When I left the ranks in 1988 I could not endure combatant life any longer.

I was very ill. I went to Mexico to find my family. During the first years, when they were still in Puerto Rico (Chiapas) we exchanged letters. From 1984, when they were moved to Quintana, I lost contact. My family did not know that I was alive. They had been informed that I had died after having been injured in combat. During the years in the mountains, I never left. Some people were given permission to leave, but I never asked. When I arrived in Mexico I had no concrete information about my family. I had no documents and the army and police control was tough, if I die, I die, I thought. Three months later I found my family in the Maya Balam camp in Quintana.

In Quintana, Santiago registered as a refugee and settled in the camp where his parents lived. There he married and became actively engaged in the preparations for return. Once back in Guatemala he held different leadership positions in the cooperative. He is always a critical and engaged debater in public meetings, and his opinions are listened to.

Julián, another important figure in the cooperative, had a similar trajectory. The circumstances of his recruitment participation in the guerrilla movement also became a process of political as well as general education. When he left the EGP files in the early 1990s and went to exile in Mexico, he became heavily engaged in the refugee organization CCPP, where he also gained leadership positions.

The cases of Santiago and Julián are not representative of the ex-combatants in La Quetzal. Even though both of them joined the rebel forces as a consequence of the violence committed by the army, and not due to a revolutionary awakening, they gradually acquired an understanding of the organization and what it stood for. They joined EGP in the early days, when the organization was small and idealistic, attempting to be a school of revolutionary learning and thinking. Moreover, their experiences in the rebel forces were converted into political leadership after they abandoned the ranks. This was not the case for the other ex-combatants who joined the guerrilla at a later stage, when the level of violence and the influx were so massive that ideological training was limited or nonexistent. According to what they described, they understood neither how the guerrilla was organized nor the cause for which they were fighting. Most of these ex-combatants are rather invisible in the public life of the community.

RECRUITMENT UNDER FALSE PRETENSES

Dolores is a Mam of thirty-one, who spent seven years as an EGP combatant. She is mainly devoted to family life: her husband Rodrigo, who is also an ex-combatant, and their three small children. I got to know her quite well before we talked at length about her experience in the guerrilla.

She referred to it from time to time, but I did not have the opportunity to sit down and have a more substantive talk, until one day when she invited me for lunch. Generally her very nice and talkative children were around demanding attention. When I arrived this day, her children had gone to their grandmother's and she was plucking a hen to cook a soup, something that implied that we had time to talk before eating. It was Dolores who started to talk about the guerrilla. The night before she had seen a film *La hija del Puma* (The Daughter of the Puma) and that film had made her think about and cry over her past as Floridalma (her "war" name).[8]

I was in the guerrilla for almost seven years, from 1983 to 1989 when they let me leave, six months pregnant. They wanted me to stay until the last month of pregnancy when they were going to send me to a clinic in Mexico to have my child. They would give me one year maternity leave. After that I was supposed to return to combat, leaving my baby in an orphanage in Mexico. After several petitions, they let us leave under the pretext that we were going to find our families. None of us (she refers to herself and her husband) had seen our families after having joined the guerrilla. We had to promise to return, but we had no intention of complying.

Dolores's eyes filled with tears when she talked. I asked her to tell me about how she became a guerrilla, which apparently had been very hard on her. She started with the beginning.

I grew up in a village in Colotenango, Huehuetenango, not far from Santiago Chimaltenango. I was number two of six children. My older brother was fourteen and I was thirteen when we were recruited by the EGP guerrilla. This happened in 1983. The situation was terrible by then. The military was present in our area, and so was the guerrilla. My father was a PAC leader, but I think that he also had some sympathy with the guerrilla. One night a man, a neighbor of my parents, came to talk with my father. I was there and could hear their conversation. Our neighbor talked about the guerrilla's need for the collaboration of peasants now that they were about to win the war. He suggested that I could become a messenger. I had no idea what that entailed; I knew nothing about the guerrilla. What I knew was that people disappeared and that frightened me. We were afraid. The man told my father that he needed my brother and me only for a couple of months, and after that we would return to our families. My father accepted. What they promised though was not what happened. They took me to their military headquarters in Ixcán, where I was a messenger for six months. This was not what they had promised. I felt completely fooled. I had understood that I was going to help with a few tasks and then return to my village. That was what happened to my brother, who was trained as a "propagandista" and returned home to do his job, something I found out years later. Once in Ixcán, I realized that they would never let me leave. Some of the combatants were given permission to visit their families. Not me—during the seven years I spent in the guerrilla I did not leave the jungle one single time.

After six months I started my military training. I learned, among other things, how to use and maintain my gun; we practiced shooting and did a lot of physical training. First I had a carabina, I don't remember the label; later they gave me a M16. After six months of training I was a full-fledged combatant. Each group had members of different languages; Mam, Q'anjob'al, Q'eqchi', Ladinos, all kinds of people. We were organized into platoons of 24 combatants. My platoon leader was a K'iche'. Almost half of the combatants in my platoon were women more or less my age. Some of the men were very young, younger than me, but some were older, as well.

Dolores did not know much about how EGP was organized beyond the platoon. She was uncertain about how many platoons there were in each company and how the lines of command operated. Nor did she know what ranks the different leaders had.

When I joined the guerrilla I had no idea about what they were doing. In Ixcán our bosses talked to us about the reason why we had to fight—in order to create a better society for the poor and such things. They also told us about another country where the guerrilla had won the war. What was the name of that country? (She tries to remember.) I don't remember the name of it any more. I was there doing what my bosses ordered me to do. At that point I was not afraid, not even when I saw people die. I thought that one day that would happen to me, but I was not afraid of dying. Sometimes I thought about how my life would have been if I was not in the guerrilla or how it would be when the war was over, but I did not worry much about it. I was so involved in the war that I did not even miss my family, or at least, I don't remember having missed them. So different from now!

The combatants were like the people here, revueltos (mixed), the majority indigenous—the platoon bosses as well. The higher bosses were not. They were from the city, white people. In the headquarters there was a "gringa" too, Lola she was called, she had a very high position, but I don't know what kind of position it was. She was a mature woman of some fifty or sixty years, I think. There were also some Cubans. Once, they brought me to the hospital. I had injured my foot escaping a bomb attack. The doctor was a Cuban, but his assistants were chapines (Guatemalans).

I asked Dolores about how she thought about her future when she was in the guerrilla.

I did not think about the future, nor did I think about leaving. I was convinced that my life was going to end in the mountains. Several from my platoon died, some were injured, but more army soldiers died. One time I participated in an operation against a convoy of soldiers. We had mined the road and a truck full of soldiers exploded. The truck blew up and so did the soldiers, there were dead and injured bodies and parts of bodies all over the place. We withdrew, but after that I was afraid. I think this was in 1988, one year before I left.

Dolores's husband Rodrigo was also a guerrilla who came from a co-operative in Ixcán.

I met my husband after four or five years in the guerrilla. One day we attended an assembly and the two of us were called upon to keep guard together. Rodrigo belonged to another platoon. The shift lasted several hours so we had time to talk and get to know one another. When we finished, each of us returned to our group. The chances to meet again by accident were rather small. Knowing that, Rodrigo did it the formal way. He sent a letter to his boss asking for permission to see me. "Amiga" he called me at that point. Rodrigo's boss sent a letter to my boss who came to ask me if I agreed to see him. I agreed and that's how we met again. We continued in this way for more then a year. We had no private dates, we were always surrounded by people and could not touch or kiss or anything. Then we applied to become husband and wife, something that also took place according to military formalities. After the wedding they gave us eight days together in a kind of honeymoon place in another part of the jungle. When the eight days were over we returned to our respective platoons. From then on I constantly worried about Rodrigo. He operated in a very dangerous place, close to the military base in Playa Grande.

During my last stay in La Quetzal I went to visit Dolores. She told me that she had not felt well lately and that she had problems with her sleep. It had started when Don Diego, one of their closest neighbors and the father of her best friend Virginia, died.

Don Diego's death affected me a lot. I could not sleep at night. I started to dream about the war, I could not get it out of my mind. I told my husband. "Try to forget it," he said to me. He does not think about the war any longer, I think his body is stronger than mine and his blood too, that's why he does not think about the war. I am weaker. I don't think about it all the time, only when I feel sad. When I am happy, I don't think about it. The death of Don Diego made me think. I wonder about how my life would have been if I had not been involved in the war. Sometimes I wake up at night, thinking about it.

When I am like that I always remember the death of two of my compañeros in the platoon. One day we were walking along a path in the jungle, we were attacked by soldiers, who threw bombs at us. All of a sudden I realized that a bomb was falling close to us. I threw myself to the ground. I don't know how my compañeros reacted. When I lifted my head to see what had happened, I realized that the one who was on my left side was thrown face up on the ground, blood-stained, his chest was perforated, there was a big hole in his chest. He was dead. This was a muchacho (boy) about twenty-five years old. On my right hand side was my compañera, a chamaca (young girl) of sixteen. They had blown her arm away, but she was not dead. I got terrified and started to run to catch up with the others from my platoon to tell them what had happened. When they returned to help, both were dead. We dug a grave to bury them, but it was not very deep, barely deep enough to cover their bodies. There we left them, the two of them together, before we ran away to hide in the jungle.

When I feel sad, the image of my dead compañeros comes to my mind—I cannot get rid of it. I have seen other people die, many soldiers, but not so close and not in the moment of dying. Sometimes when we attacked the soldiers who patrolled outside the military camps, I saw that they were hit, sometimes by the bullet from my own gun, and I heard them scream and saw them fall to the ground. But that did not impress me so much, they were further away—you could not see the expressions on their faces and, after all, you never knew if they were killed or only injured.

When I think about my life during the war I find it very, very hard, but at that time I did not think like that, I just lived. For seven years my food consisted of totoposte and powdered milk. I mixed it with cold water—that was my food. There was no other food. I had two changes of clothes, one in my rucksack, and the other I wore. Our clothes were made of very light material, a kind of "nailon" that dried very rapidly. We had two pairs of panties and two pairs of socks to wear in the boots. That was all. The women also received sanitary towels. We also had a tarpaulin, very light and made of a special material to protect ourselves against the rain and a hammock made of the same material. These could be folded to a size which fit in the sack. The hygiene was quite good when we were out of combat. In Ixcán there are lots of rivers and brooks where we could take a bath. When we were in combat there was no hygiene at all, we were very dirty.

Dolores generally talks about her guerrilla experience in a very matter-of-fact manner, even though sometimes remembering certain episodes fills her eyes with tears. As we saw from her narrative, her memories of the past haunt her, which does not seem to be the case for her husband. He explains that he rarely thinks about the years in the guerrilla, unless somebody raises the topic, and he never dreams about it. It belongs to the past, he says. However, Dolores never expressed bitterness toward her father who involuntarily let her join the guerrilla, against those who fooled her father and transformed her into a combatant nor those who made her spend seven years of her life fighting for a cause she did not understand. She seems to consider it a matter of destiny.

FIGHTING AS A WAY OF LIFE

In contrast to his wife, Rodrigo joined the EGP voluntarily. He had been in touch with them for some time, meeting them in the jungle on his way to and from the milpa. They had tried to recruit him, but he was not interested. After the massacre in Cuarto Pueblo and the counterinsurgency campaign against the other cooperatives, his home was burned down and his family was obliged to hide in the jungle, and he decided to join the EGP.

It is better to combat the enemy than to hide in the jungle, I thought. I told my parents about my plans. They did not agree. "They will kill you," they said. "I will be killed anyway," I answered, and I went. That was in 1982. I was fourteen years old. During the first months, I was a carrier of provisions for the combatants. I went to Mexico to fetch my loads. We had a camp about one hour and a half from the border. We were about sixty people in my camp—a mixture of all kinds of people—Mam, K'iche', Q'eqchi', Castellanos too, some of them from the capital city. We hid the food in the jungle. There it was picked up and carried farther on until it reached the combatants. During the first three months I was a simple carrier, I had no arms. After three months we moved the camp, but my task continued, for almost two years. Then I was really fed up. I talked to one of the bosses who came to see us. "I am so tired of doing this," I said, "you have to find something else for me—if not I will leave." One week later they called on me to go to a training camp. They took us to Mexico—to the Lacandón jungle—to a military training school called Antonio Fernández Izaguirre. We received lectures, which taught us why the guerrilla was important, they told us a lot of things but I hardly remember any of it. For me the most important was the military training. We learned how to shoot. I had a rifle, an M16. We practiced and they registered the results. We also practiced how to move in the jungle, in terrains with more or less difficult access. They registered the time we used with every movement. We also learned to make trenches and repositories to protect ourselves against bomb attacks. After four months, we returned to Ixcán.

Once in Ixcán I became a combatant. We were organized into three combat companies and a forth whose task was to provoke the army. For example, in cases where the army was burning milpas, the soldiers of the "provocation company" approached to shoot a few rounds; then they withdrew. It was our task to fight them. Each company was divided into three platoons. Each platoon had two captains (first and second) and two lieutenants. They had four squads, consisting of one sergeant and six combatants, under their command.

Rodrigo told me that he also learned to operate a rocket launcher, but he never had a machine gun. Only the chiefs of platoon had machine guns, not the simple combatants. He also told me about the turnover in his platoon. Some were killed in combat, others were so injured that they had to leave them behind. However, the most important losses were due to desertions. Many people could not endure the life of the guerrilla and thus escaped to Mexico. Rodrigo also had a combat friend who surrendered to the army. This happened after the military started to make announcements over loudspeakers and to throw flyers from helicopters, "promising all kinds of things to those who surrendered." One of the combatants in Rodrigo's platoon succumbed to the temptation. After his disappearance the army attacked incessantly, and many storage places were found and provisions destroyed. His friend had helped the army to identify them.

I don't know what happened to him. Most probably he is dead. The military generally killed their captives after having obtained the information they wanted. If not, the guerrilla would kill him. We often let the captured soldiers live. They were peasants like us. Sometimes they were injured. They were cured and then liberated—to demonstrate that both the soldiers and the guerrilla were of the people. Sometimes when we were in combat we also shot in the air to spare the lives of soldiers.

In order to illustrate how his company operated, Rodrigo asked me to imagine an attack to be made on military transport supposed to take place on a transit road.

Everything was well planned beforehand. We had to become familiar with the terrain, which had been carefully drafted beforehand. We planned our movements carefully. Often we had to wait one to two weeks before anything happened. During this time the combatants kept guard close to the road, hiding in the bushes. In order to sleep, we withdrew some ten meters and we had to take turns sleeping. When we finally started combat, it normally lasted only one to two hours. When it was over, we returned to our camp deeper in the jungle. Each platoon had a separate camp. There we were allowed to eat, sleep and rest. The camp was almost like our neighborhood here, consisting of small pole houses with hammocks in which to rest. We did what our bosses told us to do. They always told us that everything was going very well, that we were winning the war, but for us one day was like the other, always the same. I got tired of it and wanted to leave. But this was after I met my wife.

THE RETURN TO CIVILIAN LIFE

When we decided to leave, I asked for permission to visit my family in Quintana. My boss neither answered my first petition, nor my second. When my wife told me that she was pregnant I presented my third petition. I had decided that if they did not answer this time I would try to escape. After a few days the chief of my platoon came to see me. "We have decided to let you leave, but promise me not to tell the others. If somebody discovers that you are about to leave, you tell them that you will be transferred to another camp." From then on we had no support from our superiors. They treated us like strangers. The day we left they took our arms, gave us some civilian clothes, I received a pair of worn-out pants and a shirt, Dolores a dress that did not fit her condition. They also provided a man who knew the area to guide us to the border. There he left us unarmed, without food and money and without documents; this was all they gave us after seven years in the guerrilla. I felt completely naked and defenseless after having spent every moment of the last years with my gun. It was a terrible feeling. Fortunately, we were close to a refugee camp where we could find shelter. Since we had no money and no food, I was obliged to work. One of the refugees worked on the farm of a Mexican employer close by. He said that he needed hands to slash his grazing grounds, so the following day he brought me along. I was not accustomed to work with a machete. After one hour's work, my hand was raw meat. Moreover, I remained far behind the other workers, who slashed very fast. The patron saw this and approached me to ask what happened to me. I explained that I was not used to work with machete since I had worked in a coffee farm in Tapaschula (Mexico) since I started my working life. This was what my fellow workers had told me to say. The patron accepted this explanation. "You will have to learn then," he said, "but in order to learn you have to cure your hand." During four days I could not touch the machete, the fifth day I returned to work. I stayed with this patron for 20 days, but I suffered very much, because my hand would not heal.

When this work was done, we entered Guatemala again to visit my parents-in-law who had remained in their village in Huehuetenango. This was in 1989 and Guatemala was still very dangerous. We had to walk, but only during the night. Since we had no documents and almost no money, and only the clothes that we wore, we did not dare to walk during the day. When we arrived at my parents-in-law they became very, very happy. They were convinced that Dolores was dead. They had not heard from her since the day she had left some seven years earlier. . . .

I was afraid that Dolores's parents would be annoyed when they knew that she was pregnant, but they were not, they received me very well. You can stay with us, my father-in-law said, but you will not be safe here. She got her documents, her father had taken care of them during her absence, but I had nothing. If the neighbors saw me they would realize that I was a stranger and could denounce me to the commissioner. If they found me there without documents it would be my death and maybe that of the others as well. I had to leave. I asked Dolores to come with me to Mexico to find my parents. You stay here with your parents, I said, I will go to the Cienaguita camp to earn money for the ticket. I will stay there for two weeks. If you want to go with me, you come there; if you do not arrive, I'll go alone. After ten days she arrived and we went to Quintana to search for my parents.

When we finally arrived at my parents' house, my father was not at home, only my mother and my small sisters and brothers. They did not recognize me. "Who are you?" my mother asked. Not until I had responded with "I am your son Rodrigo" did she realize who I was. It was very moving. My father recognized me immediately.

Shortly after having arrived in the camp I got land. I went to talk to COMAR who had representatives there. They told me that they would give me land only if I promised to remain in Mexico permanently. If I returned to Guatemala I would lose it. They had realized that I had been a guerrilla, in spite of the fact that my father had told them that I used to live in another refugee camp. The agricultural work under the sun was terribly hard for me after seven years in the shade of the jungle. In the beginning I often desired to return to Ixcán, I really thought like that, but I could not—I stayed in the camp until the return in 1995.

It was not until I arrived in Mexico that I realized that the war was more complicated than what we were told by our guerrilla leaders—first, because I realized that we had no great military achievements, second, because we had much less civilian support and collaboration than they had claimed. I also realized that there were strong conflicts between the different guerrilla groups, especially when we started to talk about the return. EGP—or "vertiente noroccidente" as it was called at that point, wanted those who came from Ixcán to return to Ixcán.[9]

Many of the people who left Ixcán did not want to return to their communities, partly because their land had been occupied by others, partly because there was not sufficient land to sustain their children, who in the meantime had married and needed their own piece of land. What was terrible was the jealousy between the different groups. People who wanted to join another "vertiente" were looked upon as traitors. My father did not want to return to Ixcán to fight for his land. That is why we decided to return to the Petén and, of course, also because here we have more land.

A Guerrilla with Slippers and Chewing Gum

David is another ex-combatant in the EGP. Even though he joined the guerrilla voluntarily, he thinks that he was fooled by those who recruited him by giving him a false picture of the guerrilla. David was recruited at the age of thirteen when he was living in the refugee camp with his parents. He deserted after 11 months and returned to the camp.

One day I went with his mother Candelaria to the milpa to harvest chili. During the break we were toasting and eating corncobs and his mother told me, I think for the third time, about her flight with her children. David was lying on the ground listening. When she finished I said that I had heard that he had been a combatant, something he confirmed, and I asked him how he was recruited.

I was thirteen when I joined the guerrilla. It was in 1987 I think and we lived in the camp in Mexico. I was tired of the life in the camp. I longed for a change, some excitement; I wanted something exciting to happen in my life. I was recruited by one of our neighbors in the camp. He cheated me. He said that I was going to learn a lot, that I was going to learn how to use guns and I would get a better life. I had no idea what it meant to be a guerrillero, how they operated or the cause for which they were fighting. They talked about the revolution and about the new society, but I did not understand what that meant. When I was about to leave, my mother bought me a nice backpack and I packed a change of clothes, including a pair of new slippers, sweets, and lots of chewing gum. I had heard that gringo soldiers used chewing gum. They obliged me to give away all my personal belongings.

First, I spent a couple of weeks among the Zapatistas, close to San Cristobal de las Casas. Nothing happened, no training, only waiting. One day a woman came to pick me up. She took me to the Guatemalan border close to Chajúl, where she handed me over to the guerrilla. It was here that they took away all my personal belongings and gave me a uniform. From there, they brought me to the camp in the jungle of Ixcán. I think it was the headquarters because all the hierarchy, including the commander-in-chief, were there. They introduced me as a new recruit at a big assembly.

I grew very disappointed when I discovered what they wanted me to do. I had to carry provisions from the Mexican border to the combatants in the jungle; very heavy burdens over long distances. I was still quite small and not very strong. I was always hungry; they gave us too little food. Sometimes I stole food from the provisions. They scolded me, but then I had already eaten the food. After some two or three months I started to receive military training. This was very hard, but I felt that something was happening. Only twice I participated in combat. Both times we attacked detachments trying to kill the guards and then we withdrew. This created alarm in the detachment, a deployment of soldiers, both times they did not succeed in catching us, and we returned safely to our camp. Most of the time, we were just waiting. I disliked the guerrilla life very much. I think that only those at the top understood what we were fighting for. Moreover, I lost any illusion of a better society when I saw how camp life was. The bosses were privileged. They had the best food, the best uniforms, and the best boots. The combatants, who walked the most, had boots that sometimes were so worn out that they barely remained on their feet. The same happened with their uniforms, the food was bad, and so were the way they treated us. Those who protested, at least some of them, were obliged to a dig a pit. When they finished, they were shot and thrown into it, accused of being a runaway. I didn't like the way they treated people who were killed in combat, either. Then they also dug a pit, threw the corpses into it without putting them into a coffin or some other wrapping, and filled it with dirt. The commander then said a few words about the sacrifice made for the cause, or something like that. He did not mention spiritual or religious values. I felt that it was as if we were burying a dog and not a human being.

There were many Cubans in the camp, most of them worked at the hospital. There were also some Russians, I think. I don't know what they did; they spent most of the time with the bosses. The highest bosses were white, most of the lieutenants and corporals were peasants, lots of indigenous people from different groups, but maybe the majority were Q'eqchi's. There were also many women, maybe the majority of the combatants were women, and some officers too. The men said that without women they could not make war; they needed their novias (girlfriends), I think.

What I saw in the camp is also what we see now after the peace process. There is peace only for those at the top, including the guerrilla leaders; the situation of the poor people continues as before. Did you notice that almost none of the returnees turned up at the meeting with the URNG leader Monsanto last Sunday?[10] Most people came from the other communities. I saw him with his family in Santa Elena (the largest town in the Petén). His daughters looked like upper-class girls (chamacas de clase alta) and behaved like that too, and the group had 15 bodyguards! The guerrilla leaders have gained from the peace accords, not ordinary people.

David returned to La Quetzal with his parents and siblings. He is a peasant, a cooperative member, married with two children. He finds life in La Quetzal difficult, and in contrast to Rodrigo, who is quite content, he expresses certain bitterness with regard to the results of the many years of armed conflict. He had expected something better.

CHILD RECRUITMENT

Armando and his sister Clara are the only ones in La Quetzal who remained in the guerrilla ranks until the demobilization in 1997. They were part of the FAR guerrilla. Armando started to receive military training when he was around twelve years old. He grew up in a community in western Petén where his family settled in the early 1970s. His father was brutally killed when Armando was a couple of years old. Armando and his sister grew up with his grandparents who always had a very turbulent relationship. It was due to the quarreling between the two that Armando became a guerrilla soldier. This happened when they were in exile in Campeche. Armando's maternal aunt Alicia told me the following story:

My mother was always very jealous, she still is, she accuses my father, unjustly, I think, of having other women. This was what happened in Campeche when she decided to leave him. My mother left with the four children of my sister who lived with them. Armando was eleven years old then. His sister Clara was thirteen, Marco six, and Rosana barely three. She crossed the border to Guatemala and jointed the Community of People in Resistance in the Lacandón jungle of the Petén. There she expected to find my brother, who was a combatant in the FAR. However, he was not there any more. He had been seriously injured, part of his face blown away in combat, and brought to Cuba to be treated. My mother stayed in the CPR for more than one year. Then, she could not stand it any longer. The life in the mountains was too hard on her and she decided to return to the refugee camp. But the FAR did not allow her to bring the older children, only the small one. She even had to leave Marco behind. When my father got to know that she had left the children he became furious and went immediately to the CPR to bring them back. He returned with Marco; the others were obliged to stay. This is how Armando and Clara became guerrillas.

I think the guerrilla destroyed Armando. He cannot adapt to normal life, he does not want to work (no agarra machete). My father, who is now almost eighty-five, works alone on the milpa. With the demobilization Armando received a compensation of 4,000 quetzales and six piglets, to start a piggery. He bought a dress for his sister and a sewing machine for his grandmother. The rest of the money he spent drinking with his friends. He used to walk around with all the money in his pockets, showing off and inviting his friends to drink. The money did not last long. When he had no money left he sold the sewing machine and spent that money too. The piglets also disappeared. Now he has nothing left and he does not want to work. When my father reproaches him, my mother protects him; she is still very tough on my father.

When I knew Armando in 1998, a year after the demobilization, he was in his early twenties. He had been invited to join the ex-combatant cooperative Nuevo Horizonte to be established in another part of the Petén, but he preferred to return to his family in La Quetzal. That is why he was offered the compensation that his aunt referred to. When I knew him, he was a kind of misfit in the community, considered dimwitted (*sin grandes luces*) and lazy. He often used to hang around outside the cooperative store and sometimes turned up at my house in the late afternoon when I was cooking. Then I invited him to share a meal.

Armando was a man of few words. When he visited me he normally settled in my hammock, where he remained silent, if I did not keep the conversation going. He gave short answers to direct questions; otherwise he did not talk much. Therefore, it was difficult to get a coherent picture of what he had experienced as a combatant. He had spent most of the time in the Petén, but had also been combating in the area around Lake Atitlán. Apparently, he had seen or experienced a great deal of what is associated with the life of combat: hunger, thirst, and lack of sleep, dead and injured friends and enemies, but also the protection of the insurgents and the people of the CPRs who became his "family," Armando could not tell what he was fighting for or why he was fighting.

His sister Clara also lived with her grandparents in La Quetzal. When I first met her in 1998 she was a single mother with a newborn son. Like her brother, Clara was considered dimwitted, and she was rather unfocused in her conversations about the past. My attempts to get her to talk about her experience in the guerrilla were not very successful. It was my impression that she did not consider it worth talking about, as opposed to an unwillingness to pursue the topic. Clara spent most of the time as part of the supply base of the guerrilla, taking care of food and other provisions, something she talked about as quite boring. Clara had the reputation of being sexually corrupt, running after married men. On one occasion during my fieldwork she was penalized by the local authority for having had a sexual relationship with a married man. Her lover was also penalized.

Two others from La Quetzal used to be FAR combatants. One is Mariano, now in his late twenties. Like David, he was recruited when living in the refugee camp, and his experience was similar. He found out that combatant life was much harsher than he thought and deserted as soon as he had a chance and returned to the camp. Mariano never wanted to become a peasant, and he is not a member of the cooperative. Nevertheless, he decided to settle in La Quetzal, where most of his family lives. The other FAR combatant is a woman in her early twenties who joined the ranks after having returned to La Quetzal because she fell in love with and later married a combatant. They now live in the ex-combatant cooperative. So does her brother, who was a student until a month before the demobilization, when he decided to join the ranks in order to get access to land. He was too young to become a cooperative member when the family returned from Mexico. I have not met any of them, since their visits to their parents never coincided with my fieldwork periods.

Fighting for a Strange Cause?

From the above descriptions, we may conclude that those who joined the rebel forces were very young people whose recruitment was initially based neither on an understanding of nor in support of the "war of the poor."

Some, like Santiago and Julián, acquired a kind of revolutionary consciousness through ideological instruction and exchange with guerrilla leaders and combatants; others spent as much as eight years in the ranks without understanding the objectives, the ideology, or the organization of the guerrilla. What brought them into it were the army reprisals against EGP actions or, as in the case of Dolores, false pretenses. Protection and revenge seem to have been the most important motives. Those who joined voluntarily wanted to defend themselves and their families or avenge the abuses committed against them. Others, particularly those who were recruited while in exile, wanted to escape from the boredom of camp life, as Marco put it. They had a romantic vision of guerrilla life fomented by guerrillas on recruitment campaigns in the camps. They became disappointed when confronted with everyday life in the ranks and deserted as soon as they could. The saddest chapter of the local combatant history is the one comprising those who were recruited against their will and had no chance to leave. Some of them are still haunted by the ghosts of their violent experiences.

The War of Whom?

The Guatemalan guerrilla, especially the EGP and the ORPA, have argued that the strong support from the indigenous peasants is what distinguished this guerrilla from others on the continent. Some even refer to the armed conflict in Guatemala as the "War of the Maya" (Le Bot 1995: 279–96). Based on my interviews presented above, I suggest that, at least in Ixcán and the Petén, the guerrilla actually drew the indigenous peasants into a war that was not of their making. As settlers in the cooperatives of Ixcán they had achieved a level of prosperity that gave them a certain hope for a better future. They did not understand and were not interested in the revolutionary cause. And, yet, this is precisely the area where the guerrilla first sought its recruits in the 1970s.

In contrast, the urban upbringing, that is, the ideological baggage and the self-importance of Payeras and his *compañeros*, appeared to have prevented these young revolutionaries from understanding why they were so unsuccessful in recruiting the settlers to their cause. The response to the questioning of this cause by one of the few indigenous members of this first guerrilla group of fifteen was execution.

Far from liberating the settlers in the cooperatives of Ixcán and the Petén, the guerrilla in fact wittingly or unwittingly contributed to the destruction of what these peasants had built so painstakingly, to the massive loss of lives and forced exile of the survivors from the country. Certainly, in spite of the errors committed by the EGP, one cannot accuse them of conducting a war against the indigenous peasants. The massacres and destruction were in the majority of the cases committed by the army and not by the guerrilla. Nevertheless, my informants blame the guerrilla for being partly responsible, because they were perfectly aware of how their actions would trigger the army's reprisals against the civilian population, and, according to some, they were consciously sacrificing them.

The victims of the armed conflict in Guatemala were primarily indigenous peasants, whether as combatants, soldiers or civilians massacred by the armed forces. The guerrilla was completely incapable of protecting the civilians. Survivors like my informants do not forget that while the guerrilla voiced triumphant declarations of victory of war, the army was killing people who in most cases were not committed to the cause, but just happened to live in the area where the guerrilla implemented its armed propaganda. When the army arrived, the guerrilla had withdrawn safely into the jungle and left the people completely defenseless.

Judging from the stories of the ex-combatants, the majority of the guerrilla soldiers were indigenous youth belonging to different ethnic groups. The same was the case of the middle-range leaders. The upper-level leaders were Ladinos or "white people," often of urban background. With the exception of two combatants who were receptive and skilled in the revolutionary cause (certainly defined by the ideological leaders), they did not understand what they were fighting for, they just responded to orders. According to both Colom (1998) and Ramírez (2001), ex-combatants in EGP and FAR, respectively, this lack of understanding was a product of a process of uncritical and rapidly increasing recruitment due to the escalation of violence. There was not enough time or resources to train the newcomers. I suppose that certain recruitment practices and the young age of the combatants also played a role here.

For obvious reasons, this chapter has been dominated by the destructive aspects of violence. However, as Bowman (2001) has shown us, violence and narratives of violence may also be constructive, engendering imagined community and identity. As will be demonstrated in the following chapters, the common experience of violence and the common urgency to prevent violence underpinned the construction of new communities in the refugee camps.

Part II
Reconstruction of Livelihoods and Identities

Chapter 5
Exile and Return

Despite the international prestige Mexico enjoys as a country open and generous to people suffering from political persecution, Mexican immigration laws has been quite restrictive. Until new legislation was approved in 1990, Mexico recognized just one specific category of asylum: political asylum, granted only to those who were escaping from individual persecution in their countries of origin due to their political activity, beliefs, or opinions. With the arrival of Guatemalan refugees in the 1980s, Mexico received the highest number of immigrants in its history. These immigrants were different from the ones who had arrived earlier. They were poor, illiterate, indigenous peasants who arrived in Chiapas, a region that for many years had been ridden by conflicts and other difficulties, and very few of them qualified for asylum, since persecution in most cases was not directed at them as individuals.

Refugee Migration and the Enforcement of National Borders

The arrival of the Guatemalan refugees not only implied changes for the refugees, it also altered the relations between the states of Guatemala and Mexico, producing a process of reinforcement of the border. Until 1824, when Chiapas became an integrated part of Mexico, it belonged to Guatemala. Therefore, its history and its ethnic and cultural characteristics are more similar to Guatemala than it is to the rest of Mexico. When the border between Chiapas and Guatemala was established in 1882, the inhabitants of these regions did not recognize the division, because life and people were similar on both sides. Moreover, Mexicans and Guatemalans continued to cross the border, assisting each other in agricultural labors, exchanging goods and services or simply visiting relatives. According to an estimate made by church workers at an early stage of the refugee influx, 33 percent of the refugees had relatives in Mexico prior to their entry (Zinser 1991: 108).

Today, Chiapas is a strategically important region in Mexico, not only because it shares a border with Guatemala, but also because of its richness in natural resources, especially water, oil, and wood. In spite of the abundance of natural resources, the population is among the poorest in the country. The poverty that afflicts parts of the population in Chiapas is to a large extent associated with the unequal distribution of land. For many years Chiapas has been hit by conflicts, including land occupations, massive expulsions, and violent repression of peasant movements, which in turn have generated militant organizations struggling for land (Womack 1999; Nash 2001; Higgins 2004).

With the arrival of the Guatemalan refugees, Mexicans became conscious of the existence of the border, which for the refugees, in many cases, became a dividing line between life and death. The first refugees arrived in the municipality Marqués de Comillas, located in the Lacandón jungle of Chiapas, in 1980. During 1981 the exodus was intensified and by the end of that year approximately 5,000 people had arrived. During the same period, refugees also started to appear in other parts of Chiapas (see Map 3) With the scorched-earth campaign in 1982, the exodus exploded and by the end of the year the number of refugees in Chiapas exceeded 30,000. By the end of the following year the number of refugees recognized by the state of Chiapas approached 46,000, the number of camp refugees when the relocation to Campeche and Quintana Roo started in April 1984 (Kauffer 1997: 91). Camps were established spontaneously in *ejidos* (communal lands) or private properties with the consent and even support of both the *ejido* members and the land owners. The camps were distributed among seven municipalities in Chiapas, but most of those who arrived from Ixcán were concentrated in Marqués de Comillas in the municipality of Ocosingo, the largest in Chiapas.[1]

The first refugees arrived individually or in small groups, intimidated or in other ways affected by the selective repression characteristic of the late 1970s and the turn of the decade. They generally settled on *ejidos* or small farms in the tropical forest, where they found temporary employment. They remained very close to the Mexican-Guatemalan border, and thus rather close to their communities of origin on the Guatemalan side. This was the case of those of my informants who arrived in Chiapas from Ixcán in 1980 and early 1981. With the mass influx in 1982 and the arrival of relief assistance they registered as refugees and moved into camps.

Other early arrivers were less fortunate; they were captured by the migration authorities and deported back to Guatemala. The migration authorities defined them as illegal temporary migrants. During this first period Mexican policy toward the refugees largely denied the existence of a refugee problem. Mexican authorities registered an increased influx of people, but defined it as a temporary phenomenon that could be ignored and handled through deportations (Zinser 1991). According to Americas Watch (1984), 3,000 people were expelled in 1981 alone.

With the massive influx of people during 1982, the political situation in Guatemala attracted international attention. The national and international reactions against the deportations were so strong that the Mexican government decided to stop them. At the same time the government was reluctant to offer explicit refugee status, because it feared that the country would be overwhelmed by refugees and that this would create a dangerous political situation and even provoke an armed conflict with Guatemala. Since Mexico was not a signatory to international conventions on refugees, UNHCR was only permitted to enter Mexico in January 1982, after a bitter inter-agency struggle. Even though this step signaled the government's willingness to adopt a more generous approach to the refugees, Mexico remained uneasy about the events in Guatemala and the continuous flow of refugees.

With the arrival of UNHCR, the Guatemalan refugees were granted a status that permitted them to stay temporarily in Mexico. However, only those who settled in camps were treated as refugees; the others, an estimated 150,000 were defined as undocumented economic migrants subject to deportation. Many of them were seasonal laborers who decided to remain in Chiapas until the situation in Guatemala changed (Zinser 1989; Salvadó 1988).

The status given to the refugees was a restricted one. They were accepted in the camps, but there were restrictions on their movements and they had to obtain special permission to leave the camp. The Mexican government was afraid of a Guatemalization of the rich tropical rainforest. It was also concerned about the potential contamination of the political environment of the volatile state of Chiapas and an increase in social tensions through interactions with the local population.

The Catholic Church and the Refugees

The Catholic Church in Mexico, especially the Diocese of San Cristobal de las Casas in Chiapas headed by Bishop Samuel Ruiz García, played an influential role in shaping Mexico's response to the Guatemalan refugees. From the beginning of the refugee influx, the Church provided assistance to the Guatemalans and displayed a particular sensitivity to their special needs. Close relations between the diocese and the local Catholics allowed the bishop to learn about the presence of the refugees before the government agencies were alerted. As a result, when the government agencies entered the scene, the refugees were already under very active protection and assistance from the Church.

The bishop in San Cristobal instructed the parishes to work directly with the refugees and to provide food, clothes, medicine, and shelter. Large quantities of material aid arrived, partly in response to the Church's directives, partly as a result of the spontaneous generosity of many Mexican organizations and individuals. As aid piled up and the number of refugees increased, the Christian Coordinator for Aid to Guatemalan Refugees was established. At the same time, international NGOs were searching for mechanisms to deliver funds and material aid. Many international NGOs channeled their support through the Church organization or other local organizations, which had previous experience with international collaboration, something that facilitated rapid fundraising.

In the camps the refugees were not treated as passive recipients of aid. From the very beginning they were stimulated to participate in the making of their new livelihood, not only in food production and building shelters and some infrastructure, but also by creating new forms of cooperation for mutual benefit, taking advantage of opportunities open to them as a consequence of international assistance. Literacy classes and courses in Spanish were organized in the camps, and the interest was enormous. In Guatemala most adults could speak only their indigenous mother tongue, so they had been unable to engage in smooth communication in multiethnic contexts. The strategy of some of the organizations, such as the Diocese of San Cristobal, was also to recruit relief workers among the refugees, who were trained and gradually became able to run important parts of the relief programs. Generally, the Guatemalan refugees became very well organized in spite of their precarious and poor conditions, and engaged in a proactive way in shaping their conditions in the camps. Their success inspired funding agencies, especially the UN and international NGOs, to extend their support beyond emergency needs, and by this means to contribute to a more integral and coherent process of social and economic development (Kauffer 1997).

The camps were given a high degree of autonomy regarding internal affairs. The old authority structures eroded, and new elected leaders appeared who were more in line with the needs of the community. Teachers, catechists, and health workers assumed leadership positions because they could speak Spanish and could function as mediators in negotiations with aid agencies and Mexican authorities. Under this camp leadership, decisions were made only after an assembly where all adult camp dwellers were invited to participate and discuss every issue concerning the community. In order to protect the identity of the leaders, no outsiders except trusted Church representatives were allowed to attend. This was mainly due to the fear of recurring Guatemalan army incursions into the camp to kidnap or kill community leaders.

Attitudes of the Mexican State

The arrival of the refugees led to an intensified presence of the Mexican government in Chiapas. Migration control was one of the first measures to be implemented by the Mexican government in 1981. In the beginning, control was carried out at the crossroads of the border to prevent the influx of undocumented foreigners. During that year Guatemalan refugees were frequently deported (Aguayo 1985: 91–94; Fagan 1983: 179, Kauffer 1997: 95). Later, when the refugee camps were established, control posts were installed to prevent people from leaving their authorized area of settlement, a measure considered necessary to preclude participation in or even contact with the Guatemalan insurgency movement.

From the beginning, the Mexican government held an ambivalent attitude toward the refugees. Foreign affairs authorities were sympathetic toward the progressive political tendencies in Central America, and to a certain extent they favored the reception and good treatment of the Guatemalan refugees. The defense authorities, in contrast, were worried about security in the border areas and did not welcome the presence of the refugees. Between 1981 and 1984 the Guatemalan armed forces regularly violated Mexican sovereignty by entering Mexican territory, purportedly in search of guerrilla soldiers in the refugee camps. According to Aguayo (1985), 68 military incursions took place between 1980 and 1983, resulting in a number of abductions and casualties among both the refugees and the local population, in addition to material damage in the camps and beyond. The increasing number of incursions was interpreted as provocations intended to undermine Mexico's foreign policy in the Contadora peace process.[2] They represented a threat to Mexican national security and revealed more clearly the dilemma faced by the Mexican authorities. These wanted to prevent a rupture with Guatemala in spite of the incursions, at the same time that their acceptance of Guatemalan refugees meant an implicit denunciation of the Guatemalan regime.

The Mexican government also faced internal problems produced by social unrest in the border areas due to increased pressure on the land, followed by fervent political debates, raised by political groups as well as civil organization mobilizing to pressure the government to protect the refugees.

Becoming Guatemalans

Arriving in Mexico became a haunting experience for my informants in more than one sense. Becoming refugees meant incorporation into a social system where they interacted with nationals from different ethnic groups sharing a common experience of violence, flight, and exile, and with foreigners from the aid and solidarity community representing practices, ideas, and values that were novel to most of them. The encounters with these people created new space for participation and influence that granted the refugees access to material resources, new skills, and knowledge that inspired them to act and reflect on themselves and their place in the world in new ways.

A number of people recount that when they lived in Guatemala they did not think about themselves in national terms, as being Guatemalans, or in ethnic terms as being Mam, K'iche', or Q'eqchi'. They defined themselves in terms of their place of origin, the municipality or village where they were born, or their new place of settlement. Their vision was a local-centric one. Informants also reported that they did not realize the significance of nationality and national borders, because there was nothing that marked the boundary, and the landscape, villages, and people on the two sides were similar.

Even though Mexico had not signed the international convention on refugees, the Mexican border defined their condition. With the arrival of the UNHCR, the Guatemalan refugees were granted a status that permitted them to stay temporarily in Mexico. For my informants, the border became a question of life and death. Before crossing they lived in constant fear of the Guatemalan army, who considered them "subversives" and would kill them without mercy and in the cruelest way. They had seen this happen to others. After crossing the border they were no longer defined as subversives, objects of extermination, but as displaced people or refugees, entitled to assistance. The latter was associated with registering as a refugee and living in a camp.

In the camps they also realized that the meaning of being "indigenous" changed. In Guatemala, they had experienced discrimination and exploitation in interaction with non-Indians. But now, in the refugee context, being an Indian was no longer something negative: everybody was entitled to the same treatment independent of race, color, or religion. They had entered an area of influence of international law based on a concept of universal human rights that implies a specific kind of subjects—individual citizens—who are all equal. These new ideas about state-citizen relations were acquired through encounters with non-state institutions as well as with Mexican state agencies. This supports what Trouillot has argued: to identify state practices, processes and effects, we have to look beyond the central sites of national governments (Trouillot 2001: 131–32).

The stories informants recounted about their arrival in México were generally very positive. "Arriving in Mexico was like crossing from hell to heaven", one of them said. Generally they were well received by fellow peasants, who gave them shelter, food, and a piece of land where they could build a *champita* (shelter), until they were able to find work on a nearby farm or clear a piece of land to plant their *milpas*. This help was of crucial importance for survival, especially for those who left Guatemala before the refugee problem was officially recognized in Mexico and the aid organizations had been established in the border areas. In what follows I will let my informants narrate how they experienced their arrival in Mexico.

Maria B. left Guatemala in 1982 shortly after the massacre in Cuarto Pueblo.

The day of the massacre in Cuarto Pueblo we remained at the farm. I had planned to go to the market that Sunday but a neighbor passed by to tell us that somebody had observed soldiers in the area; therefore we decided not to go. We lived so near the center that we could observe the planes and the helicopters, hear the shooting and screaming, and we also saw the smoke of the houses that were burned. It was so terrifying that we decided to hide in the jungle. There, we stayed with a few other families for 20 days. Then we could not bear it any longer and decided to cross the border to Mexico. We were rather close by. We started to walk at about 12 o'clock and arrived around five in the afternoon. My son Francisco was four, Mario one and a half. While walking we passed by a house where the soldiers had been already. The house had been burnt down. Outside there was a dead body, the hens around picking. . . . I realized that the smell I had registered on several occasions during the previous days was of rotting human flesh—what a strong smell!

We crossed the border close to Boca de Chajúl (Chiapas) and arrived at a place called Loma Bonita. At that point there were no refugees there; we were the first ones. We were hungry and there was no work. Fortunately a patron from Reforma arrived and offered work. Don Lino was his name, a good man he was. He agreed to employ us for a month to find out if we were fit for work. He gave us a house and treated us well. All the families of our group worked for him, his brother, and one of his neighbors. After some four months, a lot of new people arrived. This is also when the Church arrived; by boat they sent us food. My husband stopped working for Don Lino. During the following week, quantities of refugees arrived and the first camp was built. COMAR and ACNUR (Spanish acronym for UNHCR) assisted in the building of the camp. They gave us axes and machetes to make our champitas. They treated us very well.

Rosalía had arrived a few months before Maria B. She left Guatemala with her mother and younger sisters and brothers when the army killed her father. They arrived in Mexico before the mass exodus.

We settled on Sánchez's farm, he was a good man. At the beginning we were not many people, but in March 1982, after the massacre in Cuarto Pueblo, lots of people arrived, about four thousand people altogether, I think.[3] Sánchez let the people stay in his grazing ground, but you can imagine he had not enough food to feed all these people. Through his brother, who was a lawyer, he called the attention of the organizations and we received the first help from the Church—the Diocese of San Cristobal de las Casas. Before the help arrived, the situation of the refugees was terrible. We had no food and we were obliged to eat leaves and roots from the forest. Many people fell ill, their bodies swollen, the children were particularly hard hit and many died during this first period—every day someone died. When the Church provisions arrived a storehouse was built and I was appointed as a caretaker, responsible for putting together and distributing the rations to the refugees. Once things had become better organized I was appointed to assist to the nuns in the attention of children, trying to control malnutrition and illness. We examined them, measured and weighed them, made diagnoses, and tried to help them to overcome their problems.

This was the beginning of Rosalía's career as a professional health promoter.

Candelaria is one of the few whose memory of the arrival in Mexico is not entirely positive. After a terrifying experience of persecution by the army, Candelaria and her family decided to cross the border to Mexico. They were also among the early refugees.

My husband was employed by a señor in La Reforma. He was paid with corn, worm-eaten beans, and little else. He did not receive cash. The children fell ill of malnourishment. They needed nutritious food and medicines, but we had no money to buy any. After six weeks, I went to see the boss—my husband is very timid, as you know—I told him what I thought about the working conditions and concluded that if the conditions were not improved my husband would return the farm implements the next morning and find a new boss. The boss became furious. He asked us to leave the same day—if not he would call the police. We were scared, we had no idea where to go and we had almost no money. But God helped us.

Shortly after, her husband was employed by "a very kind Mexican." The family stayed on his farm until the refugee camp was established in the area, when they moved there.

For most people, Mexico represented the end of what they often refer to as a nightmare (*una pesadilla*). However, the security situation in the areas closest to the border was far from reliable. For Don Gregorio, sixty-four, the nightmare continued in the refugee camp. He was one of those who suffered the consequences of the Guatemalan aggression toward the refugees in Chiapas. The Guatemalan army killed his son Eduardo, eighteen years old. This happened after some six or seven months in Mexico, when they lived in a camp in Chajúl, very close to the border. His son had just left the house and was on his way to the *milpa* to harvest corn. Gregorio heard shooting and went out to se what was going on. He found his son in a pool of blood, riddled with bullets. Shortly before, they had lost another son Alberto, twenty-five, who died from illness. According to his father, his death was caused by the loss of his wife and two small children, who were killed in an army ambush while hiding in the jungle of Ixcán.

Unrest at the Border Areas

Growing unrest, military incursions, and emerging tensions among the local population in Chiapas made the Mexican government increasingly impatient with the presence of the refugees in the border area. The establishment of camps created not only pressure on land and deforestation, but also competition for other scarce resources such as water and firewood. Aid was earmarked for refugees, and this created some resentment among their poor Mexican neighbors. Moreover, the presence of the refugees influenced the local labor market, since many of them were willing to accept lower salaries and poorer working conditions than what had been common before.

In April 1984, 200 Guatemalan troops attacked the refugee camp of El Chupadero, five kilometers from the border, and six people were killed. Following this incident, the Mexican government decided that in order to avoid further tensions and protect the refugees it would move all of the 46,000 refugees living in camps in Chiapas to new camps in the states of Campeche and Quintana Roo. Not only could security be improved in these areas, but the refugees could work toward self-sufficiency. This was impossible in Chiapas at that moment (Franco 1999: 78).

Although many refugees had long requested to be relocated further away from the border, the majority refused to move. This brought them into direct and bitter confrontations with the government. Over the next two years the government used a combination of persuasion, threats, and confrontation in order to relocate some 12,000 to Campeche and 6,700 to Quintana Roo. By the end of 1988, however, more than 22,400 refugees remained in Chiapas. The decrease in the number of refugees in the last census indicates that many refugees were dispersed throughout Mexico or had returned to Guatemala (Zinser 1991: 82).

For most of my informants, the removal was one of the most dramatic events during their period of exile. In spite of the tensions and aggressions created by the Guatemalan military presence in the area, most of them strongly opposed this decision and fought against it. First and foremost, they were afraid of what was going to happen to them. When they learned about the removal plans, terrifying rumors about the destinies of the removed started to circulate. Some said refugees were relocated to be killed by the Mexican army; others painted an equally frightening scenario, deportation to Guatemala and handover to the Guatemalan army. According to some informants, the guerrilla who feared to lose contact

with the refugees fomented these rumors, even though they officially supported the relocation (Delli Sante 1996).

In some areas COMAR, assisted by the army and the marines, used force
to relocate the refugees. Nicolás, forty-nine, told the following about his
experience in the Marqués de Comillas area.

When we crossed over to Puerto Rico in 1982, the Church had arrived, COMAR
and ACNUR also. Señor Gregorio Sánchez was also there, the one who was killed
afterward by the guerrilla for controlling the people too closely. We stayed in
Puerto Rico for two years. During these two years I was a health promoter, full
time, 360 days a year. With other six compañeros we attended to 9,000 people. They only gave us our rations of food; we received no salary. After two
years my family had no clothes. They needed clothes and I had to find work
elsewhere to earn some money. I went to an ejido in a neighboring area. Two
months later the relocation started.

My mother had remained in Puerto Rico accompanying my daughter, who
went to school there. When the relocation started I did not want to leave. I
had my family in two places, in the ejido where I worked and in Puerto Rico.
I decided to go to Puerto Rico to pick up my mother and daughter. On my way,
the Mexican police captured me. They thought that I was a guerrillero. "How
many people have you killed," they asked. They obliged me to drink alcohol
and threatened to kill me. I spent a bad night with security officers. The next
morning the soldiers had started to destroy the cayucos (local boats) because
people tried to escape. Finally, I was able to cross the river to see my mother
and daughter, but nobody was allowed to leave the place so I had no chance
to take them back to the ejido. After a couple of days I succeeded in escaping,
crossing the river in a canoe that passed by. When I arrived in the ejido after
more than two days walk, my wife and children were not there any longer. The
alcalde auxiliar told me that this very same day the army had picked up all the
Guatemalans to be moved to Quintana. You have to go too, he said. Of course,
I said, but I had no intention of complying. I walked around in the village. The
houses were empty. I met a Mexican I knew and he told me what had happened. They took your family with them; they are already in Boca de Chajúl
now, I think.

I stayed in the village for three more days until I found someone who could
take me to Boca de Chajúl. When I arrived there, my wife and children had
already been removed and I was told that the same had happened to my mother
and daughter in Puerto Rico. Some Guatemalans still remained, but their conditions were so bad that they finally agreed to be moved. I decided to join
them and we were taken directly to Quintana Roo. My family were not there,
they had gone to Campeche. This I was told by COMAR's camp officer, the
brother of Sánchez, a good person. Don't worry, he said, in two, three days
your family will be here. In five days they all arrived.

Nicolás's story reveals the confusion that characterized the removal of the refugees. According to Kauffer (1997), the removal operation was not very successful. By the end of 1985, when the last contingent of refugees was removed from Chiapas, fewer than half of the 46,000 of those registered as refugees had resettled in the Yucatán peninsula. The rest refused to leave Chiapas, unwilling to give up their geographical and cultural closeness to Guatemala. Due to the pronounced economic inequality and social conflict that had been exacerbated by the presence of the Guatemalan refugees, the Mexican government discouraged permanent settlement in Chiapas. This attitude translated into marked disparities between the levels of assistance provided to the refugees in Chiapas and to those who moved to the new camps in Campeche and Quintana (Riess 2000; Stepputat 1989; Freyermuth and Godfrey 1993). No new refugees were officially recognized in Chiapas after the relocation to the Yucatán peninsula. Those who arrived in Chiapas from now on were obliged to be clandestine, dispersing throughout the region, or return to Guatemala. These clandestine refugees received neither public attention nor validation of their migratory documents. Nevertheless, they were able to make a living, in spite of the absence of aid (Kauffer 1997: 111).

Relocation to the Yucatán Peninsula

The relocation to Campeche and Quintana Roo implied new ruptures and months of emergency in precarious shelters, until the construction of the new camps had been completed and people could move in.[4] With hindsight, my informants, who eventually and after strong resistance moved to new camps in Campeche and Quintana Roo, consider the move a success—an evaluation shared by several aid agencies (Franco 1999: 79). After overcoming the initial phase of precariousness and hardship, they realized that the transfer was for the better. The new camps resembled villages rather than camps. Housing standards were improved, and people got access to land to cultivate their own food and even products for sale, potable water, electricity, good access roads and transport, and, above all, a variety of possibilities to obtain cash income. Social services improved considerably, especially education and health.

UNHCR, in collaboration with the Mexican government, implemented programs to help the refugees to integrate and become self-sufficient. These programs were based on a combination of subsistence farming, casual wage labor within the states where the camps were located, and income-generating projects within the settlements themselves (Stepputat 1989). They emphasized preservation of the refugees' ethnic and cultural values, participation of women, physical and intellectual development of children, and protection of the environment. During this period, organizations and

networks of refugees within as well as between camps mobilized and uti-
lized local resources and energies for problem-solving. This was possible
thanks to human as well as financial assistance provided by international
agencies.

"Repatriation" Versus "Collective Return"

Even though most of my informants considered their stay in Mexico a
temporary one, they had no concrete plans for return until after the signing of the first peace accord in 1992. They were deeply skeptical about
the repatriation that had taken place so far. Small numbers of individuals and families had started to return to Guatemala as early as 1984,
when the army increasingly managed to isolate the guerrillas in the mountains and people felt that their home communities were no longer under
immediate threat. The precarious economic conditions of the Guatemalans who remained in Chiapas also provided a strong incentive for some
refugees to repatriate spontaneously and without any institutional support. Official efforts at repatriation began only in 1986, following the
election of President Vinicio Cerezo Arévalo, marking the return to civilian rule after three decades of military dictatorship. A Guatemalan repatriation agency, CEAR (National Commission for Repatriates, Refugees,
and Displaced Persons) was established in late 1986, and in early 1987 a
tripartite mechanism, involving the Mexican and Guatemalan governments as well as the UNHCR, was established and an agreement signed
that laid the ground rules for official repatriation. An important point
in this agreement was that it permitted UNHCR to operate within Guatemala and continue its assistance to the refugees after repatriation (Zinser
1991; Riess 2000). Several of my informants remember the visits paid by
Tereza Blandón de Cerezo, the wife of President Cerezo, and the director of CEAR, to the camps in Quintana Roo, trying to convince them that
the new government was creating the conditions for their safe return to
Guatemala. They were not well received by the refugees. During this
period they also received visits from representatives of the Ixcán Grande
Cooperative and from cooperatives in Zona Reina who had decided to
remain in the country under military control, who informed the refugees
that if they did not return immediately, INTA would distribute deeds
to the people who were occupying their land (Espinoza and Figueroa
1999: 163).

The camp refugees were not satisfied with the conditions offered in the
repatriation agreement. They felt that the Guatemalan government intended to fool them. The government representatives did not inform them
about the human rights situation in the country, which at this point was
rather bad. Neither did they inform them about establishment of the PACs

(Self-Defense Patrols) and the "model villages."[5] Through their own information networks, the refugees were well informed about what was going on in their areas of origin. Moreover, they knew that the image created of them in Guatemala was that they were guerrillas or their collaborators and that the refugee camps were insurgency sanctuaries. Therefore, most camp refugees did not accept the invitation by the government to return.

However, these initiatives from the Cerezo government called for a response from the refugees and inspired many to increase their organizational activity within the camps. The refugees wanted to determine the conditions under which their return should take place. For this purpose, a refugee organization, the Permanent Commissions, CCPP (Comisiones Permanentes de los Refugiados Guatemaltecos en Mexico), was created in 1987 in order to represent the refugees in direct negotiations with the Guatemalan government. This was a representative body, elected by direct vote of all refugees living in the camps. Each camp selected six permanent and two supplemental representatives to the commissions. The CCPP did not replace the existing leadership, who continued to administer the internal affairs in the camps. They did, however, gain considerable power. With the establishment of the CCPP, the refugees got a country-wide representation. This organization enjoyed greater leverage than the camp leaders in representing the interests of the refugees before the outside world. This was a departure from the traditional process of decision-making based on assemblies, eroding the purity of the democracy practiced in the camps and leading to a certain rivalry between CCPP representatives and camp leaders. However, it strengthened the negotiating power of the refugees, as it facilitated the development of a camp government based on consultation with representatives of the larger refugee communities in Mexico (Zinser 1989: 76–77).

In early 1989, following an elaborate process of discussion and consultation, the CCPP formulated their conditions for the return to Guatemala. They demanded that the negotiations be based on a list of six points expressing their main concerns. These included conditions of safety and the implementation of an integral reintegration program, including access to land and credit, and the right of every refugee to determine how, when, and to which place to return (CCPP 1989; Rivero 2001).

The most controversial point was the demand for collective return. The military authorities were against it because they feared the reestablishment of a support base for insurgency in communities outside military control. CEAR rejected it because of the logistical complications. Instead, they promoted repatriation in small groups, something most camp refugees saw as a threat to the safety of the individual returnee and a ploy against the community (Zinser 1991: 77).

The mutual lack of trust, especially the reluctance of the Guatemalan authorities to recognize CCPP as a legitimate representative of the refugees and a relevant negotiating partner, prolonged the process toward the negotiation table. Not until March 1991 were peace negotiations initiated between the refugee organization and representatives of the Guatemalan government and armed forces, mediated by the Roman Catholic Church and the UNHCR. After a year and a half of difficult discussions, an agreement was signed on October 8, 1992. The first return under the terms of these accords took place in January 1993.

In this agreement, the government committed itself to facilitate access to land for refugees who decided to repatriate. This was an important achievement and probably the main motivating factor for return, at least for my informants. Another essential condition, often mentioned by the returnees, was exemption from military service and the prohibition of members of the armed forces from entering the returnee communities. International verification and monitoring, particularly by the United Nations and the international *acompañantes*, was also an important element in this process.[6] With the understandably deep skepticism toward the Guatemalan state, prevention of entrance of the armed forces was to be monitored on a daily basis by the *acompañantes*, who were supposed to live in the returnee community and thus be able to witness and report potential violations to the UN Mission with authority to intervene. With the establishment of the agreement, a distinction was made between *retorno* (return), which referred to the collective returns under the terms of the 1992 accords, and *repatriación* (repatriation), the term used for the smaller groups who chose to return outside the 1992 framework and who were given the basic assistance laid out under the 1987 Tripartite Pact. For my informants this distinction is very important. They will correct anyone who refers to them as *repatriados*, explaining that they are different from the repatriated who returned in an "individualistic and unorganized manner." As we shall see in more detail later, organization plays a central role in the self-identification of the returnees.[7]

Preparing for the Return to the Petén

The returnees in La Quetzal were part of the collective refugee return that started in 1993 and ended in 1998. Planning for the collective return formally began in 1987, when the camps' refugees gathered to choose representatives to take part in the CCPP, which was going to represent them in what became a five-year ordeal of negotiations with the Guatemalan government. However, most people did not engage in the planning at this point. They did not have much confidence in the outcome of the negotiations. Not until they had learned the content of the agreement did their attitudes begin to change. The accords detailed agreements on timing, land access, credit, military service, legal rights of returnees, and the role of NGOs (Mahony 1998). For my informants, the government's commitment to facilitate access to land for refugees who decided to repatriate was the most important achievement and motivating factor for return. The commitment to warrant their security though international verification and monitoring, particularly by the United Nations, was also an important element.

In 1993 the refugees organized to negotiate the details of return and to plan how the returnee communities should be structured and developed. This process was controlled by the CCPP whose leaders were closely linked to the URNG (Guatemalan National Revolutionary Unit). The refugees who intended to return to the Petén were expected to approach the Vertiente Norte of the CCPP, the branch responsible for the planning of returns to the counties of the Petén and Alta and Baja Verapáz.[8] The Vertiente Norte started out with 27 members who became the leading force in the planning and implementation of the return of 236 families to La Quetzal, the first return to the Petén (Cedillo 1999).

The Vertiente Norte developed a community-centered model of development that integrated social, political, and economic dimensions. Rejecting what they defined as the dominant liberal model of development as one that concentrates wealth and impoverishes the majority, they intended to establish cooperative-based agricultural communities. Their model of communitarian development was built on the following principles: the recognition of human rights, inclusive and participatory democracy, and an efficient and sustainable communitarian economic base that protects natural resources (CCPP documents). It should be noted that, in spite of the stress on participation, this model was largely a product from above. Only the most politicized of my male informants—a relatively small number—participated in the planning process from the beginning. Most of them had already been actively involved as community leaders, such as education and health promoters and group representatives in the camps. A few (all men) were members of the delegations sent by CCPP to the Petén to identify possible sites of return and to negotiate the terms of purchase and the establishment of the cooperative once the farm had been selected. The rest were recruited later, at a point when most general terms of the return had been established.

Committed to the idea that development should benefit all members of the community, they encouraged various constituencies, such as women, youth, and educational and health promoters, to organize themselves as *sectores* (sectors) to participate in the planning process. The organization of refugee women—Ixmucané—established in 1993 played an important role in the return and settlement processes.

A corresponding youth organization—Maya Tikal—was established in early 1994. Even though the education and health promoters did not establish formal organizations until after the return, they were heavily engaged in enhancing their skills in order to serve in their new community. The training of health and education promoters had begun long before concrete plans of return had been drawn up, in order to provide health and education services in the refugee camps. From then on these efforts were intensified and directed primarily at preparation for serving in the returnee community.

The return to La Quetzal was realized after almost two years of preparations. The process started in June 1993, when a commission from the Vertiente Norte visited the Petén to identify land for sale and access productive alternatives and mechanisms to obtain the land. The commission returned to Mexico with several alternatives, all captured on video. These were carefully studied by the potential returnees and, after several rounds of discussion, La Quetzal was selected as to the most attractive one. People tell about their fascination with the natural beauty of the place that seemed to have everything: big, beautiful trees, wild animals, and a river providing enough water. At that point, they did not reflect much about the labor required in order to produce enough food in this dense rainforest.

Once the decision to go to La Quetzal was made, two major challenges still confronted them. First, a group of people willing to engage in this project of return had to be recruited and consolidated. Second, all the practicalities associated with the purchase of land had to be settled. At the beginning, only a limited number of families had expressed an interest in returning to the Petén. A recruitment campaign was therefore initiated by a small group of refugees interested in buying the property in La Quetzal. They traveled to different camps in Quintana Roo and Campeche where they had contacts, trying to recruit people to join their project of return.

Many of those who finally settled in La Quetzal were recruited through this campaign. They had not planned to return to the Petén in the first place. They would have preferred Ixcán, but they gradually realized that this was neither possible nor desirable. New settlers had occupied the land previously tilled by the refugees and they were not willing to give it up without fighting (Garst 1993; Egan 1999). Neither were the refugees eager to face conflicts upon their return, as certainly would have been the outcome if they started to claim the rights to the land they once tilled. Moreover, due to the expansion of many refugee families, they would need more land than they previously had in order to sustain their adult sons and daughters, who had married and become parents in exile. Those who had lived in the Petén before the "violence" preferred to settle in this region. They could not return to their old communities because they felt excluded and threatened by their ex-neighbors, who defined them as guerrilla supporters and even traitors.

The return to La Quetzal was one of the most controversial collective returns, due to the fact that 80 percent of the estate was located within the core area of the Maya Biosphere Reserve, established in 1990. The estate had been purchased in the late 1970s by a cooperative federation in Chimaltenango (FEDECOMERQ) and was occupied a few years later by a cooperative of some twenty indigenous peasant families from this area. After the establishment of a camp by the FAR guerrilla in the jungle part of the estate, followed by military incursions and counterinsurgency actions, these people abandoned the area and never returned. It is not known what happened to them.

Once the returnees had decided to buy the estate, CCPP negotiated the purchase with the owners. The next step was to apply for the credits (to be provided by the government under the 1992 Peace Accords; Riess 2000) to make the purchase, and to obtain government approval to settle on the land. They soon ran into trouble with CONAP, the government agency responsible for protected areas in Guatemala. The law that created the reserve strictly prohibits settlement in the core area, and CONAP refused to approve any settlement in the estate. The refugee organization argued that because the *finca* existed prior to the establishment of the reserve, and because private ownership of land was protected in the constitution, they had the right to settle and develop the land. They also provided the government and CONAP with a forest management plan that they maintained would protect the ecosystem of the area. This initiated a long and difficult process of negotiations between the refugees and various government agencies, the most important being CONAP, CEAR, and INTA. While the latter were eventually willing to approve settlement, CONAP remained intransigent, preventing the release of funds and credits needed to buy the land. As a result the return was postponed several times.

In December 1994, tired of struggling with bureaucratic authorities, the refugees took matters into their own hands and organized a self-financed working brigade to go to the estate to start preparing the ground. In January 1995, this work brigade escorted by international accompaniers, arrived in the area to build temporary sheds and prepare for the return. In April 1995, approximately 1200 refugees returned to La Quetzal, this time escorted by sixty international *acompañantes*, young people mostly from Europe and the U.S., recruited by CCPP. Although CCPP was the main organizer, the process of return was also supported by UNHCR and CEAR and some national and international NGOs.

This return, like the other collective returns that took place between the signing of the 8 October 1992 Agreement and the signing of the final peace agreement in 1996, still in the middle of the armed conflict, had strong political connotations. The political character of the return to La Quetzal became evident during the three days between the refugees' landing at the airport of Flores and their arrival at the estate. Receptions and demonstrations were organized at the airport by a number of NGOs, popular organizations, and trade unions, including a demonstration and a Mayan religious ceremony in the Mayan temples of Tikal and a Catholic sermon in the municipal capital of La Libertad. After countless difficulties, the arrival of the returnees in La Quetzal was certainly a great political victory for the leaders and their legal and political advisors (van der Vaeren 2000: 2–4). What motivated the majority of the returnees, however, was their land hunger.

Motives for Return

It has been questioned to what extent the return to Guatemala was voluntary. Based on a study of refugees who repatriated from Chiapas in 1997, Riess (2000) argues that for a decision to be a meaningful choice between returning and not returning, two conditions need to be satisfied. First, viable alternatives from which to choose must exist, and, second, the person making the decision must have full information about these alternatives. Unlike the returnees from Chiapas who, according to Riess "repatriated by default," the returnees to La Quetzal considered staying in Mexico to be a real alternative to returning. Many people described the decision to return as a very difficult one, characterized by ambivalence and doubts.

For most people, but especially for adult males, access to land appeared as the major motive for their return to Guatemala. They wanted ownership of land, enough land to feed their families and grow produce for sale, land that could be passed on to their children. In talking about their motives of return, expressions like "Quería volver a mi tierra, estar en tierra ajena es muy duro" (I wanted to return to my land, to be in the land of others is very hard) were rather common. *Mi tierra* did not refer to their place of birth or where they used to live before exile, but rather to any place in the Guatemalan national territory that could provide enough land to secure their livelihood. It should be noted that in Spanish there is no word equivalent to *home* in English. The word *casa* (and sometimes *hogar*) is used when referring to home in the sense of residence (house/apartment/farm). Even though *mi tierra* is sometimes used by farmers for the plot they till and live on, it is most often used in a more general sense referring to a community, region, or country. My informants talk about *mi tierra* in that general sense.

The returnees in La Quetzal had in common that they did not want to go back to their *casas* (houses) or villages in Ixcán, the region where most of them lived before going into exile. These had been destroyed by the scorched-earth campaign in the early 1980s (Falla 1992; Le Bot 1995; Schirmer 1998). Nor did they want to return to their own piece of land, because it had been occupied by people brought in by the army after the refugees left, who would refuse to hand it over to its previous owners or tenants. The most frequent reason given for not wanting to return to the place they came from, however, was that that land was not big enough to sustain their expanding family, sons and daughters who had grown up, married, and become parents in exile. I found a high degree of pragmatism with regard to the location of land to "return" to. It is also noteworthy that a number of informants said that, if they had been offered property rights to land in Mexico, they would have remained there.

The decision to return to Guatemala was talked about as a very difficult one, characterized by ambivalence and doubts. Some of my informants said that their doubts were so overwhelming that they registered and resigned several times before they eventually decided to join the return to La Quetzal. The fact that the Mexican government decided to grant permanent residence and the option of citizenship to those who decided to stay contributed to their hesitancy. Approximately one-third of the camp refugees decided to remain in Mexico and become Mexican citizens (Zinser 1991).

I observed certain age and gender differences regarding the topics emphasized in talking about the decision to return. Generally, adult men, who had been more actively involved in the negotiations and preparations for the return to Guatemala, were the most positive toward return, while women and adolescents were more reluctant. Women more often than men stressed their fear about the lack of security. We should remember that the return to La Quetzal took place one and a half years before the signing of the final peace accord, and the armed conflict was still not settled. The fact that an agreement had been signed (8 October 1992), denying the army entrance to the returnee communities and allowing the presence of foreign accompaniers to monitor the security situation, did not fully comfort them, since they had little confidence in the will of the Guatemalan authorities to comply with the agreements. They were well informed about the situation in Guatemala and knew of repatriates who had been harassed, kidnapped, and even killed upon their return.

Moreover, women seemed to be more concerned about what they had achieved in Mexico. They talked about the quality of housing and basic infrastructure, such as electricity, piped water, and good roads. Another common theme was the variety of produce; they had all kinds of fruits and vegetables in addition to the basic corn and beans. Not only did they produce enough for their own consumption, but they could also easily sell their surpluses at good prices. Moreover, they stressed that there were plenty of job opportunities for young people. Their unmarried sons and daughters had worked in nearby cities and in this way contributed to the family income.

As in other refugee contexts, the adolescents were perhaps the most unenthusiastic about the return. They had been born or had lived most of their lives in Mexico, and their visions of Guatemala were generally very negative, associated with violence, persecution, poverty, and backwardness. What Yolanda told about her reaction to the return is quite representative of what other young people expressed. Yolanda had been sixteen years old in 1995, and, like many of her female friends, she had been working as a maid in a Mexican family in Cancún. She liked it there, the employer family treated her very well, and she had become accustomed to urban life. When I asked her about her attraction to this life, she mentioned comfortable housing, television, varied and tasty food, and *paseos*—on Sundays she used to stroll in the streets of Cancún with her friends. When her father decided to return she became terribly distressed, but at the same time she realized she could not remain in Mexico without her family around.

I hated to leave Mexico. I cried during the whole flight to Flores and did not stop crying for several days. When we arrived here in the jungle I despaired, nothing except the galeras (rickety sheds) where we all were stuffed together. How I missed Mexico! For a long time everything seemed hopeless, but little by little I got used to it, and now I rarely think about the past.

When Yolanda told me this she was twenty, about to marry a local school teacher and cooperative member, and committed to a future in the returnee community.

When there were conflicting views within the family as to whether to return or not, the wish of the male head of household often appeared to be decisive. Maria's laconic comment illustrates this. "Life was much easier in Mexico and I would have preferred to stay, but my husband wanted to return. What could I do, I could not stay behind, could I?" It should be noted, however, that in a few cases families and even couples split; some members decided to return, while others stayed. This was, for example, the case Graciela, who left her husband to join her widow mother and married brothers and their families when they returned. Graciela had two sons, one with her husband and one from an earlier relationship, who used to live with her mother. When it became clear that her husband would not allow the son from the previous relationship to live with them, she decided to leave him and return with her mother to Guatemala.

My findings support previous studies which indicate that the desire to return varies tremendously according to individual and collective experiences as well as social, political, and economic contexts in the country of origin as well as in the country of exile (see Allen 1996; Long and Oxfeld 2004; Markowitz and Stefansson 2004). "Home" cannot with certainty be reduced to place of origin, but may be something that is made and remade on a daily basis (Hirschon 1998). I found that, in an addition to security in the sense both of protection from violence and of sustainable livelihoods, what Hage (1977) calls "a sense of possibility" was characteristic for my informants' notion of "home." "Sense of possibility" challenges the passive notion of "home" as mere shelter and attaches to it the opportunities for change and improvement. For these returnees, "home" is where they have family around, where they have enough resources to make a good living and where they can be with people with whom they share certain experiences and visions for the future.

Exile as a Transforming Experience

In this chapter we have seen that the experience of armed conflict and exile that led to a dislocation of economic and social life, in the case of these Guatemalan returnees also led them into situations where they learned to relate to each other and to their surroundings in new and different ways. In most cases, those who became refugees were people who lived close to the national borders with no marked cultural differences following the border line. People crossed the border because they felt threatened in their society, and for most of them exile did not mean deprivation and victimization, but the contrary, recognition and even empowerment. My informants hold contradictory notions about their experience of exile. Time and again they stressed that in spite of implying hardship and suffering it also taught them a lot that they would not be without. In the following chapters we will see that the experience of exile has inspired new notions of belongingness, and, rather than loss of identity and culture, often said to characterize displaced people, a process of redefinition was initiated in exile whereby new concepts of community and self developed.

Chapter 6
Constructing a New Community

The settlement and construction of the village of La Quetzal were quite different from the more spontaneous occupations (*agarradas*) so common in the rainforests of the Petén during the previous decades. The returnees settled after almost two years of detailed planning assisted by a number of different development agents, the most important being the UNHCR and national and international NGOs. Upon their arrival, the returnees were already organized as a cooperative and had mobilized other segments of the population, acquired land (even though the formalities regarding property rights had not been settled), and worked out a number of plans as a basis for the construction of the new community. They had made plans regarding not only the production and use of natural resources, but also urbanization, comprising a variety of infrastructural and service projects, all beautifully adapted to the ecological conditions of the rainforest. Considerable time and resources had been contributed by the many NGO technicians and advisors assisting the refugees in the preparation process. The plans looked excellent on paper and were well intentioned, but were too idealistic and theoretical as far as implementation was concerned.

The Arrival in the Jungle of the Petén

If the collective return can be described as a political success, this was not the case for the practical arrangements. The first encounter with their future home place was not what the returnees had expected. When the bus convoy arrived in Retalteco, 14 kilometers from La Quetzal, they could not continue because there was no road, only a poor logging trail. When they finally arrived in La Quetzal the next day, 8 April 1995, the estate was still an uninhabited, dense jungle. Except for the remnants of a small number of families who had lived there in the late 1970s and early 1980s, there were few traces of human intervention. The community had to be constructed anew. The forest had to be cleared, and space was needed to construct homes, gardens, and public buildings. The challenges were countless for this conglomerate of people recruited from seven different camps in Campeche and Quintana Roo, many of whom did not know each other beforehand.

Due to the delays referred to in the previous chapter, the working brigades who were responsible for preparing the site for settlement had neither time nor adequate equipment to do their job. In addition to building of a temporary camp, the brigades should have measured and deforested the settlement area and identified the areas to be used for agriculture. They had barely been able to raise the precarious collective sheds, where people had to live crammed together for months before they could clear their lots to build their own houses.

A few days after the arrival in La Quetzal, most of the people and organizations that had been assisting during the preparation for return and installation in the new community disappeared, visiting the returnee community only sporadically. As far as the advisors associated with URNG were concerned, they had achieved their objectives once the demonstrations and ceremonies in the Petén had been completed and the returnees had arrived in their new settlement. They were not much concerned with the practical questions of the survival and construction of a new community. Only representatives from two NGOs and two *acompañantes* (accompaniers) remained in the community after the first week (van der Vaeren 2000: 13–14).

The encounter with the jungle was difficult in more than just the practical sense. Some of my informants recounted how anxious they felt about their security situation; they could not relax, because the jungle of the Petén reminded them of the past. The sense of insecurity increased dramatically when they discovered that the FAR guerrilla had a camp not far from their area of settlement. Josefa remembers:

The first year here was terrible. I was very scared, especially when we discovered that the guerrilla was around. I could not sleep at night. Every night I was back in Ixcán with the soldiers, killing people and trying to capture me and my children. I was in such poor shape that my little daughter died, she was only eleven months. After her death I was overcome by a terrible sadness, I became so weak that I could not rise from my bed. Finally, they took me to the hospital and the doctor gave me some medicine that helped me a little. I think it was Doña Margarita (local midwife and traditional healer) who finally cured me. Now I have stopped dreaming and I rarely think about Ixcán.

Thanks to some external support and their own organizing capacity, the returnees were able to make a living in spite of the overwhelming difficulties. After only a week they could send their children to a school, organized by the education promoters in the sheds raised to house the working brigades. A provisional health clinic was also soon established and during the first year personnel from an international NGO helped run it.

During the emergency phase, the women were to a large extent in charge of the everyday running of the camps, while the men started to clear sites to build their houses, a priority task due to the extremely poor housing conditions in the temporary shelters. The clearing went very slowly; it had to be done with axes and machetes, since there were only two power saws available in the community. They had no chance to clear the agricultural land for the first planting season in May-June 1995, nor for the second in November. They had to postpone it to May-June the following year with the first harvest three months later. This meant that they depended on food aid much longer than they had foreseen and had to endure a rather deficient diet.

Cristobal remembers his first months in La Quetzal.

I had many illusions arriving here, I had seen pictures, everything green and fertile, monkeys playing in the trees, it seemed very joyful. When we finally arrived I found it equally joyful, until the first rains, then everything became very sad. We had almost no money, and no land to plant our milpa; we were not able to clear land in time. First we had to clear the sites to build our houses. As the rain started to pour down, the road was pure mud and we continued to be stuffed together in the sheds, we became very depressed. "How are we going to survive here?" I said to my wife. "Let's leave this place, let's go back to Quintana," said my wife and my children. "If you want to leave, we leave," I said. "I have to find out how to pass immigration to return to Quintana. Let us think about it a couple of days and then decide." So we did and when we were to decide my eldest son said, "If we return to Quintana we can only bring what we can carry; we will lose everything, we better stay here." We all agreed.

I tried to figure out how to earn some money. I had a bicycle, a very nice, new one that I brought from Quintana. People admired it. I brought the bicycle to Retalteco with the idea of selling it; I had to carry it on my back most of the time to prevent it from being covered with mud. To make it more attractive, I pretended that it was not for sale when somebody asked. After a while I hinted that if someone offered me 300 quetzales I would consider selling it anyway. That's how I earned my first money in Guatemala. What shall I do when I have spent this money? I wondered. I decided to use one hundred buying conos de hilo (cones of synthetic fiber) to make hammocks. I had learned to make hammocks in the camps. Twenty days later I had made two hammocks and went to Bethel to sell them. Before I left Guatemala I could not speak a work of Castilla, but this was not a problem any more. Nevertheless, I was scared stiff when knocking on people's doors to offer my hammocks. It went very well. I got 150 quetzales each. Part of it I used to buy more hilo, and, like this, we kept going until the road was repaired and I could sell my surplus of corn. Others were not so lucky, there was not enough food and many people fell ill.

Expectations Confront Reality

Many of my informants said that they had quite unrealistic expectations regarding their new home, even some of those who had visited the site previous to the return. They had acquired a rather idyllic picture: enough water, abundance of land, flat and smooth, certainly covered with dense forest, but with beautiful trees and lots of birds and animals. They were prepared for certain transitory hardship, but not for the extremely difficult conditions they had to endure before things started to improve. Neither were they prepared for the isolation, a situation that worsened drastically once the rainy season started a few weeks after their arrival. At that point, the only means of transport for people and goods was by horse or on their own backs. After a while not even tractors could move on the poor logging trail. My informants tell dramatic stories about how they struggled to transport sick people on stretchers with mud above their knees. Many of them felt that they had been fooled, and more than once regretted that they had left their relatively comfortable conditions in Mexico.

One of their slogans for the collective returns was "Struggle to return, return to struggle." That is what most of them decided to do instead of resigning and leaving. Their fight for the road is illustrative. During the negotiations for return the refugees had been promised that the road connecting the estate to the neighboring village would be upgraded before their arrival. The existing logging trail was only drivable some three months a year during the dry season. The project was delayed pending permission from CONAP, who opposed it for environmental reasons. After a number of attempts to obtain the permission, the refugees lost their patience. By the end of May, some forty women with their children occupied the regional CONAP offices in the Petén, while a male delegation demonstrated in front of the central offices in Guatemala City. After three days of occupation and difficult negotiations, supported by UNHCR and CEAR, the returnees obtained the permission. However, due to weather conditions and a number of bureaucratic difficulties, the road was not ready until April 1996. The road implied an important turn in the life of the community; they were no longer isolated in the jungle.

Social Organization in the Returnee Community

Arriving at the community of La Quetzal is not very different from arriving at any other peasant community in the jungles of the Petén. The thatch-roofed houses on both sides of the access road bear witness to poverty and precariousness, in spite of being surrounded by exuberant vegetation giving the homesteads an agreeable appearance. In the center of the village the impression of precariousness continues; the public build-ings are simple constructions mostly of rough wood planks with corru-gated iron roofs. However, the number and size of the buildings attracts one's attention, especially if one knows that they have been raised during a period of four or five years, with local and very simple means. There are four school buildings, a large two-story building that houses the store-rooms and offices of the cooperative, and a large, very tall construction referred to as the bus station. If you by chance comment to the villagers that La Quetzal is similar to other villages you have passed by, they will probably strongly disagree with you and refer to their organization as a very important distinguishing factor. "We are organized, the others are not." If one remains in the community for a day or more, it is absolutely impossible to avoid noticing at least one expression of this: the frequent announcement of activities over the powerful loudspeakers in the coop-erative shop.

To understand the social organization of the returnee community, we need to make a distinction between the cooperative UMI (Unión Maya Itzá) and the community of La Quetzal, even though local people as well as outsiders often use the name of the cooperative to refer to the com-munity. This is probably because the cooperative is so pervasive in the economic and social life of this village.

The Community of La Quetzal

Whereas the community of La Quetzal comprises all the inhabitants living in the village, regardless of age or sex, the UMI consists only of its members, defined according to its statutes. Most of them are adult mar-ried men; a few are adult and single. However, not all adult men in La Quetzal are cooperative members. Since 1997 the inhabitants have been divided into two categories, according to their relationship to the coop-erative: 168 are cooperative members and approximately 45 are *pobladores*, also called *parcelistas*, most of the latter former members of the coopera-tive. Distinct from the rest, they were legal owners of their land before going into exile who decided to renounce their membership in order to be in a position to claim new free land from the government as compen-sation for land lost due to the "violence." Such compensation is guaran-teed in the peace agreements.[1] When the *parcelistas* withdrew from the cooperative, their membership was in most cases transferred to a son, or, in two cases where all the sons were already members, to an unmarried daughter. Together with one woman, whose husband has lived in the

United States since years before the return, they are the only female members; the cooperative is largely a male business.

The *pobladores* have been allowed to keep the two hectares of land, distributed to each family shortly after the settlement in the community, to sustain their families while waiting for the new land. They also benefit from some of the services provided by the cooperative, but receive neither the additional agricultural land that was distributed to the cooperative members in 1999 and 2000, nor the benefits from the extraction of timber from the rainforest, which is planned to be the main economic activity in the future. On the other hand, the *pobladores* are exempt from cooperative commissions and most of the heavy work obligations of cooperative members, but do participate in the work organized by the community. The first group of *pobladores* acquired land in a village in the municipality of Sayaxché by mid-2000 and started to prepare the site for their move there in the first half of 2001. The situation of the rest was by then still rather insecure.

THE COOPERATIVE UNIÓN MAYA ITZÁ

The UMI is the backbone of the returnee community. It was established in June 1994 by twenty of its current members almost a year before returning to Guatemala, to facilitate the purchase of land and other preparations for the return. The decision to organize as a cooperative was based on a number of considerations. It was a form of organization recommended by leaders and advisors of the refugees, but also welcomed by the refugees themselves, at least as far as the service part of it is concerned. They had experienced the advantages of this kind of organization with regard to social services, marketing of products, and negotiation with state and non-state agencies. Moreover, in order to obtain credit to buy the land, they were obliged to establish some kind of association qualified to claim legal status (*personería jurídica*). With the assistance of FEDECOAG (Federación de Cooperativas Agrícolas de Guatemala), an NGO that supported the return process, they were able to obtain this status in less than a year, something quite exceptional in Guatemala, where this kind of bureaucratic procedure often takes several years.

The cooperative is governed by the general assembly, which delegates the responsibility for the daily running of the institution to a directive board—*junta directiva*—elected once a year.[2] The *junta directiva* consists of five ordinary members, plus one representative of each of the committees of education and auditing. The level of activity within the cooperative is very high, and the number of committees appointed to administer cooperative affairs is steadily increasing as new projects are established. By the end of 2000, I counted fourteen committees in addition to the board and the committees of education and auditing. They were responsible for the following activities: labor, agriculture, forestry, marketing, poultry, vegetables, apiculture, tailoring, *xate*,[3] credit, transport, water, ecotourism, and elaboration of projects. The labor committee is, for example, responsible for planning and recruiting people to carry out collective work for the cooperative, while the poultry committee is responsible for running a poultry project and the transport committee for the use and maintenance of the bus and the cooperative vehicles (a truck and a pickup truck).

Legally, the rights and obligations of the cooperative members are defined by the cooperative statutes, which are identical to the statutes of other agro-industrial cooperatives in Guatemala. According to these statutes, the members have voice and vote in general assemblies. They may be elected to commissions, have to participate free of charge in cooperative work and projects, share the benefits of incomes and services, and share responsibilities regarding debts and losses. Regarding land property, however, UMI differs from most cooperatives in Guatemala; there is no individual ownership of land. The cooperative owns the land, and the member has only usufruct right to a certain piece or portion of it. This right can be transferred to one heir, but the land cannot be sold. According to the statutes, the cooperative is only committed to elect three committees in its annual general assembly: a directive board to administer the organization, and the auditing and education committees. The latter is in charge of educating the members in the philosophy and functioning of the cooperative as well as promotion of formal education. It is evident then that UMI has more committees than required: a level of activity and organization far beyond what is common in agro-industrial cooperatives in Guatemala.

THE SECTORES

In addition to the committees within the frame of the cooperative, several committees work at the community level, comprising certain segments of the population. These are referred to as *sectores*. These are six altogether: women, education promoters, health promoters and midwives, parents of families (*padres de familia*), youth, and catechists.

Perhaps the most important *sectores* are the promoters of education and health. As we have seen in the previous chapter, health and education have been of highest priority since the arrival of the refugees in Mexico. Training of promoters was intensified during the planning for the return and directed particularly at providing such services in the returnee community. By the end of 2000 there were eighteen education promoters (three of them women) teaching at the pre-primary, primary, and secondary levels (*ciclo básico*).[4] There were twelve health promoters (two women) in addition to the eight midwives, who used to be traditional midwives, all of them trained by national and international NGOs.

The *sector* of "parents of family" operates as a link between the education promoters and the parents of schoolchildren. Their role is to organize meetings where concrete problems related to the schools, as well as more complex issues such as the role of education in community development, are discussed. This committee also coordinates collective work to be carried out by the community such as constructing, equipping, and maintaining the school buildings; it operates as a support group for the promoters in negotiations with state and non-state institutions, and attends a monthly meeting with the school supervisor of the Ministry of Education.

The largest *sector* by far is the one associated with Ixmucané—the women's organization established in Mexico in 1993 to enhance women's participation in the returnee community. While very few women are cooperative members, most adult women are members of this organization. Despite representing half the adult population in the community they are defined as a *sector*. The refugee women played an important role in the preparation of return as well as during the emergency phase in the new settlement. However, as we shall discuss in more detail later, they face a number of problems and tensions regarding public participation as the community becomes more established.

The youth are also defined as a *sector* associated with the organization Maya Tikal, founded in Mexico in 1994. The situation of the adolescents is especially precarious, since they are not members of the cooperative and there is not enough land to incorporate them as members when they marry and establish their own families. This is one reason so much emphasis has been put on education. Most young people would prefer to make a living removed from the hardships of peasant agriculture. However, their possibilities are limited by the fact that there are very few scholarships and no family money available to complete secondary education. After having completed the *ciclo básico*, they still need two years of secondary school to be accepted for tertiary studies. They must go to the municipal or provincial capitals to do this, something very few families can afford. This is perhaps the most important explanation for the steady increase in labor migration that I found during the last part of my fieldwork.

Finally, the thirteen catechists (all men) constitute the *sector* in charge of the everyday running of the Catholic Church. The local church is part of the parish of La Libertad, but the parish priest, who serves a large district, visits the community only once every two months to celebrate mass. The catechists run the pastoral work. Every Wednesday afternoon and Sunday morning they arrange a Celebration of the Word. They also prepare children and youth for communion and confirmation and arrange courses for parents and godparents before baptism. So far La Quetzal is a predominantly Catholic community. However, there are seven evangelical families who until recently used to hold their services in each other's homes. In October 2000, they built a chapel and organized a religious festival, with the presence of believers from a number of sister congregations in the region. This event attracted a number local Catholics, many of whom said that they liked what they had witnessed.

With the exception of the women and youth *sectores*, the majority of the people constituting the *sectores* are cooperative members; a few are *pobladores*. Some of the *sectores* are affiliated with formal organizations or institutions operating at the regional or national level. This is the case of the education promoters who are members of AMERG (Asociación de Maestros Rurales Guatemaltecos), the health promoters and midwives associated with AMASAR, and the catechists.[5]

It should be noted that there are no associations constituted on the basis of ethnicity, even though La Quetzal is a multiethnic community, where some 90 percent of the people are of various indigenous origins. Eight of the 21 Mayan languages in Guatemala are represented in La Quetzal: Q'eqchi', Q'anjob'al, Mam, K'iche', Popti', Chuj, Ixil, and Ch'orti', in addition to Spanish (locally referred to as Castellano or simply Castilla), which is the lingua franca, spoken more or less fluently by the majority of the population. People do not seem to be preoccupied with ethnic differentiation, and ethnic categories are not much heard in everyday interaction. Nevertheless, as we will see in more detail in the next chapter, people are perfectly aware of them and are able to classify all their neighbors accordingly.

Local State Institutions

La Quetzal holds the status of *aldea* (village), and is thereby integrated into the state system represented locally by the *alcalde auxiliar* (assistant mayor). As the legal representative of the state, the main task is to monitor the local state of affairs, keep the register of births and deaths, and resolve local conflicts or infractions that are too small to bring to the center. In this case the *alcalde auxiliar* is the local representative of the municipal mayor of La Libertad. The people of La Quetzal have elected two *alcaldes auxiliares* to share this unremunerated position, because they consider it too much of a burden for one person. In addition, the *alcaldes* have two young male secretaries to assist them. The tasks of these secretaries can include, for example, doing the writing when the elected representatives are illiterate, as is not uncommon, since this post is often held by elderly people (always men). A small building has been erected in the center of the village to accommodate the *alcaldes auxiliaries*, one of whom is present every afternoon between four and six o'clock for people to present their cases. This institution does not hold a strong position in La Quetzal; most cases brought to the *alcaldes* are, as we shall see later, of a more personal character where members of only one or two families are involved. Problems and conflicts involving more than two families are generally discussed and resolved in other forums: the cooperative, with its multiple committees, or the general assembly, where all adult community members are invited to participate.

A local development committee (*comité de promejoramiento*) is another institution at the level of *aldea* required by the state. This committee, whose members are elected locally and authorized by the municipal authorities, is supposed to contribute to the generation of development projects. During my fieldwork the committee was involved in the promotion of a regional electrification project together with corresponding committees in other villages of the region. In many *aldeas* in the Petén the *alcalde auxiliar* and the development committee are the only local institutions except for the Church.

In order to coordinate activities, representatives of the cooperative and the *sectores* meet once every two weeks. Each of the four neighborhoods has elected two representatives to attend these meetings. Their function is to assure smooth communication between the leadership and the grassroots, especially keeping people informed and giving them the opportunity to express their opinions in communal matters. These representatives organize meetings in their respective neighborhoods when they consider it necessary. Even though all the representatives so far have been cooperative members, these meetings are open to all inhabitants, including *pobladores* and women. This is one of the very few arenas where women are invited to express their views on community affairs. Except in their own organization Ixmucané, women have only minority representation in two other *sectores*, the health and education promoters.

Thus, the level of involvement in public affairs, particularly in the case of cooperative members, is very high. Approximately two-thirds of the cooperative members hold at least one commission at any given time. People attend meetings—men much more frequently than women—several times a week, sometimes more than once a day. The cooperative, with its *junta* and 16 committees, involves many people, as do the different *sectores*. The community is also visited by many people who require the attention of members of the *junta*, the different committees or *sectores,* such as representatives of NGOs and other donor or potential donor organizations, visitors from other communities who come to "learn about the experience of the returnees," journalists, and so on. Moreover, since the work of the committees—at least some of them—requires contact with outside institutions and actors, the committee members, most frequently the committee president, have to pay visits to the municipal or provincial capitals, in some instances even to Guatemala City.

If one walks through the center of the village, especially in the afternoon, it is common to see people meeting in four or five different places. Attending a meeting takes time: first, because few people turn up on time and the meetings do not start until those who are expected to attend arrive; second, because discussions tend to be long, since everybody should have the chance to express an opinion and then reach a consensus without voting. If it is necessary to vote, decisions are made by simple majority by a raise of hands. Even more time-consuming than the meetings is the participation in collective work for the cooperative, something I will return to below.

Planning and Implementing New Livelihoods

Due to the organized and detailed planning referred to earlier, little has been left to chance in the construction of La Quetzal. The cooperative leadership, advised and supported by a number of development agencies, entered the scene with a model of communitarian development. A first step in the implementation of this model was to make a territorial survey (*ordenamiento territorial*) with the objective of designing an integrated management plan for the total estate, finding a balance between agricultural production, management, and conservation of the forest, and establishing the agricultural frontier. The technicians, together with the returnees, attempted to find definitive answers to the burning questions: Which part of the estate can be distributed and how much land can be allocated to each cooperative member? What kind of perennial crops can be cultivated on this land? How can the natural resources best be used for community development? How does one live off the rainforest without destroying it? (van der Vaeren 2000: 214)

The farm was carefully measured to localize borders, rivers, mountains, swampland, and the urban center. Types of soil were classified and samples sent to a laboratory for analysis. A forest inventory was also made to identify the potential economic prospects of the jungle. However, the numerous institutions involved in this process used different technical approaches as well as different ways of communicating their findings to the local population. Some attempted to involve the local population in all phases; others made expert assessments and presented their result at the end. The reception of the results of the technical studies was varied. Some results relating to existing practices, such as classification of soils, were easily understood, even though the methods used were different. Others that were not part of peasant practice, such as analysis of cartographic unities, created confusion and frustration.[6]

The distribution of land was a particularly controversial question. In spite of certain basic principles regarding land distribution established in Mexico, such as the principle that at least half the estate should be conserved as forest area, many people came to assume that the farm would eventually be divided so that each family could have enough individual land. As we have seen in the previous chapter, access to and ownership to land was the main motivating factor for return for most people.

The territorial survey revealed a number of miscalculations, among them that the estate was smaller than declared in the property documents (5,924 as against 6,209 hectares) and that the quality of the soils was much more uneven than calculated previously. This new information regarding ecological conditions made it necessary to reassess the issue of land distribution. The decision that each family should be given the opportunity to produce its own food was upheld; this was an unquestionable condition for most returnees. The question was how much land should be distributed to each member, given the production potential of the land and taking into account the constraints associated with its location within the Maya Biosphere. This led to tough discussions and controversies among the cooperative members as well as between the returnees and their advisors. Those who had not been closely involved in the planning of the return appeared not to have understood or taken seriously the constraints of being located within a protected area, and some even proposed expanding into the core area of the Biosphere. This was unacceptable to the leaders and the advisors, who had a hard time convincing their opponents.

It was eventually decided that five hectares per cooperative member should be assigned for agricultural purposes, two plots of two hectares each for *milpa* and one hectare of swampland for rice production. The first plots were distributed in January 1996, the swampland in April 1999, and the second *milpa* plots in early 2000. Due to the distribution and variety of soils, the latter were not located in the same area as the first *milpa* plots. This produced frustration among the peasants, who argued that it would be more difficult to look after the crop during harvest, to prevent theft. Moreover, land in three different areas implied more time spent walking. Due to the relative scarcity of land, the peasants could no longer continue their slash and burn agriculture. They were allowed to slash and burn the land before starting to cultivate it; then they had to stop this practice. After the first harvest of corn they were advised to rotate corn and manure beans, one harvest of each, in order to be able use the land continuously, something that implied long-term dependence on technical extension services.

Given that 80 percent of the estate was located within the Maya Biosphere reserve, only a minor part could be used for agricultural purposes. It could, however, be used for timber extraction, subject to approval by

CONAP. Economic development in La Quetzal is therefore primarily associated with the exploitation of the forest, not with the production of basic grains and perennial crops. A forest inventory was conducted in 1996/1997 by technicians from Centro Maya,[7] with the participation of members of the forestry committee of the cooperative and with a large number of the ordinary members doing the practical work. The different tree species were classified according to their marketing possibilities (van der Vaeren 2000: 230–31). On the basis of this inventory, a plan of forest management was drawn up. According to this plan, the total forest area assigned for management was divided into 25 plots. A different plot could be exploited each year over a period of twenty-five years, at which point the process could start over again. The trees on the first plot should then be big enough to be logged. Furthermore, only the species demanded by the industry or the local market should be felled.

The question of the regeneration of the forest was a delicate one. Studies exploring natural regeneration, based on the projected number of trees to be spared as seed carriers, showed that the regeneration capacity was not satisfactory as planned and that artificial regeneration or enrichment of the forest would be necessary. All the activities related to the exploitation and administration of the plan were to be taken care of by the cooperative members, who also considered the possibilities of initiating manufacturing projects such as sawmills and carpentries, thereby creating local employment opportunities.

It took four years before CONAP approved the management plan. The first extraction of timber could not be made until the dry season 1999/2000. Two thousand quetzales were distributed to each of the cooperative members; the rest was used for investment in the cooperative. As an initial step toward local wood conversion, the cooperative, in collaboration with a Guatemalan NGO, offered carpentry courses to its members starting in late 1999. The cooperative also sent a delegation to other cooperatives in Guatemala to explore their experiences with sawmills. However, when I finished my fieldwork, the prospects for local timber processing still belonged to the future.

Peasant Production

When I finished my fieldwork in early 2001, people in La Quetzal were still primarily subsistence producers, in spite of their enormous efforts to *progresar*. They had certainly achieved a lot, but their economy and welfare at the household level had not improved. At that point they had acquired the five hectares of land that was to be distributed for individual use. Corn was by far the most important crop as well as the primary staple food. Tortilla is the main item in the local diet; a meal without tortillas is not a real meal. Beans are the other main staple. My informants claim that the land in La Quetzal is not suitable for bean production, so they must purchase a major part of what they consume.

Corn is produced mainly for household consumption, while the surplus is sold to itinerant merchants arriving in the community. Agricultural production in La Quetzal is carried out in much of the same way as always, except that burning is no longer practiced. Cultivation is done with machete, hoe, and planting stock. Chili and pumpkin seeds are produced primarily for the market, but are also consumed by the household. These crops are common in other parts of the region, but they are new in this particular place and to these peasants, who are still searching for crops that can yield cash income. The returnees produce enough corn to eat and some to sell, but cash incomes are too low to cover what is needed to lead a decent life according to their own standards.

These standards are set with reference to their living conditions in the refugee camps in Mexico. They are still far from reaching such conditions, and many of my informants claim that they are worse off now then when they arrived in La Quetzal. Prepared as they were for a certain period of scarcity in their new settlement, they had purchased what they could afford before the return. In addition, they had been assisted through donations. This implied that they brought rather abundant supplies of certain goods such as clothes, bedding, household utensils, and radios. These things are gradually being worn out without being replaced, because most people are obliged to use all their income for everyday survival. I noticed an increasing anxiety regarding their private economy. After more than six years in Guatemala, the returnees are still poor and vulnerable, an element of frustration and disappointment for many people, especially the women, who feel most responsible for the clothing and education of the children.

Once the forest management plan moves forward, people expect to obtain additional cash income. They received their first small portion in 2000. At that point a number of people were rather desperate due to extreme drought, bushfires, and insect attacks damaging their crops. It is likely that the continued support for the communitarian development model will actually depend on the success of the forest management plan. The income from the forest so far, through sales of timber from the areas cleared for settlement and peasant agriculture, has been used for productive investments by the cooperative such as the grocery shop, two buses, and a truck, rather than being distributed to individual members.

SOCIAL AND SEXUAL DIVISION OF LABOR

The cooperative members divide their time between farm tasks and their collective obligations, such as construction work, digging of ditches to prevent the spread of forest fire, and logging, which during 1998 amounted to 80 working days per member. Even though people define the work carried out in the *milpa* as the most important one—"that's what keeps us alive"—they claim that this work becomes subsidiary to the collective one, in the sense that it is very difficult to avoid being present when called upon by the cooperative, unless one is able to send a substitute.

My informants were much concerned about the relationship between the individual and the collective work, as well as about the output of the latter. A number people felt that they had to spend too much time on the cooperative at the expense of their private activities. One problem with the cooperative work was that it did not feed directly back into the household, even when the cooperative had considerable income, as in the case of timber sales in 2000. The income was used mainly for cooperative investments, and only a small portion was distributed to the members. On two occasions toward the end of my fieldwork, cooperative members in a general assembly meeting questioned the investment policy of the cooperative, calling it "hyper-capitalist," and denounced what they called disregard of the welfare needs of the people. This provoked heated discussions about the distribution of money to cooperative members.

The men in La Quetzal are first and foremost agricultural producers, and their everyday life is to a large extent adapted to the imperatives of the agricultural cycle. The exception is the education promoters, who receive a salary.[8] They are also peasants or members of peasant households and carry out ordinary agricultural work (or household work in the case of women). However, they work less on the fields than other men, because they do not have the time, since they also have to comply with their work obligations as cooperative members. Those who do not have adult sons or other family members to help are obliged to hire hands during peak periods. Their participation in the commissions of the cooperative represents a controversial matter, as we shall see below. The work of the health promoters is unremunerated and less time consuming, but since it is defined as a service to the community, these promoters are exempt from parts of the collective work.

In the peasant household, labor is strictly gender-specific. Women, with the help of their daughters, are responsible for housework, children, and domestic animals, and men for agricultural and collective work. As is well known from other rural societies, women are the first to get out of bed in the morning, already before dawn to prepare food for their families. Subsequently, they light the fire, clean the *ixtamál* (the corn to be used for tortillas), rush to the mill—located in each neighborhood—to grind the corn, and return to the house to make the tortillas. This process is repeated three times a day, morning, midday, and late afternoon. When breakfast is ready, the husband and children get up, eat, and the men go to the cornfield or to participate in some assignment for the cooperative. Normally, the men leave between 6 and 7 o'clock. During labor-intensive periods, they often stay in the field until mid- or late afternoon. In this case they bring a lunch box or their wives bring a meal to the field for them. Sometimes women lend a hand in the field, especially during harvesting. They go to the field in the afternoon when they have finished their tasks at home. During less intensive agricultural periods the men often return for lunch and stay at home. If they have no meetings to attend, they may carry out repairs on the house or tools, or simply rest in the hammock.

Women stay in and around the house most of the day. When the male household members have left for the fields and the older children for school, the women clean the house and surroundings, feed the animals, and wash the clothes. Laundry is normally done three times a week and is one of the most time-consuming activities, not only because of the quantities of clothes due to the size of the families, but also because clothes get very dirty in this dusty and muddy environment. Clothes are washed in the *lavadero* of the neighborhood, where several women gather at certain times to do their washing, chatting, laughing, and apparently enjoying themselves.

The rigidity of the existing sexual division of labor limits married women's opportunities for community participation. Since very few men are willing to assist their wives in the home, and those who do are objects of gossip and mockery, women's public participation often requires tough negotiation, detailed planning, and helpful female relatives. Thus, even though gender equality and the participation of women in the community are advocated by community leaders as central elements in the model of communitarian development, these are barely noticeable in practice. We have seen that women are weakly represented in local organizations, the cooperative, church, and most *sectores*. Adding to this is the lack of recognition of women's communal labor. Gender relations will be discussed in more detail in Chapter 8.

Nonagricultural Activities

Lack of money is a permanent preoccupation of the returnees, and they adopt different strategies to obtain cash income. The most popular one is the establishment of a small shop at home, something that does not produce much income, but has the advantage that it can easily be combined with housework and childcare. There are now ten small private shops across the community in addition to the cooperative grocery store. The supply is normally much more limited than what the cooperative offers, but prices are the same and the private shop has the advantage of being close to people's homes and is a meeting place where neighbors stop by, exchanging the latest news.

A number of people, some of them women and children, also collect the wild plant *xate* (*Chamaedorea*) for sale. The collection of *xate* is an important source of income for a number of families. It can be combined with household and agricultural tasks since the plant grows in the jungle not very far from the community. The cooperative, through its *xate* committee, organizes the marketing. The *xate* is exported to Europe and the United States to be used in flower arrangements.

Handicraft production is not very common, but a few people make hammocks, a skill learned in the refugee camps in Mexico, and *morrales* (knitted bags) for sale. Even though a number of women know how to weave, this practice has almost disappeared because they do not use handwoven cloth and there is no local market for it. Others sell domestic animals, fruit, or other farm products to local consumers, visitors, and itinerant merchants who occasionally travel to the area to purchase peasant products. Finally, some work as day laborers for other peasants, for example, members of *pobladores* families who work for the teachers.

During the first two years of my fieldwork, labor migration was not common among the returnees, even though some of the younger men had returned to Mexico for shorter or longer periods to work as agricultural laborers or as construction workers in the tourist towns on the Yucatán peninsula. In 2000, the number of migrants had increased considerably and some had even managed to enter the U.S. illegally. Most migrants were young, unmarried men, but there were also some women.

Leisure and Entertainment

Life in La Quetzal is not only work and organizational activities. Even though young people claim that the community is utterly boring, some leisure activities and entertainment certainly take place, perhaps the most common simply referred to as "ir al centro" (go to the center). A favorite meeting place in the center is the cooperative shop, more specifically the big open porch outside the shop. People gather there during the day, but especially in the late afternoon when the bus arrives from the provincial capital, normally between six and seven o'clock. Mostly men but also whole families arrive in the center to do their errands or simply entertain themselves, to see who is around. The cooperative shop (as well as some of the other public buildings) has electric lighting a couple of hours in the evening, something that adds to its attraction. One evening a week, a TV screen is put up in the porch to show a film. This is one of the most appreciated entertainments, appealing to men, women, and children of all ages.

In La Quetzal, as in most villages in Latin America, football (U.S. soccer) is the favorite male entertainment. Every afternoon, when weather permits, groups of young men gather at the football field to play. Various local teams compete, and tournaments are organized during the annual fiesta, when teams from other villages in the region are invited to participate as well. Hunting and fishing are other popular male leisure activities. Early on Sunday mornings, one can observe small groups of men entering the jungle with their dogs. They prefer to spend the day by the river instead of going to church. Women, in contrast, are often more bound to home Sundays than other days because they prepare a special meal, for example, chicken stew, which requires a great deal of preparation. Otherwise, women often visit close neighbors, especially if the neighbor is her mother, sister, or sister-in-law.

On Sunday mornings and Wednesday afternoons, the catechists organize the Celebration of the Word. In the church there are not many opportunities to socialize because the sermon requires silence and attention. After church, however, people meet and walk to the shop together to have a coke and some biscuits or chips, and chat. Some of the men who pass by the shop on their way to church meet someone and remain there instead of continuing. Several informants claim that the sermons led by the catechists are too long (normally more than two hours) and quite boring. The number of attendants is not high; there are more women than men. Few young people attend. When the parish priest arrives from La Libertad to celebrate mass once every two months or so, "everybody" attends and the church is overcrowded. The priest, a Salvadoran liberation theologian, is very popular; he is an engaging orator who easily catches and keeps the attention of the public. Moreover, he often brings musicians with modern sound equipment accompanying their songs, which makes a big difference. People enjoy the masses, "son muy alegres" (they are very lively).

The priest is of the opinion that people in La Quetzal need more *alegría* (joy). During my fieldwork I attended two meetings between the parish priest and the catechists to discuss the selection of a new patron saint, something that would be accompanied by a patron saint fiesta. Since the returnees used to live in different places, they have no common reference as far as a patron saint is concerned. The image they now have in the church is a Virgin the bishop of Chetumál gave to one of the camps in his diocese, but people do not identify much with her.

The priest voiced rather pragmatic opinions regarding what a suitable patron saint should be. In the first place he recommended choosing one who had a special devotion for the oppressed and persecuted; second, and as important, it should be one whose festival fits the agricultural cycle. A patron saint fiesta before the harvest, when there is no money, would be a very sad fiesta, he argued. He advised them to choose one that could be celebrated after the harvest, when people had sold their products and had time and money to spend. When I left they were still discussing this topic.

The Celebration of 1 November, the Day of the Dead, is different from what can be observed in other rural communities in Guatemala, where people meet in the graveyards to honor their deceased kin. The local graveyard in La Quetzal is not a meeting place on this day because it has only a few graves, those of people who have died after 1995. A mass is organized where the names of the deceased kin of each family are read aloud. These are people whose resting places are distributed throughout Guatemala and Southern Mexico. Otherwise, close kin used to meet privately over a good meal. In some houses, they make an altar to share the food and the drinks with the spirits of the dead that are believed to pass by. This is most common in the houses of the Q'eqchi's.

Currently, the only big fiesta of the year is 8 April, the day of the arrival in La Quetzal. This is a joyful fiesta that goes for three days and something that the people greatly anticipate. A mass celebrated by the parish priest, a football tournament with participation of a dozen teams from the region, a dance with invited orchestras, and a contest to select the Queen of La Quetzal and the Queen of Sports are among the many popular events. During these days many visitors arrive in the community. Kin from near and far, including some of those who remained in Mexico, migrant workers, and students come to stay for a few days. Friends and collaborators from different organizations are also invited to a special ceremony to celebrate the latest development achievement, and members of their closest neighbor communities come to participate in the dance night. The permission to sell beer, which is not allowed the rest of the year, adds to the high spirits of the participants. Most inhabitants participate in one way or another in the preparations for the fiesta and virtually all in the celebration. It seems that the commemoration of the date of return contributes to consolidating their sense of cohesion and belonging. Their condition as *retornados*, which is the main label used to distinguish themselves from the repatriated and those who remained in Guatemala during the armed conflict, is associated with this date.

Return to the Future

The returnees in La Quetzal do not fit the image of refugees as passive, traumatized victims of war, which is the image that is commonly spread by the media as well as by aid organizations (Malkki 1997). In exile they acquired new skills and knowledge and learned to assess new situations and opportunities and take advantage of them. This made a return to the peasant life they had once known unattractive to most of them. They returned with the idea of building a new kind of community based on democratic values and participation, and new forms of economic and social solidarity and mutual aid. They want to build a prosperous and well-functioning cooperative, and to have good schools and health services and a progressive church that is concerned with the worldly as well as the spiritual problems of its members. At the same time, they want to participate in the economic and political life of the nation. We have seen, however, that these innovative aspirations are limited to certain areas of life, while others seem more resistant to change. The latter include family and gender relations, something I will return to in more detail in Chapter 8.

The returnees hold a view of themselves and their community as a model for others to follow. They believe that they have gained insights that those who remained in the country do not have. Knowledge of their rights and the capacity to organize is often mentioned as one of the most important achievements. They speak up when politicians and government people visit the community, expressing their discontent and saying what should be done, and they have organized a number of actions to bring attention to their needs. They are familiar with development discourses and talk the "right language"; they are not passive recipients—many of them are public speakers who appear to have clarity about their needs—something that motivates donor agencies to support. The returnees have been and still are favorite targets of aid. Their organizing capacity is also something the returnees emphasize when they distinguish themselves from the *repatriados* or those who remained in the country during the conflict. These rather unorganized people have not acquired the level of knowledge and skills necessary to relate to government and nongovernment agencies in a proactive way, and the support they receive is limited.

It should be evident that the achievements of the returnees would not have been possible with "organization" alone. When they registered as refugees in Mexico they became "the concern of the international community." The organizational capacity and fighting spirit that characterize the returnees have been developed and maintained through interaction and alliance with the international community. This alliance, which is also the basis for more general international attention and sympathy, has been an invaluable resource in their relations with the Guatemalan state, as it gives protection against abuses and helps to obtain what they have been promised. This relationship will be discussed in more detail in Chapter 9.

Chapter 7

Community and Identity

In this chapter I will focus on identity processes among the returnees and different groups of returnees, how they perceive and classify themselves, who they are in relation to relevant others, and the implications of this for the way they relate to each other and the outside world. I will also discuss how all this has changed over time, and the way the returnee community presents new ways of being Guatemalan and also new ways of being indigenous and Ladino. An important part of the chapter deals with ethnic identification as compared to other social identities, demonstrating that, in most public situations in this multiethnic community, ethnicity does not matter. However, this does not mean that classification and identification along ethnic lines are no longer observed.

In the following we will see that my informants associate ethnic differences with cultural markers, especially with language. Anthropologists have gone a long way in relativizing the importance of cultural differences by stressing that it is only when cultural differences make a social difference that they contribute to the creation of ethnicity (Eriksen 1993). This does not mean that they suggest that culture or cultural differences are unimportant; rather, it is the uses to which they are put that give them social relevance. However, the cultural content of identities changes as does the social relevance of cultural contents. The case of the returnees illustrates how cultural resources that a particular group brings with it are transformed through contact with other groups, but they are also put to new uses in the new context and thereby their social significance is changed.

All identity formation is dynamic and many-sided. This implies, for example, that we cannot assume a priori that all members of a category are culturally similar or relate in the same way to their ethnic label. We will see that there are considerable variations regarding this, especially as far as gender and age are concerned.

More Equal Than Different

"Nosotros somos revueltos" (We are mixed). This is a statement often heard when the returnees characterize their community; and they will probably detail it as follows: "Here we have Mam, Q'anjob'al, Q'eqchi's, Castellanos, all kinds of people—people who speak different languages—but we understand each other and we all speak Castilla." In La Quetzal people from different ethnic groups are mixed in more than one way. This mix is the product of a specific historical process that started with the migration from the Highlands to Ixcán in the1960s and 1970s.[1] Before that most people lived in monoethnic and monolinguistic communities and could speak only their own mother tongue. Even though many cooperatives, especially the ones in Ixcán Grande, were multiethnic, the degree of mixing was different from what it is today, since people spent much of their everyday life in small, dispersed monoethnic hamlets or centers and married partners with the same ethnic background. Nevertheless, men from the different groups, especially those in leadership positions, interacted with each other within the wider context of the cooperative and the Church. Knowledge of Spanish became an important criterion for good leadership, language teaching was promoted, and there was a certain impetus toward egalitarian democracy, where distinctions of language, religion, or color should no longer be made (Le Bot 1995: 128–29).

This process of development was interrupted by violence and exile, but not so with the interethnic mixing. In the camps in Mexico, the refugees from Ixcán became even more *revueltos*, especially after the transfer to the camps in the Campeche and Quintana Roo. They met new people from other parts of the country belonging to a variety of ethnic groups, including people who did not speak a Maya language and, thus, were defined as Ladinos and later Castellanos. Even though certain ethnic concentrations, regarding accommodations, were reproduced in the camps, distances between the different clusters were shorter, and through their involvement in the daily running of the camps, the refugees interacted with people from the different groups.

Exile also brought them into contact with representatives of Mexican state agencies and representatives of the international aid community. Through registration as refugees they discovered that they were Guatemalans, that they belonged to a nation-state, and that their condition in exile depended on that. This challenged their local-centric perspective of themselves and the world. We have seen that a similar redefinition also happened in other areas. In Mexico they were no longer defined as subversives to be exterminated or dirty Indians worth no respect. They were treated as persecuted and displaced people deserving assistance, and they learned that all human beings deserved the same respect independent of race, color, and religion.

The representatives of aid organizations introduced the refugees to the language and practice of democracy and universal rights associated with individualized citizens—who all appear equal. They learned about the existence of human rights, women's rights, and citizen rights, about national constitutions and international conventions, and they learned to claim their rights. Even though one may question to what extent these new ideas were understood and taken on by common returnees, we have seen they are reflected in the way the new community is structured. It is not a mere reconstruction of the cooperatives they left in Guatemala in the early 1980s. There is an attempt to create a new kind of community based on what has been learned in exile, combined with certain traditional knowledge and customs, which are largely confined to the domestic sphere. The most politicized also emphasize their desire to see themselves as actors in a process of transformation of Guatemala toward a just and participatory democracy.

Through the experience of exile the returnees have acquired a different understanding of the world, of themselves, and of the "national reality" of Guatemala. I will argue that the communitarian model has served as a frame for the redefinition of ethnic identity and the organization of social relations, where ethnic identification has become secondary to being *returnees* with a common past of violence and exile, and with a common project for the future: the creation of a new kind of community based on democracy, equality, and justice. In what follows I will discuss how this is articulated in everyday interaction in the community and beyond.

Ethnic Differentiation

We have seen that La Quetzal is a multiethnic community where most people are of indigenous origin, something that distinguishes it from most other settler communities in the Petén (where most settler communities are Ladino), and it is multilingual. In addition to Spanish, which is the lingua franca, spoken fluently by the majority of the population, eight Mayan languages are spoken in the community. Only five of them (Q'eqchi', Q'anjob'al, Mam, K'iche', and Jakalteco) can be said to have an impact at the community level, which means that they are spoken beyond a limited family group. Of the remaining three, Chuj is only spoken in two families and Pocomchi' and Ixil are not practiced at all since there is only one person who has each of these as a mother tongue. They are married to a K'iche' and a Castellano respectively and speak Spanish. Spanish—Castilla as it is called locally—is the mother tongue of some 10 percent of the inhabitants, those who fled to Mexico from the Petén.

We have already seen that ethnicity is not a central organizing principle in La Quetzal; none of the many associations at the community level is constituted on the basis of ethnicity. Nevertheless, the ethnic variety characterizing the community is reflected in the different associations. The main Mayan groups and the Castellanos are, for example, represented in all the different *sectores* (teachers, health promoters, midwives, and catechists). This is to some extent a legacy from the camps, where recruitment of people to be trained was made on the basis of appointment or election within a section or a neighborhood, where most people usually belonged to the same ethnic group. Moreover, the spokespersons of the aid organizations encouraged interethnic representation.

Language as an Ethnic Marker

In spite of the apparent lack of importance given to ethnicity, the returnees are perfectly aware of ethnic positions and are able to classify all of their neighbors accordingly, when asked to do so. This was not only the case of adults; I registered the same among schoolchildren. The main criterion used in this classification is language. Statements such as "He/she is Mam, Q'eqchi', or Q'anjob'al" are made with reference to their ability to speak a particular language. Those who do not speak an indigenous tongue are referred to as Castellanos, unless their parents are known to speak one. The term Ladino, so frequently used to contrast the indigenous in other areas of Guatemala, is not used by the returnees when referring to nonindigenous members of the community. This is because they associate this label with "los ricos" (the rich) and "here we are all returnees and poor." The ethnic differentiation is only observed internally and in certain situations and contexts. Outside people from La Quetzal are referred to—and refer to themselves—as *retornados*.

When I asked don Luís, one of the Castellanos, about why he and his family decided to settle in a predominantly indigenous community, he stated:

We decided to return with those who shared our suffering in Mexico. People here are tough and skillful, we understand each other. Here we may have conflicts and disagreements, but we solve them. I do not trust those who remained in Guatemala. In my old community, disagreements led to accusations of being a guerrilla, you could not trust people. Here it is different. . . . The disagreements are not between indigenous and nonindigenous or between people who belong to one or another group. We may disagree about many things but those who are for or against something are "revueltos.". . .

It was difficult in the beginning, in the camps, before we knew each other. We stayed with lots of Mam people—the men wearing pants with red stripes—they could only speak their language and we only Castilla. They did not like us, they were suspicious. We all have our errors, and we had to change our attitudes. For example, I used to say chante or Indio when I talked about an indigenous person. This was normal when I lived in Guatemala. I have now learned that this is discriminatory. We discussed what to do about it and agreed that we should no longer say Indio or Ladino, but use our languages: He is a Q'anjob'al, or he is a Mam, or he is a Castellano. This is what we do now.

Sometimes the classification based on language is not so clear-cut. One may hear comments such as "She is a Mam, but does not speak the language." This is because people know that her parents are Mam-speaking and that she has grown up in a Mam home and acquired certain customs associated with this group. On the other hand, nobody classified Mariano as a Q'eqchi', in spite of his speaking the language fluently; it is the language he speaks with his family, he is married to Q'eqchi' with two daughters and living in an almost monoethnic Q'eqchi' neighborhood. Mariano is a K'iche', I was told, something he confirmed when I asked him. Even though he does not use the language daily, he speaks it with his brother and other K'iche's living in one of the other neighborhoods.

Gregorio was born to Mam parents but did not learn the language because his father, who was adopted by a Ladino family as a child, did not learn the language and customs of the Mam. In spite of being aware of his origin, he refers to himself as Castellano and so do his neighbors. When I asked him why, he told me that it was because he speaks only Spanish and grew up in a Spanish-speaking home in the Ixil area of Quiché. He learned to speak Ixil, a language he spoke with his Ixil wife, before going to exile. In exile they switched to Spanish, even though his wife was and still is not fluent in this language. They wanted their six children to master Spanish. Two of their sons studied at the Maya Q'eqchi' Don Bosco teacher training college in Cobán and learned Q'eqchi' and were influenced by the ideology of the new Pan-Mayan movement. They identified themselves as Maya Ixil, drawing on the ethnic background of their mother, in spite of not speaking the language. However, in La Quetzal they were still defined as Castellanos.

I also registered certain "reinvention of ethnicity" among some of the Castellanos. Members of the family of Isabel sometimes referred to themselves as Chorti'. According to Isabel, her mother was a Chorti' but she married a man who prohibited her from speaking the language and passing it on to her children. Therefore Isabel, who is now in he fifties, never learned it. She also married a Castellano, and her daughters who are Ixmucané activists sometimes refer to themselves and their family as Chorti'. The interaction with NGOs and international aid agencies have taught them that sometimes it is an advantage to be indigenous rather than an ordinary poor person, which is no priority target in any aid agenda.

Other Ethnic Markers

Before describing how the languages are used in everyday life, I will draw the attention to other ethnic markers that to some extent are used to identify people. One of them is surnames. In contrast to the other groups, the Q'eqchi's have indigenous surnames that in most cases are markedly different from those of Spanish origin. Quix, Choc, Caal, Coc, Poov, Max, Ixim, and Xol are typical surnames in this group. Only among the K'iche's did I register a few indigenous surnames: Saquic, Lux, and Ixmáy; the rest had typical Spanish surnames such as Pérez, Ramírez, Velásquez, López, García, and Morales. In the other groups, these kinds of surnames are mixed with Spanish first names such as Pedro, Domingo, Nicolás, Matéo, and José, used as surnames. Juana Matías Pablo, Juana Hernández Simón, and Juana Sánchez Méndez are examples of combinations of surnames found among the Mam informants. Similar combinations were also found among Q'anjob'al and Chuj and to a lesser extent among Jakaltecos. All those who are identified as Castellanos have typical Spanish surnames.

Another marker is dress. Q'eqchi' women are the only ones who systematically dress in what is referred to as indigenous clothes. Independent of age they use traditional clothing, a skirt made of *corte*—a patterned cotton cloth, traditionally handwoven but today often industrially made—with a design that is characteristic of this group and a light plain blouse with short sleeves, now made of industrial fabric. Among the other groups the older women often wear *corte*, wrapped around their waists and fastened with a cotton band. The patterns of the cloth do not vary according to ethnic group; rather, they vary according to what was available at the camp or the cooperative shop. However, the style of wrapping of the skirt does indicate some differentiation; each group has its particular way of folding or wrapping. Those who still have their *huipil* (traditional woven blouse) normally women over fifty, take good care of it, and use it on special occasions, for example, when they go to church. They claim, however, that *huipiles* are too warm for the climate of the Petén; moreover, they are too expensive to buy—only a few women have maintained the weaving skills necessary to make them. Therefore, they normally wear a T-shirt or a western blouse with their *corte*. Younger women and girls are completely westernized in their way of dressing, as are the men from all groups and all ages. None of those who are categorized as Castellanos wear clothes that would identify them as indigenous.

Interethnic Relations in Everyday Life

The family and segments of the neighborhood are the only monoethnic spaces in the community. This has to do with the migration history of the returnees and with certain marriage and settlement patterns. We have seen that, despite the fact that most returnees have been part of multiethnic communities ever since they moved from the Highlands in the late 1960s and early 1970s, their everyday life with regard to their family and neighborhood has been largely monoethnic. Groups of neighbors fled together and also tended to settle together in the camps in Mexico. This pattern was to a certain extent maintained through the various moves between camps in Chiapas and the Yucatán peninsula and is also reflected in the ethnic composition of the neighborhoods in La Quetzal.

Three of the four neighborhoods, La Laguna, Maya Balam, and Cuchumatanes, are named after refugee camps in the state of Quintana Roo, while the fourth, Campeche, is named after a camp in the state of Campeche. Each neighborhood consists of two *supermanzanas* (supersquare), the basic local unit. In each *supermanzana* there are 32 50 x 50-meter square plots of land meters with their respective homesteads around a central communal area (100 x 100 meters), where among other things the local outdoor laundry and a roofed meeting area are located.[2] Even though all the neighborhoods, especially at the level of *supermanzana*, have ethnic concentrations—clusters of neighbors often related by kinship—some are more ethnically homogeneous than others. This is particularly the case for La Laguna, an almost exclusively Q'eqchi' neighborhood. Only three of the 59 households in La Laguna are not headed by a Q'eqchi'; one is headed by a Mexican, another by a K'iche', and the third by a Mam, all married to Q'eqchi' women.

The frequency of mixed marriages is by far the lowest among the Q'eqchi's, only five of the 59 households in this neighborhood. This ethnic concentration can be partly explained by the fact that the majority of the inhabitants in La Laguna fled to Mexico from the cooperatives in Zona Reina (Ixcán), a predominantly Q'eqchi' area. For reasons referred to above, a certain degree of homogeneity tended to be maintained during the migratory cycle. However, the returnees use additional arguments to explain why the Q'eqchi's are considerably less mixed than the others: They are more *tradicionales* and tend to stick more together than the rest. This is a view most Q'eqchi's would agree with. However, the cluster of ten Q'eqchi' families in the neighborhood of Campeche shows that this is not always the case. Upon return, these families chose to remain with their previous camp neighbors who are mainly Mam and Castellanos, thus prioritizing friendship over ethnic affiliation. It should be noted, however, that there are no mixed marriages in these families. While the Castellanos are concentrated in Campeche and the K'iche's in Maya Balam, groups of Mam, Q'anjob'al and Jakaltecos are found in all the neighborhoods, except La Laguna, though the proportion varies.

The Traditionalism of the Q'eqchi's

In addition to their indigenous surnames and their way of dressing, the traditionalism of the Q'eqchi's is primarily associated with what is referred to as their *costumbres*, certain practices and rituals characterizing tradi-tional Mayan communities, which are no longer observed by the rest. Some agricultural activitiesr, such as clearing of new land and planting, are carried out collectively and most Q'eqchi's would not start a new agri-cultural season without performing rituals that assure that permission from the higher powers has been granted, as well as the blessings neces-sary to achieve a good harvest. These rituals are now in most cases lim-ited to the home; they are no longer carried out in the field as they were only a few decades ago. Cristobal, a man in his early forties, describes how he performs his rituals before planting.

When I am going to plant, I always make an altar in my house, where I put the seeds that I am going to use. I decorate the altar with fruits and guaro (hard liquor), and I light candles that burn all night. I stay awake all night watch-ing and praying. My wife also stays awake until very late. She has to prepare the food for the next day—the tortillas for the breakfast. At dawn, those who are going to help me come to eat before going to the field; tortillas, beans, eggs, sometimes rice or spaghetti, whatever we have, not always the same, and we drink coffee. When we have eaten, I say my prayer, burn incense and distribute the seed to the workers; each of them has brought his morral (color-ful knitted bag) to carry the seeds. When I plant one hectare I need six or seven men, when I plant two I need twice that number. We normally work until midday. Then we have a good meal prepared by my wife and some other women that come to help her. Normally we serve caldo de pollo (chicken soup), sometimes we also kill a piglet and we serve boj.

Cristobal explained that he never starts an agricultural season without making his altar and performing the rituals.

When I received the new land to grow rice I had to cut down the trees. The trees are living beings that are killed when we cut them. We have to ask for permission, otherwise God will become angry and bring a bad harvest, or he will bring animals which will damage the plants. He may even bring poisonous snakes that can kill us. Therefore, we always have to ask God for forgiveness before starting. Sometimes, when the milpa is not so good, I also do rituals in order to improve it. I try to teach my children to do the same. I think it is important that they learn that the nature is the creation of God. God expects us to ask for his permission, those who do not ask cannot count on the bless-ing of God, they are subject to the game of chance.

Cristobal confirmed that God in Q'eqchi' would be *tzuultaq'a*, the word used for the "mountain spirit" when referring to traditional Maya religion. However, he seemed quite surprised when I asked if *tzuultaq'a* is the same as the Catholic God and said with a firm voice, "Yes it is the Catholic God!" Cristobal is a devoted Catholic and a catechist. Apparently, he does not accept the image of God as a kind of hybrid, a combination of the Catholic and the Mayan almighty, held by some of the old people from this group.[3]

Only two Q'eqchi's, young men in their twenties, no longer perform the rituals Cristobal refers to; neither of them had their father in the community. It is often the father who insists on performing the rituals and once he dies, the sons continue. Pablo, one of these young men, explains why he stopped.

The first season here, I planted without doing the ritual because I did not have the things required to do it. Then I realized that it made no difference, the harvest was really good and I did not suffer any misfortune. I also knew that my father-in-law who returned to Ixcán stopped, nothing has happened to him either. That's why I stopped.

However, Pablo continues the tradition of collective work in much the same way as described by Cristobal.

Jesús, a young Q'eqchi' who is also a catechist, said that he learned to practice the planting rituals from his father when they lived in the camps in Mexico. He has continued ever since. Unlike other Q'eqchi's, his group continued to practice their *costumbres* in exile. They even maintained the *cofradías* (saints' brotherhoods), discontinued when they returned to Guatemala.

We had to stop the cofradías when we settled here. The problem here is that we are a mixture of different groups; the catechists from the other groups did not accept our customs. They believe that they are pagan traditions. They did not accept that we were going to play marimba, drink boj and dance in the church. The conflicts regarding this were so strong that some proposed to build a separate Catholic church for the Q'eqchi's. Most people were against this proposal, including myself. I think it is better to have one church and to struggle to make it more tolerant.

The Q'eqchi's have also tried to introduce some other collective rituals. During the drought in 1998 they organized several processions to a mountain a few kilometers from the community, where they burned candles and incense and said prayers. The processions were headed by the image of the Virgin and musicians with their instruments, and gathered some people from other groups, including some catechists. Other catechists did not want to participate; they considered it a pagan ceremony that should not be patronized by the Church. As soon as the rain started the participation of the other groups stopped.

Every year, before the annual commemoration of the return to Guatemala, the Q'eqchi's start practicing traditional Mayan dances to the sound of marimba. A group of Q'eqchi's own the only marimba in the community. They meet two to three times a week in different houses throughout the neighborhood of La Laguna, where they are offered *boj* by the host. When the fiesta is approaching, some of them go to Cobán to rent costumes for the fiesta, a big expenditure for the participants. During the fiesta and for a couple of weeks after, the dancing group is invited to different houses to perform. There, they are offered food and *boj*. Most of the spectators are Q'eqchi's of all ages, but a number of other people also drop by to watch. "The other groups like our fiestas, but they do not want to spend money," one of the dancers explained.

Abelardo is deeply concerned about the maintenance of the customs, the rituals before interfering with nature and asking permission and forgiveness. He used the same vocabulary as Cristobal. He is also quite concerned about the customs related to marriage, trying to explain to me why it is so important for the Q'eqchi' to stay together.

Some customs were not good and they had to be changed. I think it is important that young people are allowed to decide with whom they are going to marry, not as it was before when the parents decided everything. When this is said, things should follow the same proceedings as before. It is very important to have ones family close and that the couple involve their families; the same with the godparents. Imagine that I beat up my wife; she can go to her father or godfather to complain. Her father will come to me to ask me for an explanation. He will probably give me advice about how to get along. He may for example help me to remember the early days of our relationship when I was in love and running after his daughter. He will tell me how to take care of these emotions in order to have a happy marriage. My experience is that there are problems only the first years of marriage, until you have two or three children. Then things tend to become quieter. . . .

I think that the other groups have lost their costumbres. They do not work together and they are much more revueltos. They marry spouses from other groups, people whose customs they do not know, and they have to speak Spanish to understand each other. Sometimes the children do not learn to speak the language of the parents. Among the Q'eqchi's, very few marry women from other groups, although there have been some lately. In these cases, the women learn the language and integrate into our way of living.

Most people use one or more of the above criteria to describe the differences between the Q'eqchi's and the rest. This does not mean that language is the only criterion used to differentiate the remaining groups; there are others, but they are less tangible. When I asked people about the differences, they often answered, "we have different customs." When asked to be more specific, people most often referred to practices related to engagement and marriage, childbirth, and food preferences. However, what they refer to as "ethnic differences" are often traditional ideals that are far from always observed in everyday practice. They tell you how things should be, according to certain traditions, not how they are.

Nevertheless, certain differences exist and have to be dealt with. One is related to marriage practices, most clearly revealed in the negotiations leading to interethnic marriages, increasingly more common in this multiethnic context. In these negotiations reference is made to "our custom," but it is not always clear whether it applies to the family or to the ethnic group.

Regarding food preferences, often mentioned as another distinguishing factor, differences are not easy to detect either. All the groups share the everyday diet of tortilla and beans, and these dishes are made much in the same way by all of them, including the Castellanos. What varies is to some extent the food served at fiestas or special occasions such as Christmas and Easter, or fiestas related to marriage and baptism. At these events it is not so much the kind of food served, such as *caldo de pollo* (chicken soup) or *tamales*,[4] but the way of preparing it—the ingredients used and the seasoning. Again, in this context, the main distinction is made with reference to the Q'eqchi's. They are said to use more herbs and hotter spices than the others. They also use *achiote* to color their *caldos*, and in every Q'eqchi' courtyard you will find a couple of *achiote* shrubs.

The third difference that is emphasized is related to childbirth, especially the position of the woman while giving birth. Some are used to giving birth lying in bed, others in other positions. Therefore, women tend to consult a midwife of their own group when becoming pregnant. Raquel a young Q'anjob'al married to the son of a Jakalteca midwife, told me that she had been assisted by her mother-in-law during pregnancy. When her labor started she realized that this was not a good choice.

According to the traditions of my mother-in-law women give birth lying in bed. After having been in labor for a long while, I realized that I would not be able to give birth like that, I felt that I was fainting all the time. It was terrible. According to our tradition, and that is also the tradition of the Mam, we give birth kneeling, the midwife behind receiving the child. My husband hurried to bring Doña Carmen (a Mam midwife). When she came, she ordered me out of bed, explaining that if I stayed in bed the child was going to die. I kneeled like she told me and after a while my daughter was born. I barely felt any pain. This time (Raquel is 7 months pregnant) I will deliver in the same way, but with the assistance of my mother-in-law. Since she was present when my daughter was born, she realized how it should be done.

With the formal training of midwives and the collaboration between the midwives and the other health personnel, midwifery has become more standardized. However, certain traditional practices, such as different delivery positions and certain postpartum practices, have been maintained.

Interethnic Marriages

In La Quetzal households are family-based, in most cases composed of a nuclear family. Some are extended by one or both parents of one of the spouses, an unmarried or divorced daughter with her offspring, or children of the spouses from an earlier relationship. In 138 (71 percent) of the total of 195 households headed by a married couple, the spouses belong to the same ethnic group. The ethnic distribution is as follows: Q'eqchi' 65, Mam 22, Q'anjob'al 21, Jakalteco 13, Castellano 11, K'iche' 5, and Chuj 1.

Of the 195 households, 57 (29 percent) are headed by mixed couples. As we have seen above, the degree of mixing varies. In only five of the mixed couples is there a Q'eqchi' spouse, the three men referred to above and two women. The latter are married to Q'anjob'al men. The Jakaltecos are the most mixed; the number of couples with one Jakalteco spouse is higher than the numbers of couple where both are Jakaltecos, 16 and 13 respectively. Among the Mam the number of mixed and nonmixed is identical, 22. Among the Q'anjob'al the numbers of nonmixed and mixed are 22 and 10 respectively. The Castellanos also mix. There are eleven couples where both spouses are Castellanos versus eight with only one. Three Castellano men are married to K'iche', Q'anjob'al and Ixil women respectively, while three Castellano women are married to Jakalteco men and one to a Q'anjob'al man. Perhaps the most remarkable mix is the one between Castellano and the indigenous, since these groups have traditionally avoided intermarriage.

When I asked the Castellano parents how they reacted to the choice of an indigenous spouse, all of them answered more and less the same way: that they respected the choice of their children; that in this community all are equal, returnees, and poor; and that what is important is that the spouse is a good person, hardworking and honest: whether he or she is a Castellano or *habla lengua* (speaks an indigenous language) does not matter.

The percentage of mixed compared to nonmixed couples is certainly correlated (negatively) with the size of the group. When the children of the Chuj couple start to marry, the percentage of mixed marriages will most probably be 100 percent. There are no other Chuj people in the community or in the wider area, and the parents find it quite normal

that their children marry a partner from one of the other groups or someone from another community for that matter, if that is what they want.
Only some Q'eqchi' parents said they would dislike their children to
marry someone from another group, because they would like to conserve
their language and customs, which they consider a more difficult task in
a mixed couple. Most other parents were willing to let destiny prevail; they
believe that young people should choose their own partners. The majority have suffered the consequences of arranged marriages where they had
no say, and they would like to avoid that.

Mixed marriages are products of exile. Very few of those who were married when they left Guatemala have partners who do not belong to the
same ethnic group. Daily interaction with people from different groups
combined with the emphasis on equality and common history of violence
and suffering created alliances across ethnic boundaries, and also marriage alliances. After return, most marriages have been contracted between people within the community. Recently, a few persons have found
partners in neighboring communities. This may be quite problematic, as
illustrated in the following story told by Candelaria (Q'anjob'al), who has
a daughter-in-law from a neighboring community.

Elina is the daughter of an itinerant merchant who used to come here to sell
fruits and vegetables. She became friends with my daughter Fabiana, and she
would often visit us at home. That's how she met Mauro and joined him. She
is not a good wife, she is quarreling with him all the time. The problem is that
she despises us because we speak our language (hablamos lengua). Since she
only speaks Castilla she calls herself Ladina. I think her attitude is very silly. Are
you from the capital or from this area? I asked her one day. I am petenera (a
woman from the Petén), she answered. Then you are not a Ladina, you are
indigenous! I said. Everybody around here is indigenous whether they speak a
language or not. Imagine! She thinks she is better than us because she is not
a returnee. On the contrary, I tell you, in her village they are much worse off
then we are, ignorant because they are not organized. It would have been better for Mauro to marry a returnee. The returnees understand each other better
whether they speak a (Maya) language or not.

What happens to the children of the mixed marriages that are becoming increasingly common? When people are asked to classify these children, they define them as *mezcla* (mixture); they have the blood of both
parents, it is said. Normally these children will grow up in a Spanish-
speaking home, because the parents use the lingua franca to communicate. Whether the children will speak a Maya language depends on their
wider everyday surroundings. Since the residence pattern so far have been
largely virilocal—the newly established couple settling together with or

close by the husband's parents and siblings—and most marriages are still ethnically endogamous, the children will generally grow up surrounded by kin who speak their father's language. Moreover, since most grandmothers are poor Spanish-speakers, they normally speak their mother tongue in the family. In this way most children learn a Maya language, even though not all of them use it extensively. Children of mixed marriages—between a Q'eqchi's and a spouse form another group—normally settle in the Q'eqchi' neighborhood, even when the husband is a non-Q'eqchi'. This is, for example, the case of the Mexican, K'iche', and Mam "heads of household" that I referred to earlier. All of them have learned the language of their wives and use it in everyday life. The daughters of the K'iche' also speak the language of their father and his wife can understand it. Moreover, they wear a *corte* wrapped in the K'iche' way and an embroidered blouse, in contrast to the wives of the Mam and the Mexican men who wear Q'eqchi' dress. "My husband does not want us to use our dress, he wants us to use the one from his group so people remember that we belong to a K'iche' family. Julio (the Mexican) and Alfredo (the Mam) do not care," the wife explained to me. Her husband, who is in his late fifties, belongs to another generation than the other two men, who are in their twenties and more liberal. Moreover, the women in their families of origin do not use traditional dress, so they have no proper dress codes to defend.

Some cases are rather complex as Leticia's story illustrates. She defines herself as Q'anjob'al, her father is Chuj, her mother Q'anjob'al.

Since I am Q'anjob'al and my husband is Mam we speak Castellano at home. My husband tries to teach Mam to my son (Leticia's son from a previous relationship) and speaks Mam to him. I speak Q'anjob'al with him and also with the little one (their baby daughter). My parents speak different dialects of Q'anjob'al—my father speaks San Sebastián and my mother Soloma—which are quite different, but they understand each other.[5] My brother Mario and I speak the dialect of my father, but we have no problems understanding my mother. My husband speaks Castellano with them. The situation of my sister-in-law is more complicated, since she and my brother live with my parents. Like my husband, she is also a Mam; she understands the language but cannot speak it. Neither can she speak the dialects of my parents, only a few words; she does not seem to understand much either. She could speak Spanish but she rather keeps silent, she is very shy. Their children are now learning the language of my parents, they can understand, but do not speak much yet.

One day I was invited to a birthday party in a Jakalteco home. The youngest son, Miguel, was fifteen and family and neighbors from the community were invited to celebrate. A number of children were present; the majority were sons and daughters of the married offspring of the house. At one point I was sitting together with Diego, Miguel's father, observing the children playing. They were speaking Spanish. I asked Diego about his opinion regarding this. His answer revealed a high degree of pragmatism.

It is a good thing that the children are able to speak Castilla, we should not forget that many in our generation have suffered a lot from not speaking it. I would certainly like my grandchildren to speak Jakalteco and many of them do, but not all. What happens is that some of my children have married spouses who speak a different language. They speak Spanish at home, and their children get used to it. What should we do about that? Should we prohibit our children to marry people from other groups, should we return to the authoritarian system we had before when parents decided to whom their children should marry? I do not agree with that. It was easy in Jacaltenango. Almost all the people who lived there were Jakaltecos and spoke the same language. Now that we are mixed, things are different. We cannot return to the past.

Diego's position is shared by most parents. They hold a very pragmatic view of the use of Mayan languages. They would like the new generation to speak the language of their parents, and attempt to teach them, but not at any price. They would not prevent their children from marrying the partner of their choice as they identify themselves as *revueltos* and consider ethnic segregation as belonging to the past.

Use of Language

From the above we see that the family and the neighborhood are the principal arena for the use of Mayan languages. When husband and wife share a language, as is still the most common, this language is transferred to children who continue to use it at home. Since there are monoethnic clusters in most neighborhoods, people also use their mother tongue in everyday life beyond the family unit. This is, for example, the case when women shop in the neighborhood store or wash their clothes in the communal laundry. There, they often meet their neighbors who speak the same language; sometimes they even make appointments to meet. If their shopping or washing coincides with the presence of women from another language group, they will communicate in Spanish. Since most *supermanzanas* sharing the laundry have residents from more than one ethnic group, one may hear two or even three different languages in the laundry area during the peak hours of the afternoon. I also registered that neighbor women often went to church and meetings together and sat together during the events. This enabled them to communicate in their own language at the same time as they were listening to Spanish. One result of the experience of living in multilinguistic contexts is an ability to switch between languages. For example, when I visited someone's home, those who were participating in the conversation with me—there could be three or four sitting around a table—would speak Spanish. However, they addressed an adult in another part of the room who was not part of the common conversation, or a child who was about to misbehave, they would do it in their mother tongue.

Even though all public meetings and assemblies are conducted in Spanish, these are also spaces where people speak their respective languages. In face to face conversations the use of Mayan languages is widespread and people switch between Spanish and their mother tongue all the time when moving around and talking to different people. People normally address a person in their mother tongue if they belong to the same ethnic group, if not they will speak Spanish. In big assemblies, I often observed that a person addressed the one sitting to his left in a Maya language and the one to the right in Spanish or vice versa.

Due to their participation in the cooperative and the different *sectores* men interact more with people from different ethnic groups than women do, and are more accustomed to speaking Spanish. This is reflected in the gender difference regarding the mastering of the lingua franca, but only among people of a certain age. Young people speak fluent Spanish whether they have it as a mother tongue or not. However, men also switch between Spanish and their mother tongue, depending on the context and to whom they are talking. I observed, for example, that several Mayan languages were spoken when larger groups of men were collaborating in collective work in the cooperative. I only observed organized use of Mayan languages in two public contexts. One was in the church, when attendance was particularly high and the catechists sometimes initiated the Celebration of the Word in Spanish. After a while they would invite the congregation to split into smaller groups, led by Maya-speaking catechists who would then elaborate on the text in two or three of Mayan languages, in addition to Spanish. On these occasions there would always be a Q'eqchi' group, since knowledge of Spanish is poorest among women and old people of this language group and they generally are the most numerous. Sometimes there would be a Q'anjob'al or Mam group or both, depending on the number of people present from the respective groups. The other context was the anniversary of Ixmucané. The organization prepared a two-day course focusing on the situation of the women five years after the return. The assembly was divided into four groups, one conducted in Q'eqchi', one in Q'anjob'al, one in Mam, and one in Spanish, each led by a leading member from the respective group. In this way they attempted to enhance the level of participation, incorporating those who did not dare to speak up in a large assembly.

Bilingual Education

Language has been one of the main concerns raised by the new Pan-Mayan movement in Guatemala.[6] A national program of bilingual education (PRONEBI) was introduced in 1984 during the military government of General Víctor Mejía and strongly supported by USAID. Its mandate was "providing preprimary and primary education in bilingual and bicultural form to the school age indigenous population of the country." Beginning in 1986, forty pilot schools were established, providing instruction from preprimary through fourth grade. By the mid-1990s the number had expanded to some eight hundred in eight language regions (Richards and Richards 1996: 214).

The introduction of bilingual education has been a rather controversial issue. According to Becker Richards, PRONEBI is largely controlled by officials of indigenous origin who advocate a firm Mayanist orientation that is perceived as a threat not only by the more integrationist-oriented people of the state apparatus, but also by teachers and parents, especially in rural areas. Many of the teachers lack reading and writing skills in Mayan languages and, in some cases, also oral proficiency as well. They see instruction in a mother tongue as an extra burden for themselves and an educational obstacle for their pupils. They reject the official bilingual education as "too Mayan" and accuse the official technicians of having lost touch with the realities of rural life. Maya intellectuals and activists such as Cojtí Cuxil and Sam Colop, on the other hand, reject the official program because it is "not Mayan enough" (Richards and Richards 1996: 215).

If the bilingual program is resisted by parents and teachers in monolinguistic rural areas, we should not be surprised that it is controversial in the multiethnic context of La Quetzal with eight Mayan languages in addition to Spanish. Four of these languages—Q'eqchi', Mam, Q'anjob'al and K'iche'—are spoken by local teachers as their mother tongue, but none of them have reading or writing skills in these languages. A bilingual program was initiated in 1998 by a private university in Guatemala City with the support of USAID. It has provoked frustration among the parents, especially those whose mother tongue is not spoken by the teachers. Their children are obliged to choose one of the languages taught at the school. For most returnees, who are first generation Spanish-speakers and have suffered humiliation and discrimination for not mastering the dominant language, this insistence on bilingual education is seen as a distraction and deviation from what they consider the most important task of the school—to prepare the children for a more prosperous future than their parents have in the modern world. Parents of the children in the secondary school were especially indignant because the English classes had been discontinued to be replaced by Mayan languages. "Imagine! My daughter who is a descendant of Chorti's, is obliged to learn another language. Mayan activists who master both languages (Spanish and their mother tongue) and live from their activism do not understand the problems of the poor," one mother explained to me. "We have spoken our language for hundreds of years, now they pretend that our children shall read and write it. For what purpose? We have no books in our language to read and who should they write to? Here we are all revueltos. What they need is to write proper Castilla," was the opinion of another. The teachers share the view of the parents. They believe it would be good for the children to learn to read and write their mother tongue, but under the existing conditions, without trained teachers and a lack of pedagogical material, it does not make much sense. They would prefer that these resources be used to improve existing education.

Few people in La Quetzal know about the Pan-Mayan movement. The teachers had heard about it, but they were not well informed, nor did the information they had inspire much enthusiasm. The following reflection by one of them, Diego (Jakalteco) is quite symptomatic.

I have heard about them; they are those who reject the Catholic religion and want us to practice Maya religion and old Maya cultural traditions. We do not agree much with them. I personally do not agree with them at all. I think they have more support in the Highlands where each group still lives in separate places, where they have always lived, not here where we are all returnees and revueltos, different groups, different languages. We do not want to return to the past. . . . My grandmother practiced Maya religion; she lit candles, sacrificed small animals, and things like that. She respected God very much, not the Catholic God, the Mayan God. She was also very respectful toward the animals; she never beat them or hurt them, and did not allow us to do so either. We are all Catholics, my father too, but not my grandmother; she practiced Maya religion until she died. . . . The Maya customs are lost here. There are only a couple of people who practice the religion (he mentions a few Q'eqchi' names, one of them Anastasio, a catechist). I think Anastasio has double religion, some of the other Q'eqchi's as well, but among the other groups, the practice of Maya religion has disappeared completely.

When I asked him if he considers himself Maya, he answered,

Yes, 100 percent I am 100 percent Jakalteco, and the Jakaltecos are Maya, the other groups too, but not the Castellanos of course. You know, here we use the languages to identify the groups, sometimes we say that we are indigenous, but we do not say that we are Maya.

When I reminded him of the name of the cooperative he offered the following answer:

This name was chosen by the CCPP delegation that went to La Libertad (the municipal capital) to register the cooperative, when we still lived in Mexico. They had not thought about a name, and when they were told that the Petén originally was the territory of the Maya Itzá and somebody proposed that they could call the cooperative Maya Itzá, they thought it was a good idea, even though none of us were descendants of the Itzá.

Most people in La Quetzal see themselves as indigenous; they want their children to speak their mother tongue and to learn certain traditions, the "good traditions," for example, those related to food, and life-cycle rituals such as engagement, marriage, and childbirth, but not at any price. Most of them have suffered for not speaking Spanish, something they learned in exile. They have also suffered the burden of illiteracy. Therefore, they give high priority to their children's school attendance and their mastering of Spanish. They argue that bilingual education only distracts attention from what they consider the most important for progress, mastering Spanish.

New Ways of Being Indigenous

The returnees did not want to return to the past, to Maya religious and government traditions. They have rejected the attempts by some Q'eqchi's to revitalize the traditional hierarchies of *cofradías* as belonging to the dark side of their history. They want to be modern, have a well-functioning cooperative, schools, and health centers, a progressive church concerned with the worldly problems of their members, not only the spiritual ones, and they want to participate in the economic and political life of the nation. The refugees and returnees who are supported by human rights groups with a popular leaning identify themselves primarily as returnees and poor peasants, not as Maya or indigenous. Those who are familiar with the Pan-Mayan movement fear that its focus on indigenous people in opposition to Ladinos may recreate new forms of conflict and racism.

Chapter 8

Changing Gender Relations

Gender and Change

Social change is often associated with transformations in the conditions of work. If the transformations build on existing gender divisions, they may only cement differences that are already there and not represent a major challenge to dominant gender roles and perceptions. Historically we have seen that this is what happened to my informants when they moved from the Highlands to the cooperatives in Ixcán and the Petén. The equal distribution of land, and the participation of the peasants in Church and community institutions and activities represented an impetus toward egalitarian democracy, where there should be no distinction based on language, religion, or color. However, this participative democracy was mainly for men, while women continued in their traditional roles, which were reinforced by general improvement in their living conditions. In exile things started to change. We have seen that the refugees soon were drawn into a number of activities related to the running of the camps as well as to the preparation for the reconstruction after the return.

The aid and solidarity workers assisting the refugees did not accept the traditional division of gender roles. They actively promoted the participation of women in extra-domestic activities, not only young, single women but also married women with children, and to some extent they succeeded. Gender roles and perceptions were challenged, and many women started to question certain traditional practices and attitudes. We have seen that women came to fill new roles in the planning forreturn and during the first difficult years after the settlement in La Quetzal. In what follows I will discuss how these changes came about, and what happened once the emergency phase ended.

Bourdieu has shown how certain ideas and practices are more resistant to change than others. This is the case when values, ideas, and practices are shared by all social actors in a given society, and are so taken for granted that they are not made explicit, and thus not questioned (Bourdieu 1977; Stølen 1991). In La Quetzal certain gender ideas and related practices seem to be of this order. I suggest that this is the case for the notion that women and men by nature belong to different social domains. In this context it implies that the man is conceived of as the head of household, the one mainly responsible for the economic and social welfare of the family members, and their representative in the public world. His wife is conceived of as primarily of the home, in charge of household chores and child care and under her husband's control and protection. This pattern is well known from many other parts of Latin America and the rest of the world (Ortner and Whitehead 1981; Melhuus and Stølen 1996; Stølen 1998).

The high valuation of virginity, chastity, and control of female sexuality also appear to be particularly resistant to change. Sexual control and legitimacy seem to hold a central place in the local gender code. A woman's sexual behavior determines to a large extent her social value, is decisive for her attractiveness in the "marriage market," and thus influences her possibility of becoming a respectable mother, wife, and housewife. Female premarital virginity and chastity also influence the reputation of men as husbands—and sometimes even as fathers and brothers—while a man's sexual behavior, on the contrary, has marginal impact on his social standing. Under such circumstances women need to be protected and controlled in order to maintain their sexual stainlessness.

The fact that women must be controlled, while men need not and indeed should not be, draws attention to the power aspect of gender relations. Women are often held to be subordinate to men in the sense of being victims of the exercise of power by men. Of course, and this should not be forgotten, the exercise of power in gender relations may be repressive. However, the fact that women often agree with the practices that subordinate them, that they resist the exercise of power, or that there often exist friendly relations between women and men, cannot be understood in terms of the exclusively repressive view of power. I suggest that the male dominance I observed in La Quetzal is based not only based on male control and repression but also on values and perceptions shared by both women and men regarding what women and men should do or not do and how they should behave (Connell 1987; Stølen 1996).

Women's Participation

"All these years of exile have been our school, we have grown and learned a lot, now we are not the same women as before, now we dare to speak up, to participate in community affairs and to struggle for our rights." This quote from a document of the women's organization Ixmucané reflects how many returnee women, in particular those who are active in the women's organization, talk about their experience of exile as a kind of passage from ignorance to enlightenment and from oppression to liberation.

We have seen that, even though exile meant hardship and suffering, especially in the beginning, the refugees were far from being passive victims of their circumstances. In the beginning the process of participation and involvement was highly gendered. Even though most training activities were open to both men and women, women in general, and particularly married women, failed to attend. On the one hand, they were busy running everyday life in the family under the very precarious conditions of the camps and had limited time to engage in extra-domestic activities. On the other hand, some say that they were limited by the reluctance and opposition of their husbands, who did not permit them to participate in activities where men, other than those belonging to the closest family and neighborhood, were present. A number of women also stressed their fear and shyness of taking part in gatherings with strangers where they were expected to speak, something they were not accustomed to, particularly when they could not speak their own language. Thus, even though new opportunities were open to women in the camps, only a limited number were ready to take advantage of them.

At first, little was done to overcome the constraints that prevented women from public participation. It should be mentioned, however, that a number of my informants, younger women who had some knowledge of Spanish, were selected at an early stage of exile to assist in the camps. This was, for example, the case of Rosalía, who shortly after arriving in Chiapas, was singled out and trained to assist the San Cristobal nuns in fighting malnutrition and illness among small children.

Gradually, different organizations assisting in the camps became aware of and concerned that special initiatives were required to increase women's participation and improve their condition. In 1992, ten years after the majority of the refugees had crossed the Mexican border, UNHCR carried out a study to determine the needs of women. Approximately 600 women in 60 refugee camps were interviewed. Among other things, this study detected extremely low self-esteem among a high number of women. Even younger women considered themselves to be too old, too tired, or too incompetent to engage in training activities. Many women also suffered from malnutrition and depression. On this background, UNHCR took the initiative to organize workshops to strengthen women's self-esteem and to establish a woman's organization. The workshops focused on nutrition, health, education, and human rights. Particularly the workshops on human rights, run by Catholic nuns, represented a source of inspiration and an eye-opener for many women. Female informants often remember these workshops, especially how amazed they were to discover that they had rights as human beings and as women: "When I lived in Guatemala, I had no idea that we had rights, I had not heard about the existence of human rights, and less about women's rights. All this I learned from the Catholic sisters" (Maria M., 52).

Most men were less enthusiastic about these courses than they had been about the more practical training courses offered earlier. In the camps men had faced problems complying with their role as proper providers and had gradually accepted that women added to the household's cash income by participating in income-generating projects, largely because they responded directly to specific and immediate survival needs. The courses aimed to raise women's consciousness were more controversial, and many women relate how they faced problems at home as a consequence. Their husbands and fathers felt uneasy about these new ideas about women's rights and changes in the relations between men and women, and they did not understand the need for a separate women's organization. Yet perhaps the major constraints to participation were to be found in the women themselves, in their lack of self-esteem and confidence in their own capabilities, as illustrated in Candelaria's (48) story.

Thanks to the workshops organized by the Mexican sisters, we started to think about our lives and our situation, our rights as Guatemalans and as women too. We learned about human rights and women's rights. We did not know that women are of great value in society, we thought that only the men are of value and that this is why they dominate. The same thing with the army; they have no right even to scratch our skin with a knife, but we did not know anything about this. We also learned about the laws of Guatemala. They told us that we have the right to have a house, a piece of land, potable water, light, roads. As inhabitants of a country we have these rights. Imagine! I had no idea! Before going to these courses I did not dare to speak, I suffered all the time, because I was so afraid of speaking. The workshops helped me a lot. I think that much of the suffering we have endured is because of our ignorance. Ignorance makes you afraid and feeble.

The support from the CCPP leaders was very important for the mobilization of women and the establishment of a women's organization in the camps. This support was probably not motivated by a concern about gender inequality or the importance of a specific female perspective for the construction of a new community. The leaders were, however, interested in the political and economic advantages of mobilizing women, first, because it enhanced their legitimacy as a representative organization and second, because the participation of women ranked high on the agenda of many aid and solidarity organizations, eager to provide funds for development projects.

The process of becoming organized implied new challenges for women, since it was not accompanied by changes in gender roles in the family. Women had to keep up their traditional responsibilities. However, some collective initiatives, supported by aid agencies, were taken to ease domestic burdens, such as mechanized tortilla making and cooperative child care, things that allowed women to participate more actively in community affairs.

The Creation of the Women's Organization Ixmucané

In March 1993, the refugee women returning to the Petén established their own organization called Ixmucané.[1] The documents from the founding meeting reflect the euphoric optimism that characterized the first years of Ixmucané, especially the period before return.

During these moments (referring to the process of preparation for return) the woman plays an important role. She is more active, participates in whatever activity is assigned to her, and feels ownership and security in relation to what she does. She prepares herself continuously and feels each day more informed about all that happens in the process of return. During these moments she dares to leave her kitchen and let her housework wait to be able to engage in organizational work. . . .

With the process of return she is learning about her rights: she searches for equality between man and woman as a means to obtain better development in the family as well as in the community. So far we have obtained few but important victories. Our compañeros have understood that we are important for the development of the land we live in and we have obtained positions of trust such as health promoters, midwives and human rights workers.

The founding documents convey a view of women as woven into the family and local community fabric rather than as autonomous individuals. The organized women defined themselves as a "social sector" or collective body, representing a specific perspective necessary to foster development. They were also concerned with personal development, for example, literacy training in Spanish, not as a means of self-realization and individual mobility, but rather as a means to community development.

Ixmucané was largely a product of international organizations, the Catholic Church and NGOs. This does not imply that the women did not put considerable efforts into it. The external backing was, however, what gave them the impetus, courage, and legitimacy to fight for their cause. "Without the support from the organizations we could not have achieved much, in spite of having many ideas and plans," stated a local Ixmucané leader.

Torres (1999) interviewed a number of women in the refugee camps a few months before the return to the Petén in April 1995, and was impressed by their level of action and consciousness. In gaining a political role in the camps, women felt they had greater control over their lives through their improved technical and oratorical abilities, she argues. This was certainly the case for the Ixmucané leaders and activists, whose voices are the ones included in Torres's work. They demonstrated an extraordinary engagement and fighting spirit that inspired not only the funding agencies but also the majority of the returnee women to take part in the initiatives. However, there was a significant divergence in the level of consciousness and engagement within the organization, between the leaders who were deeply engaged in changing the role of women as part of a political process of changing the society, and the majority, whose major concern was to improve their economic situation rather than to change gender roles in the family and the community.

Ixmucané certainly played a crucial role in the preparation for return, as well as during the first difficult months in the Petén, when the efforts of everybody were needed to make things work. Women were particularly active during first period of settlement, referred to as the "emergency phase." While men were busy clearing the forest and preparing for construction and planting, women took a leading role in running the provisional camp, dealing with the agencies assisting them, and distributing food and other emergency aid. Once the emergency phase in La Quetzal was over and the community became more established, women as well as Ixmucané itself faced unexpected challenges.

Female Exclusion Resumed

As we have seen in a previous chapter, women's participation in community affairs is largely limited to the activities organized by Ixmucané. Women are defined as a *sector*, along with minority segments of the population such as the health and education promoters and the catechists; very few are cooperative members. When the cooperative was established, membership was open to all adults, men and women. However, out of a total of 168 members (October 1999), only three are women, two of them single and one married to a labor migrant in the United States.

Why are there so few female members? In order to understand this, we have to look more closely at the local gender code. We have seen that in the dominant local gender code women are of the home, men of the field and beyond. Men are defined as the heads of household and providers for their families, while women are seen as caretakers of home and children. Since only "heads of household" can become cooperative members, married women with their husbands living in the community are excluded. In this cultural context, it is absolutely unthinkable that a woman can replace her husband in this role. However, there are a few widows who are heads of households without being members either. This is related to the fact that cooperative membership requires labor input from the members;

during my fieldwork some 80 man-days a year. The collective work may include constructing cooperative buildings and roads, cataloguing forest resources, slashing and clearing communal areas—all defined as male tasks. Women are considered, and consider themselves, unfit for this kind of work.

The work women actually carry out for the cooperative, such as cleaning the cooperative buildings, cooking for participants in meetings and events, or decorating the assembly areas, is not defined as "work" and thus not accounted for in the labor records of the cooperative members. Therefore, if you are a female member of the cooperative, you need a man to do your share, either a close relative who does it for free or paid labor.

Since the cooperative is the owner of the land and women are not members, they are excluded from direct access to land and other natural resources as well as from the economic projects run by the cooperative. Moreover, women are very weakly represented in other community associations as well, partly because they are not elected and partly because they are not willing to be elected. This means that women remain absent from power structures and decision-making processes at the community level in much the same way they always have been. Only through their husbands can they gain access to resources and have influence over the most important decisions regarding their common future. This implies, among other things, that women are extremely vulnerable in the case of death or abandonment by their husbands.

As Ixmucané members, women are represented in the biweekly assembly organized to coordinate activities between the cooperative and the different *sectores*. This is their only formal channel of participation at the community level. A number of women attend the general assemblies organized by the cooperative, but they rarely speak, even when their opinion would be crucial, as in the assembly organized to discuss planning a housing project to be implemented by an NGO. The NGO representatives displayed their drawings, and invited the participants to come with their questions and comments. As usual in these assemblies, the women had gathered at the back of the big hall, at the extreme opposite of the podium. They went forward to examine the drawings, to return to their place in the back where the discussions were very lively. I stayed with the women during most of this assembly and heard that they had lots of questions and comments, but none of them presented them in public.

Trapped in Women's Projects

The lack of participation by women in community affairs has been a constant preoccupation of the Ixmucané leadership as well as of the organizations assisting the returnees. During the first few years, all the NGOs and government institutions supporting development initiatives in La Quetzal created and implemented activities and projects aimed at improving the conditions of women. Most of these have been income-generating projects, run collectively through the women's organization. Participation in the activities of Ixmucané was seen as an aim in itself. Women would escape from their everyday routines, be together with other women, exchange experiences, and gain new insights. However, given the precarious economic situation in the community, they realized that certain economic incentives were necessary in order to motivate women, and to earn the goodwill of their men. The income-generating projects were believed to fulfill both aims: to motivate women to participate in collective activities and at the same time generate income that could be used to improve women's conditions. These projects have not been success stories. I will examine a few of them in order to understand why.

In 1997 an NGO supported the establishment of a poultry farm for Ixmucané members, providing the construction materials for two chicken coops, a number of hens, a few months of feed concentrates, and technical assistance. The cooperative allocated a piece of land to the project. The idea was that the farm should be managed by the women and become self-sustaining after a few months. The first problem faced by the women was that a number of activities—such as deforesting the site to raise the necessary infrastructure and guarding the poultry during the night—were required to make the farm operative. In the existing sexual division of labor, these activities are defined as men's work.

Another problem was that the marketing potentials were very limited, first because most households in the area have their own laying hens, and second, because there are local merchants supplying eggs for the limited demand. The local women did not have the knowledge, the means of transport, nor the confidence to compete with them. Incomes were too limited even to provide enough for a steady purchase of feed. The remarkable thing was that, when the delivery of feed concentrate by the NGO was delayed, the women did not feed the hens with their own corn as a temporary solution; they would rather let the hens die. Nobody seemed to feel responsible for the project. Following an internal evaluation made by the women, they deemed the project unsuccessful; they divided the hens that survived among themselves and closed the project in spite of the pressure to continue by the NGO, who had to report to the international funding agency. This project, like some other women's projects, was redefined—egg production was replaced by chicken-breeding—and continued by the cooperative, delegating the everyday running of it to a commission established for that purpose. It then became quite successful.

During the same year, a beekeeping project for women was established with the support of another NGO. The plan was that the NGO would provide the beehives and bees as well as technical and organizational assistance. The cooperative, this time consulted beforehand, agreed to help out with the heavy physical work such as clearing the site to locate the hives, transporting the hives to their location, and transporting the product from the site to the community. Ixmucané was to be responsible for managing the hives, organizing the labor, and the financial part. The honey would be marketed through the cooperative shop and the cooperative would also market it outside the community. So far there has been little to sell. The first year was so dry that flowering in the jungle where the hives were located was drastically reduced. This led to considerable loss of bees, and the hives had to be moved to an area some 60 kilometers from the community to save the surviving bees. The distance implied that the women could not take care of the management of the hives—"women do not travel like that"—and management had to be delegated to paid labor.

By late 1999, the ecological conditions had improved and the hives could be moved back to their old site. Ixmucané organized a meeting with the NGO, which I attended, to discuss the future of the project. Some one hundred women turned up, and even though very few expressed themselves, it was clear that the interest in continuing the project was rather slight, given the poor results so far. Many women also said they were afraid of the bees and of walking into the jungle where the hives were to be located. The Ixmucané leader chairing this meeting was quite frustrated over this lack of interest and insisted that if the organization withdrew from the project they were not going to sell the hives and share the money. By the end of the meeting it was decided that Ixmucané should withdraw from the project. Those who were interested in continuing were invited to sign up and establish a project group outside the organization. Ten women did sign up and the NGO promised to help move the hives back to the site close to the community and to market the produce. By the time I finished my fieldwork, this group had been reduced to five women and one man, who were very interested and dedicated to the project. This group will hopefully be able to earn an income from this project. Even though weather situations may create difficulties in the future, apiculture has the potential of becoming a highly profitable activity in this area, given the relatively low investment costs and the limited labor input required (van der Vaeren 2000: 266–67). Moreover, it can easily be combined with other activities, a crucial condition for the participation of women. The fact that the group has a male member also makes it more self-sustaining, since he can take care of tasks that cannot be carried out by the female members.

Based on the experiences of the failures of these and other large collective women's projects, which are certainly not peculiar this community, several efforts were made to make smaller and more manageable collective projects for women. One was a sheep project, supported by yet another NGO, to be managed by a smaller group of women. It was created much in the same way as the others, with the cooperative providing the land and support to establish the infrastructure, the NGO giving the technical assistance, and a group of women doing the work involved in the management. A piece of land had been allocated on the outskirts of the hamlet where the sheep could graze during the day, and a shelter built to protect them during the night. The women could alternate taking care of the sheep, letting them out in the morning, closing them up at night, and providing them with water, tasks considered quite bearable for women. Due to the limited extension of land at their disposal, however, the food within the reach of the sheep was rather limited. The women had to start collecting branches from the trees to feed them, which became increasingly more arduous (something I experienced when I accompanied them in this work). Since the cooperative was not willing to provide a larger area of land to improve the feeding situation, it was decided that the project should be terminated. The animals were sold and the income— 28 Quetzales (approximately $U.S. 4)—was distributed to each member. This marked the end of the project.

Understanding the difficulties women had in combining family obligations and participation in community activities, an NGO proposed financing the establishment of a daycare center. They believed that this would create the necessary conditions for women's community participation. The NGO financed the building of a house and provided pedagogical material and training of personnel to run the establishment, expecting that the project would be sustainable after a certain period of external backing. This was not the case. Once the NGO ended its support, the project collapsed. It turned out that most women were reluctant to leave their small children to persons who were not close relatives, especially if they had to pay for it; nor were they interested in a rotation system where they could alternate in caretaking. Daycare was arranged during the intense preparation for return and the emergency phase after resettlement, when everybody was mobilized and collective engagement was strong. Once daily life was back to normal the tradition that the mother should take care of her own children was again reinforced among most women as well as among men. The daycare building was used to house the local clinic for a few years until a new building for that purpose was finished. Ixmucané did not want to let the cooperative use the building for its own purposes unless rent was paid. When the cooperative refused to pay rent, the house was closed, and when I finished my fieldwork it had been unused for more than a year.

Why Do Women's Projects Fail?

Why did the projects fail when the women were in charge? First, it should be said that it is not only women's projects that have failed. The same has been true for certain cooperative projects, perhaps for some of the same reasons: lack of market for the products and services produced (e.g., ecotourism) and lack of understanding by the funding agencies of local practices and values that are not easily changed. Returnees, and especially returnee women, have been favorite targets of aid among international donors and a number of more and less competent NGOs have queued up to assist. Planning has often been fast and superficial, based on experiences in other parts of the country or the world or on preestablished aid agendas of donors or NGOs, rather on an understanding of local needs and constraints. The returnees have been offered more projects than they could handle, and during the first years, failure to comply with the preconditions did not prevent them from obtaining new projects.

The poultry project is a typical example. This project was planned and implemented without a proper understanding of the marketing possibilities. Lack of market outlets would probably have also been a constraint in the sheep production, had it not been for the scarcity of land that made sheep breeding too labor-intensive and thus too difficult for the women to handle. Without access to land, women's projects are limited to activities that do not require large sites.

What distinguishes the problems faced by women's projects as compared to men's projects is related to the organization of labor. This in turn has to be understood with reference to the dominant sexual and social division of labor, and is closely related to dominant ideas about masculinity and femininity. While men can carry out most or all of the tasks associated with an income-generating project, this is not the case for women. This implies that women's projects, as they have been planned so far, are dependent on men.

It turned out to be very difficult to carry out productive projects by an organization like Ixmucané whose membership lived under the domestic imperative. Married women's participation in meetings and project activities largely depended on their daily routines at home, something that was not always compatible with the project needs, for example the need for water of a flock of sheep or a vegetable garden.Most women did not react as predicted in the Ixmucané documents: "leaving her kitchen and letting her housework wait to be able to engage in organizational work." It is true that many of the projects failed due to lack of adequate care, but this was not (or at least not only) due to women's lack of experience and competence, an argument used by men who took over several of them and made them work. Men were not constrained by the illness of their children, by the imperative of having the tortillas ready on time, or by the behavioral codes associated with female respectability, constraining women's freedom of movement.

During my three years of fieldwork I saw that the mobilizing capacity of Ixmucané decreased, with growing organizational fatigue among the women. This may have had to do with the lack of success of many of the projects. Even though the objectives of the organization included a wide range of questions related to the improvement of women's conditions, most women's involvement was motivated by expectations of improving their income. When this did not happen, their level of engagement and enthusiasm decreased, and it became gradually more difficult for the activist minority to motivate the rest. In order to encourage attendance the organization offered sweet bread and *atol* (drink made of corn), which were distributed at the end of the meeting for people to take home.

By the end of my fieldwork, Ixmucané still existed, and those in leading positions were still actively participating in workshops and courses arranged by NGOs outside the community. But internally the organization had little influence. When larger meetings were arranged, for example, on the anniversary of the organization, many women attended, but the activity and enthusiasm from its early days were lacking.

The Power of Gender Imagery

Today most men in La Quetzal, who consider themselves "progressive and developed," would not refuse to allow their wives or daughters to participate in activities organized by the women's organization as long as they can keep up the "level of service" at home. At the same time, very few men are willing to give a hand in child care or cooking. A man making his own tortilla is a favorite example of male misery. The rigidity in the sexual division of labor and the definition of what is work and what is not are central constraints on women's participation. If women with children have no female relatives who are willing to lend a hand, they can only leave their homes for short periods if at all. The building of a daycare center was not a solution to this problem.

Both men and women are very concerned about how women perform as mothers and housewives. To have the food ready on time is very important, something that requires women's presence at home. Even though most people are against physical punishment of adults, to have the meal ready on time is so important that men and women agree that if a wife does not comply, it is understandable if her husband beats her up. Since they have no modern appliances, housework is very time-consuming.

Men's work is carried out in the *milpa* or in the village as part of the work obligation of cooperative members. By supporting and defending

the rigid sexual division of labor, men monopolize all productive resources. As cooperative members, they control the land and its use; they
also control income-generating projects other than agriculture and forestry. This monopoly is extended to institutions which are not under the
cooperative umbrella: for example, the Catholic Church, where all thirteen catechists are males. Women are eligible for the catechist positions
but are not elected. To be a catechist is very time-consuming, and, even
though women are the most faithful in church activities, most do not feel
confident enough to lead a celebration, which would be required of a
catechist from time to time. They are, however, expected to do their "non-
labor" work: decorate the church with flowers and keep it neat and clean.
In the Celebrations of the Word women's role as mother, wife, and housewife is praised as a prime female attribute; as are sexual purity, chastity
and humbleness. The parallel to "la Madre de Jesús" is explicit.

Some of the young mothers tried to instruct their sons in helping with
domestic chores, but found it quite difficult. The story of Reina, an Ixmucané activist and a mother of three sons, is quite illustrative:

Alfredo (seven) is already "muy machista" (very male chauvinist). I have to
threaten him and even beat him to make him help me carry water. He says he
cannot carry water because he is not a woman. "Don't you have two arms?"
I ask him, "don't you have two arms like a woman? If you have two arms you
can carry water." In my house, my brothers always helped my mother carry
water. They also used to sweep the house and the courtyard and even make
tortillas. In the house of my parents-in-law it was quite different. My brothers-
in-law never helped in the house, and my husband never helps me. Therefore,
it is very difficult to convince my sons that they have to help.

From this we may conclude that, as far as gender relations are concerned, the experience of exile has been less transforming than people
seem to believe. By and large those who control the important institutions
and organizations are men who, whether wittingly or not, arrange things
so that women have little access to resources or voice in important decisions. The labor division in household and family remains much the same
as before. The public-domestic dichotomy seems to have been reconstructed and women are still confined to the domestic sphere as it was
prior to exile.

If we focus on other aspects of gender relations, however, a different
picture is revealed. The changes that are most emphasized by both female
and male informants are those regarding health and education, which
we have referred to earlier. Access to health services, including preventive measures such as pre- and post-partum control and vaccination, has
reduced infant mortality rates dramatically. Most women over thirty-five

have lost one or more children due to illnesses that were not related to the violence. Today children no longer die from high fever, cough, or diarrhea, so common in the past. Neither do adults die from easily curable illnesses. If they cannot be cured at the local clinic, they are brought to the hospital in town. Access to education, particularly training in Spanish, is another change emphasized by many people time and again. This has certainly enhanced people's confidence and self-esteem and also the way men and women relate to each other. In what follows I will discuss some other changes in gender relations that have contributed to improve the situation of women.

Marriage Practices

Most women over forty recalled that they had married men who they did not choose themselves. Some had never seen the husband they would share their life with before the father and in-laws had settled the marriage contract. The only thing the woman could do was accept the decision. For some, this was the beginning of a terrible relationship, especially if the husband turned out to be a heavy drinker. For the majority, however, it was the beginning of a relationship where husband and wife learned to live together in a "customary" way. Very few had an idea about or expectations of a "love marriage." In some cases, the girl was so young that she was not yet a woman (*todavía no era mujer*): she had not menstruated and did not know about sexual relations.

Lourdes, a Q'anjob'al midwife in her late forties, was twelve when her stepfather arranged her marriage.

I am a huérfana de padre (a girl whose father is dead). My father died when I was a baby. My mother married again and had four more children. My stepfather did not like me, that is probably why he married me off so young, he wanted to get rid of me. I was only a child, twelve years old, very thin and short; I had barely had my first menses. I was very ingenuous. My mother tried to oppose my stepfather when he wanted to marry me off. She realized how apprehensive I was. My stepfather did not care about what she had to say, and even less about how I felt. My husband was much older then I, twenty-four or five, I think. The day he brought me to his house he tried to molest me (common expression for having sexual relations), but I managed to escape. He lived in a two-story house with his parents. I climbed the stairs and hid in a corner where it was difficult for him to catch me. Since everybody was sleeping in the same room he had to be careful. My father-in-law told him to leave me alone for a while. My husband went to my stepfather to claim that I did not want to hacer vida (have sex) with him. My stepfather came to see me. He said that if I did not obey my husband he would tie me to the rafter and

lash me. I continued to resist for some three or four months. One day he captured me and I could not escape. That's how I became pregnant with my daughter Micaela.

Marriages are no longer contracted in this way. The marriage arrangement is still made between the parents, but at the initiative of the potential groom, who has normally agreed with his bride-to-be beforehand.
Only in cases of premarital pregnancies do parents force or try to force
their daughter to marry. The parents of the boy would also put pressure
on him. With the practice of blood tests to verify paternity—learned in
the refugee camps and practiced since—it is no longer easy to escape
paternal responsibilities unless one literally disappears from the community, as has happened in a few cases.

Most parents try to follow the will of their offspring regarding marriage
partners. The normal procedure is that boys and girls fall in love and
agree that they want to marry. This is followed up by the boy and his parents paying a visit to the girl's home on a few occasions until the two
families reach agreement regarding the approval of the union, the practical arrangements of the wedding, and, in some cases, some aspects of
married life. Most unions are neither registered by the civil authorities
nor blessed by the church. They are arrangements between families, sealed
by the celebration of a fiesta where kin and neighbors are present. If the
fiesta is organized in the home of the bride, the groom takes her home
when the fiesta is over. If the celebration is in his home, she will stay with
him when the guests leave.

Most people do not regret the loss of imposed marriages, although some
old people think that contracting marriage has become too easy. Some
of the old men recalled that they had to work six months for their father-
in-law to be able to marry his daughter, and they were obliged to *gastar*
(spend) to buy presents for the bride and her parents.

Yolanda's story about the process that led to her marriage with Fernando is illustrative of modern marriage practices. Yolanda and Fernando
had known each other in the camp in Mexico and were close neighbors
in La Quetzal. Her narrative starts with the first visit paid by her boyfriend and his parents.

Even though our parents knew each other quite well, this was a very formal
and serious visit. After talking about anything and everything (buyes perdidos)
for a while, our fathers started talking about us. They informed each other that
they knew about our relation and our desire to formalize it and that they agreed.
After that my father said that he wanted to discuss some matters related to our
customs that he wanted them to know. I remember that he mentioned three
things. First he said that in our family we are not madrugadores (getting up

early), we get up between 5 and 6 in the morning. "I want you to know that Yolanda is not used to getting up before that," my father said, "she is not one of those who gets up at 3 or 4 o'clock, and I would not like you to oblige her to do so." The next was about our food customs. My father said, "Since we belong to different groups our ways of preparing food differ (Yolanda is Mam, Fernando Q'anjob'al). Therefore you cannot expect Yolanda to be familiar with your way of preparing food. She will have to learn." Finally, he talked about work. "I beg you not to send my daughter to work in the fields. She is not used to this kind of work and I would not like that you oblige her to do so." This was more or less what my father said in this first meeting. Fernando's father answered that he understood my father's concerns and that he would see to it that they were respected. Even though Fernando and I were there our fathers did most of the talking. My grandparents—the parents of my father—were present as well.

The next week Fernando and his parents paid a second visit to discuss the details of the wedding. Fernando's father proposed to arrange the fiesta in his house. The Q'anjob'al and the Mam share the custom that the groom's parents provide the food for the wedding. Where to arrange the fiesta is a matter of conversation. My father accepted this proposal and my parents-in-law returned home. When they had left, my grandfather said that he was not at all happy with this arrangement. If Lorenzo (her father-in-law) is going to arrange the fiesta in his house, it seems that we only go there and give away Yolanda to them, this does not seem right to me. This is against our customs, my grandfather said; we should have the meal here. My father agreed with him and my mother too. My father then went to Lorenzo's to tell him about this new proposal. Lorenzo agreed but said that he would like to talk with his wife before making a final decision. The next day he passed by to tell us that they had accepted my grandfather's proposal.

When I visited Yolanda in her new home, she was alone in the house of her parents-in-law cooking for the whole family and taking care of her husband's two small sisters. She told me about her day that started at five (and not before!) filled with a variety of household chores. She did not work in the fields; nevertheless she worked a lot, because she had taken over the housework and childcare for her mother-in-law, who therefore could spend more time in the fields. Yolanda also told me that she had withdrawn from the cooperative. She was one of three female members of the cooperative; she had been its vice-president and represented the institution in a number of regional and national contexts. Finally, I realized that her plans to join the teacher training program had not materialized. When I asked her why, she said that she did not dare apply (*no me animé solicitar*), something very unlike the Yolanda that I knew.

According to Adriana, her sister-in-law, who is a teacher, Yolanda had regressed following her marriage. She maintains that Fernando as well as his mother does not approve of her studies or her community involvement. They want her to be a traditional mother and housewife. This does not surprise Adriana. "Men want their wives to be at home serving them," she explained to me. What surprises her is that Yolanda had adapted to her new situation and seemed happy with it.

The procedures described by Yolanda are more or less similar to those of other young couples, though minor details regarding the number of visits and the organization of the wedding may vary. Some of the old people report that marriage customs changed when they moved to Ixcán. Before that it was rather common for the groom to work for the father-in-law for three to six months, in some cases up to a year, before he was allowed to take his wife with him. The custom was (and still is) that the new couple lives with the groom's parents and siblings during the first year. It is believed that the wife has to be socialized by her mother-in-law to learn the likes and dislikes of her husband. This implies, among other things, sharing the bedroom with the rest of the family. Sometimes a young man built his own house next to his parents, as Fernando did, something young couples see as an ideal situation.

There are several ways in which couples get married in La Quetzal. The most common today is to be married by *costumbre*, which implies the type of agreement between families described by Yolanda. This kind of marriage arrangement has persisted over time, even though the content of it has changed. What is new is that this customary union is not being confirmed by civil or ecclesiastical contracts. While most people over forty have been through civil or ecclesiastical ceremony, this is rarely the case for younger couples. The main argument for this is economic: "People don't want to spend money on it or people cannot afford it." Civil union is associated with expenditures for traveling and paperwork in the municipal capital; church weddings require considerable spending in food and drink. All the people who are present in the church during the ceremony expect to be invited. A customary wedding, in contrast, is limited to the families of the couple and their closest friends and neighbors. We should remember that most returnees no longer have the big families they used to have when living in the Highlands.

Mixed Marriages

Yolanda and Fernando belong to different ethnic groups. Yolanda's parents told me that this was not a problem as long as both of them were considered good and trustworthy and belonged to reputable families. Moreover, both were of marriageable age. This is a common attitude among parents today. The recognition of certain *costumbres* of the respective groups is expected and often discussed in the meetings between the two families. We saw that Yolanda's father expected certain considerations in the relationship between his daughter and her in-laws, something he also stressed in the conversations with Fernando's parents. She should certainly respect them and their customs, but he expected them to respect some of hers as well.

Not all parents readily accept the choice of partners of their son or daughter and may try to prevent a marriage. In such cases their offspring may refrain from marrying or, as in the case of Valeria (Q'anjob'al) and Macario (Q'eqchi'), they may take matters into their own hands. Valeria's mother Candelaria explains what happened:

One Wednesday afternoon Valeria was to come with me to the church. Since she was a bit delayed changing and preparing herself, I went ahead. She never arrived at the church. We did not know were she had gone. We found her the next day; someone told me that she was in the house of this muchacho (boy) Macario in La Laguna. My husband was not at home, so I went to see what was going on. There she was. I was very annoyed. "Why did you steal her (robarla)? Why did you not come to my house to ask for her?" This I said to the boy and to his parents too; they were also there. He did not say anything. "I am sure you did not come to ask for her because your parents did not want to accompany you," I continued. Since he is their only child, I suppose that they wanted him to marry one from their group. He is a Q'eqchi' and the Q'eqchi's do not like to mix with the other groups.

When my husband found out he became furious. He went straight to the alcalde auxiliar to denounce the case, he wanted my daughter to return home—at that time she was a minor, barely fourteen—and he also wanted the boy punished. When my son Severino heard about this he also became upset. "Now the damage is done," he said, "what do you do with Valeria if she returns home? Who will marry her? And don't forget that you have more daughters that you want to marry away. If you make so much of a mess, the boys will not approach them," he said. After this, my husband withdrew the charges and let her stay.

Candelaria said that she would probably have opposed the union between Valeria and Macario at the moment, not because Macario belonged to another ethnic group, but because of her daughter's age. The family had made many sacrifices to keep her studying, and she would have tried to convince her to finish her *ciclo básico*. Moreover, she disliked the idea of her daughter marrying a man without the approval of his parents. "Opposing your parents in these matters always brings problems," was her conclusion. I have never heard Candelaria complain about the fact that none of sons are married to Q'anjob'al women.

Valeria left school and in less than a year she was a mother. Her husband

and in-laws did not want her to continue in school, and neither did Valeria. Cohabitation with her parents-in-law has not been easy. Macario's mother does not speak Spanish, and she is a woman of tradition who expects hard work and submission from her daughter-in-law. Such expectations are not uncommon, but for Valeria who grew up as a schoolgirl, with sisters close in age to share labor obligations and a mother who according to herself is a "modern" woman, the transition was very hard. Several times she has returned to her parents for short periods, according to herself (and her mother) because her mother-in-law mistreated her and Macario sided with his mother rather than with his wife. So far she has always returned with her husband when he has come to ask for forgiveness. Valeria has no plans to formalize the relationship; she told me that she does not know how long she will stand it (*aguantar*). Her mother does not think she will marry by civil or by church. "He does not want to spend," was her comment.

This case also draws attention to the importance of virginity for a good marriage. The reaction of Valeria's brother Severino is symptomatic. Once Valeria has spent the night in Macario's house, her attraction as a potential wife is drastically reduced and she may become a burden to her family. Thus, the protection of a girl's virginity and chastity is not only an individual matter—it is also a family concern, well known from other parts of Latin America (Melhuus and Stølen 1996; Stølen 1998). Therefore, parents are often unwilling to accept the return of a girl who has eloped. This is especially tragic in cases where the girl really has been "stolen," brought to a man's house against her will. This had happened to several of my older informants.

When it comes to war-related sexual abuses of women, however, Guatemalans seem to be more tolerant than what is reported from some other war zones, for example, the Balkans where women abused by "the enemy" quite commonly were rejected by their families (Moser and Clark 2001). One example is Nicolás's niece, who was kidnapped at the age of fourteen by an army officer during a massacre in Ixcán. She was kept in an army settlement in this region until the officer retired fifteen years later and returned permanently to his family in Guatemala City. Then he brought her and their five children to her grandparents in Huhuetenango. According to Nicolás, she was well received by her kin, in spite of not being able to speak with them; she could no longer speak Q'anjob'al.

Gender Rights and Justice

Another change that women (and men too) refer to when asked about changes in gender relations is that women dare to speak up. They no longer have to *aguantar con paciencia* (endure with patience) abuses and injustices committed against them. This, however, does not mean that such things have stopped. What has happened is that women have acquired new values and consciousness regarding what is right and wrong, in addition to certain new possibilities for stopping or even punishing the abusers. Many women associate the consciousness-raising with the courses received in the camps, where they also learned to use the limited institutions to claim justice. The example of Elvira is illustrative. When she was sixteen she went to a training course for refugees, where she fell passionately in love with one of her teachers, a much older, married refugee from her own camp. He said he was about to get divorced, and offered her marriage, and she went to live with him without the consent of her parents. She was pregnant when he abandoned her. Elvira denounced him to the camp authorities. When she was about to give birth he was arrested. Elvira remembers:

My labor had already started when the judge[2] called me, but I went to see him, to present my case. I told him everything that had happened between us. I told what my novio (fiancé) had said to me, what he had promised, even that he had taken an oath on the seriousness of his intensions. He denied everything. At that point the labor pains were so strong that I could not endure it any longer. The judge understood my condition. "Take this woman and bring her to a midwife," he said to my novio," pay the expenses, because the child that she is bearing is yours." When the judge realized that he was not going to comply, he called on my father. "Take your daughter, find her a midwife and pay for the expenses. After the birth we will find out who is lying. If this man is lying he will have to pay, if your daughter lies she will have to pay."

"I do not want this shameless woman in my house," my father said. The judge tried to convince him to give me a space in the porch of the house, but my father did not accept. My mother was also present, but she did not dare to say anything. She knew that it did not make sense to speak up against my father. The only thing she could achieve by doing that was a beating.

The day after my daughter was born I was called upon by the judge again. I went with my little girl. Her father was there. He had been in jail while I gave birth. The judge explained to him that if he did not recognize his fatherhood, they would conduct a blood analysis to find out if the girl had his blood or the blood of another man. If the analysis showed that she had his blood, he would not only have to pay the expenses of the birth but also a fine. Confronted with the threat of paying a fine, he relented and asked for forgiveness for not having acknowledged her before. Now that he had recognized her, he asked me to give her away to him. He had even come with his sister, who brought a feeding bottle with milk. My father agreed; he wanted me to give up my daughter. Representatives from ACNUR and COMAR were present and asked me what I wanted. "I don't want to give her up," I said. "This little angel has not come to this world to suffer; she is not guilty of what has happened. We are the guilty ones, he and I," I said. "She is not going to grow up without a mother." "If you don't give up your daughter I will not accept you in my house, my father said. "You will have to leave." "I will not give her up," I repeated; "if that means that I have to leave your house, I will leave." The case ended like this.

Elvira had a terribly hard time not being allowed to live with her family after her baby was born. She went to Cancún, where she was lucky to find employment as a maid in a family that accepted her baby and treated both of them very well. She stayed with them until her father came to pick them up to bring them to La Quetzal. Her father repented of what he had done to her and she has forgiven him, even though she says that she will never forget that he abandoned her when she needed him the most.

It is interesting to note that Elvira did not relent, faced with the deceit of her boyfriend. She knew that she could report him and he would be obliged to take responsibility for what he had done. Impunity was no longer the rule of the day. In the camps, the refugees learned not only about their rights, but that there were channels through which they could claim them.

One thing that Elvira emphasized when she told me about this episode was that the organizations (she refers to UNHCR and COMAR) asked her what she wanted regarding the future of her daughter and that the judge gave priority to her desires above those of her boyfriend and father. This was a new experience for her, as she was used to having to adapt to the decisions of her father.

Domestic Violence

It has been argued that domestic conflicts and violence against women tend to increase in postwar situations due to the fact that people are traumatized and emotionally unstable. (Zur 1998: 56; Indra 1999). This does not seem to be the case here. This may be due partly to changing attitudes toward violence, as a product of people's own traumatic experiences combined with the antiviolence attitudes of those who assisted them in exile, especially the Catholic Church. The refugees learned about justice and rights, and were encouraged to stand up for them; they were encouraged to denounce injustice and violence, even in the domestic sphere. This practice has to some extent been reproduced in the returnee community.

In La Quetzal, local justice is taken care of by the *alcalde auxiliar*, operating at the community level. During my fieldwork a number of family conflicts were resolved by the *alcaldes*. In one case a young man had beaten up his wife because his brother had tried to rape her. The wife had been sleeping with her two children when her brother-in-law entered her house and bed. When she realized what was going on she screamed, and her husband who was visiting in a house next door came to rescue her. Instead of punishing his brother, who was quite drunk, he assaulted his wife. Not only did he beat her up, he also dragged her by her hair around the house. She was badly injured. Eventually she managed to escape and went to her neighbor and *comadre*, the godmother of one of her sons, who nursed her for several days until she was able to get out of bed. Her *comadre*, an Ixmucané activist, convinced her to report the case to the *alcalde auxiliar*. She did so, and both her husband and her brother-in-law had to meet before the *alcalde* and explain themselves. They were punished with two days of ditch-digging in the outskirts of the center.

This case caused a lot of discussion and gossip in the community. Most people agreed that it was very bad that the husband had mistreated his wife unjustly. They also agreed that the behavior of the brother-in-law was absolutely reprehensible. But opinions were divided as whether it was right for her to report it. Some felt the woman had betrayed her husband by denouncing him; after all, no permanent injuries or killing had taken place. Generally, people think that family problems should be resolved within the family, preferably with the help of parents and godparents. The trouble is that, in a number of cases, the godparents do not live in the community and parents tend to side with their offspring. Who will then defend a woman whose parents do not live in the community? Based on this reasoning, some found it justifiable that she reported him. Moreover, it was not the first time she had been beaten by her husband. The *comadre* was of the opinion that the punishment given was too light, compared to other offenses. She maintained that the light punishment for wife-battering revealed the *machista* attitudes of the *alcaldes*, who believed this was not a serious infringement.

The brothers felt so humiliated by the punishment that they refused to do the communal work. Their father took it on and worked four days digging ditches. The wife returned to her husband. At first he treated her badly, as did her mother-in-law, but after a while things began to normalize. The important thing is that he has not beaten her since then.

Even though most people condemn wife-battering, they contend that husbands must beat their wives in certain situations where the woman has not complied with what is considered her motherly or housewifely duty, for example, if the husband returns tired from a hard day's work at the *milpa* and the food is not ready, or if there are mere suspicions or rumors of infidelity. A man who does not react with violence in such situations is considered a nitwit.

Women in contrast cannot reciprocate if the husband neglects what is considered his duty. That would humiliate him and undermine his authority. If this happens, his use of violence is understood. This does not mean that a woman always agrees with her husband or does as he commands. She might do as she wants if she finds an acceptable explanation as to why it had to be her way. The important thing is that she does not appear as dominant in their relationship. This is the role of the husband and father, something that most men and women, young and old agree upon.

It should be mentioned that the school also plays an important role in combating domestic violence, particularly physical punishment for children. This kind of punishment, which has been quite common at home, is now completely abolished at school. The argument used by the teachers is that if one wants to prevent violence from emerging again, it is necessary to start with the children. A child who has not been beaten will be less inclined to use violence against others. This is a new way of thinking for many parents, who have been used to physical punishment as a normal thing. Questions of discipline are a recurrent theme and a source of fervent debates in the meetings between parents and teachers. Young couples say that they refrain from physical punishments, at least premeditated ones.

Sexuality and Reproduction

With few exceptions, married women do not seem to associate sexuality with pleasure and lust. Most couples start their sexual life in a common bedroom shared with the husband's parents and siblings. Intercourse is rapid and silent, the man ejaculates, and it is over. Women often refer to intercourse as *molestia* (a nuisance) and recount how they are pleased when the husband *no molesta mucho* (does not bother much) or *me respeta* (he respects me) which is another way of talking about not having sex. It is essential that there is some *molestia*, however, because lack of sexual interest by the man is interpreted as a bad sign: "Maybe he has another woman—because men always need sex." It is still a widespread view that a wife should be sexually available when the husband wants her, and according to most female informants this happens too often. One problem many women refer to is that their husband does not respect their *dieta*, the local term for the two first months after childbirth.[3] According to both traditional practice and the recommendation of the midwives, no sexual intercourse should take place during this period. Some women have had sex four to five days after childbirth, something that caused not only pain but also risk of infection, given that men's intimate hygiene is far from impeccable, and they have struggled with infections for long periods afterward.

The fear of unwanted pregnancies also impoverishes sexual enjoyment.

Women want to have children; four or five is considered a good number, but it is still quite common to have eight to ten. Today women have access to contraceptives, pills, and injections that protect them for up to three months. Nevertheless the use of contraception is not general. Some say that they are afraid of damage to their health; many tragic stories circulate. Moreover, married women need permission from their husbands to get contraceptives at the clinic, while the unmarried need permission from their parents.

Some of the Ixmucané leaders as well as the midwives are concerned about women's sexuality and reproductive health. They know that that these factors constitute a traumatic part of life for many women, and they would like to do something about it. However, they find it difficult to discuss these topics in other than medical terms. So far the issues have not been raised at the Ixmucané workshops; the leaders believe that they are still too controversial and would create resistance by a number of women and men, who would question the function of their organization even more. My impression based on conversations with many women is that they would welcome information and the exchange of experiences in this area. However, the topics are controversial and should be dealt with accordingly.

The high valuation of education and efforts to become educated create preoccupations and dilemmas for young women, who also want to be married and have children. The latter is seen as the essence of being an adult woman, and many young girls said that they would sacrifice their further education when they marry if the husband and in-laws expect it. That was apparently what happened to Valeria and Yolanda.

One afternoon two young girls, Cecilia and Elsa, came to visit; they needed help to fill in an application form for a scholarship. Both of them had finished the *ciclo básico* and wanted to pursue their studies in the provincial capital. Even though both looked forward to continuing their studies, they expressed worries about their possibilities of getting married: "Soon we are getting too old. You know, here the best marrying age is considered to be between fourteen and seventeen years, if you conserve yourself well, a couple of years more. You probably know that Yolanda was called *la vieja* (old lady) a long time before she married" (at the age of twenty-one). I did know, and I also remembered that several women had emphasized the importance of marrying early. A girl who reaches fifteen or sixteen without being engaged is most probably a *puta* (prostitute), they had argued, meaning someone who is not a virgin, thus less attractive as a potential wife.

Cecilia and Elsa were very ambivalent about their future. They wanted to study and be educated, but at the same time they were afraid of becoming too old to get married. "Life as a spinster is no life," one of them said and looked knowingly at me. They became very surprised when I told them that I was not a spinster. Not only did I have a husband, he did not prevent me from working away from home. "How do you dare to leave him alone? Now that you are here, he will certainly find another woman," Cecilia said with conviction. Elsa nodded. "I hope not", I said; "you know that I have come here a number of times and he has not replaced me yet." "You are lucky, this would be impossible here, if a wife is not around the husband finds another woman, the men here are like that," was Elsa's firm conclusion.

I remembered Rosalía, the health promoter referred to earlier, who was one of the very few married women who had a paid job. Rosalía was a special woman. She had been working outside the home ever since she arrived in the refugee camp in Chiapas in the early 1980s, first as a volunteer and later as a paid NGO employee. Rosalía had only one daughter because, according to herself, she used contraceptives to prevent having more children, but according to her neighbor, because after two miscarriages she no longer became pregnant. Her daughter, a secondary-school student, was studying in a boarding school in Mexico. Rosalía wanted to give her a solid education so that she could prosper in life. Rosalía was an object of gossip among the women in her neighborhood. Even though they admired her for her capacities, they considered that she was too much involved in her work to serve her husband properly. Moreover, she had male colleagues and often spent the night in other communities, something that made them question her respectability as well. They expressed pity for her husband. When he "joined another woman" during my last fieldtrip they found it quite normal. "What else could she expect?" Rosalía settled in another community. I had no chance to see her before I left to get her version of what had happened.

Continuity and Change in Gender Relations

Changes in gender relations have been less comprehensive than many people seem to believe. In the camps, especially during the preparation for return, and during the emergency phase in La Quetzal, new conditions and shifting relations created spaces in which women could organize and participate actively and decisively in community affairs. Judging from the documents produced by the women's organization, there was a high level of optimism and strong desires for change of gender relation. When the returnee community became more established, the old structures, where the roles for women and men were more rigidly defined, were gradually reestablished. Once again women were excluded from the institutions and organizations that control the most important resources and decisions in the community, and this is not because their participation is directly denied. Their exclusion is a result of choices and decisions made based on values and perceptions about gender roles held by both men and most women regarding how men and women are and should behave. The rigidity of the existing sexual division of labor, combined with the absence of modern household appliances, ties women to their homes unless they have other women in the household to help out.

In most cases public participation by women is limited to what is compatible with taking care of children and housework. This is one important reason why women's collective projects are more vulnerable than projects aimed at men or both men and women. Thus, the reconstruction process in many ways has contributed to weakening rather than strengthening women's organization and participation.

Nevertheless, we have also seen that certain advances made in exile are irreversible. Access to health and education has created new opportunities, especially for young people, and individual freedom and the right to decide about one's future have increased for both men and women. Young people no longer marry a person they do not know or do not like, as was the law of the day only a couple of decades ago. Most people marry the person of their choice even when the partner belongs to a different ethnic group and does not speak the same language or have the same customs. Even though domestic violence still exists, it has been reduced and a woman can get her assailant punished even when he is her husband. We have seen that denouncing a violent husband is not something that everybody approves of even though most people condemn wife-battering. However, the fact that an increasing number of women actually take the decisive step of making a denunciation seems to have a preventive effect, at least in some cases. I believe that condemnation and punishment by the local legal authority will gradually change people's attitudes and behavior regarding violence.

Chapter 9

The Returnees and the Guatemalan State

Every Monday morning at 8 o'clock, the primary school children in La Quetzal gather outside the school building to pay respect to the Guatemalan flag. The headmaster, a local returnee resident, gives a short speech reminding the children of the importance of belonging to the Guatemalan nation and of their responsibility, representing its future to make this nation a good place to live. Painted in big letters on the wall behind the children is the name Jacobo Arbenz—for many Guatemalans the sole truly democratic president in the history of their country and the only one who sought to improve the situation of the poor. Every week during my fieldwork in La Quetzal I would observe this scene from my window in the house next door: Jacobo Arbenz and the flapping flag accompanied by the thin voices of the children singing the national anthem.

This is but one of the many manifestations of the returnees' efforts to reintegrate into the Guatemalan nation-state after their years in exile. The name Jacobo Arbenz, visible to anyone who visits the community, demonstrates their identification with a different kind of society and government from the ones that forced them to leave Guatemala in the early 1980s.

In this chapter I will take a closer look at the relationship between the returnees and the Guatemalan state. This relationship is characterized not only by antagonism and mistrust, attributes perhaps most frequently associated with the returnees, but also by a struggle to become included, to become a community of citizens of the Guatemalan state through the extension of state institutions and through new administrative techniques of community organization. The latter is, among other things, reflected in the way their new settlement is being constructed.

State-Society Relations

As noted by Nugent (1994), there is a tendency in the literature on state-society relations to assume a model of state and community as two essential and bounded entities in opposition to each other.[1] The first is essentially expanding, transforming, and coercive; the other is essentially conservative and actively resistant to the imposed transformations. A number of studies, including Nugent's study from Peru (2001), challenge this view, showing that resistance is only one of several possible "junctures" of state-community relations. Such relations may also be characterized by marginalized communities actively involved in producing themselves as a community of citizens (Hansen and Stepputat 2001).

This is the perspective of Stepputat, who, on the basis of a historical analysis of the relations between the Guatemalan Indians and the state, argues against the view of Carol Smith that resistance and antagonism are what characterize this relationship from the conquest to the present. According to Smith, the state never gained legitimacy within the Indian communities, the state could control the communities only by force, and attempts to impose new institutions on them were not successful (Smith 1990: 11–17). Stepputat argues that state/society duality is not a colonial legacy but a product of certain techniques of governance introduced in the nineteenth century. It is associated with the post-colonial state, more specifically with the reforms of the government of Rufino Barrios in the late eighteenth century that privatized and individualized land, and introduced forced labor for those who did not possess enough land to be considered productive. Since then, the relationship between Indian communities and the state has been characterized by negotiations about their conditions of exclusion and possible reinclusion rather than antagonism and resistance as suggested by Smith (Stepputat 2001: 287–91).

My findings support the argument put forward by Stepputat. In the previous chapters we have seen that relations between the returnees and the state are multifaceted, contradictory, and changing over time. If we look at them from a historical perspective we will see that they are characterized by both resistance and active attempts at inclusion, and we will also see that contradictory attitudes and practices may exist simultaneously, as is currently the case in La Quetzal.

Changing State-Peasant Relations

Until the armed conflict in the 1970s, the state had only a limited direct presence in the lives of my informants, as in the lives of indigenous peasants in general, even though they were strongly affected by state policies. This was due mainly to the poor development of material infrastructure and institutions and the lack of centralization of power that characterized the Guatemalan state. Throughout history, the relationship between indigenous peasants and the state has been mediated by different non-state actors such as the Catholic Church, landowners, and local Ladino elites, and eventually the international aid community (Smith, 1990; Stepputat 2000; Stølen 2004). The fact that most of Guatemala's peasants have been illiterate as well as unable to speak the dominant language also prevented direct communication with representatives of the state, most of whom spoke only Spanish.

In my informants' narratives in Chapter 2 about life in the Highlands, we saw that they associated the state institutions with the powerful people (*los del poder*). This started to change when they joined the state-sponsored colonization programs in Ixcán during the 1960s. The settlement projects offered a unique economic opportunity, and after a few years of hard work and many sacrifices, the peasants began to experience a degree of prosperity that they had never known before.

Although relations and negotiations with state institutions were mediated by the priests, who operated as project coordinators, local cooperative leaders were gradually drawn into the mechanisms of dealing with the various institutions. Already at this point my informants had started to develop new ideas about the state, seeing it as not only violent and repressive, but also benevolent and productive. After all, it was the state that had handed over to them the land they were allocated. State institutions like INTA and the Department of Cooperatives assisted in surveying and granting land titles to the cooperatives, as well as providing technical assistance in the production of new crops. Once the cooperatives had constructed school buildings, the Ministry of Education assigned teachers to the cooperatives. During the first years of settlement, even the army was seen as quite benevolent and supportive.

These new perceptions of the state were, however, interrupted by the armed conflict. With the escalation of violence that culminated in their flight to Mexico, the state, represented by the army, became their most feared enemy. For almost fifteen years, until the return in April 1995, the returnees were physically excluded from the national territory by the repression of the Guatemalan state.

We have seen that crossing the Mexican border and incorporation into the "international refugee system" not only made them more conscious about their belonging to a nation-state, it also provoked changes in the interstate relations between Mexico and Guatemala, something that in turn challenged state-society relations in both countries (Gallagher 1989; Malkki 1995).

Through their interaction with the Mexican government, the NGOs, and the international organizations in the camps, the refugees were introduced to new forms of organization and governance as well as new ideas about the modern state. They learned about the existence of human rights, women's rights, and citizen rights, the existence of national constitutions and international conventions, and how to claim their rights. The universality of rights of citizens wherever they may roam is one of the hallmarks of the modern nation-state (Stepputat 2001: 284). The knowledge of rights was new to most people, even though some of the ideas about democracy and participation were known to those who had held leadership positions in the cooperatives in Ixcán and the Petén. During the many meetings, courses, and workshops in the camps, the returnees engaged in defining the conditions and forms of services the modern state should provide and negotiating the limits to state control and surveillance, a knowledge that became crucial in the negotiations leading to their return to Guatemala.

The interaction with the Guatemalan state during the exile was characterized by profound mistrust and resistance. In Chiapas the refugees suffered from army incursions into the camps and continued to live in an atmosphere of fear. Their resistance to removal to new camps in Campeche and Quintana also revealed that their trust in the Mexican authorities was slight, in spite of the protection and support they had received, something that started to change when conditions in the new camps improved. Democratic elections and the return to a civilian government in Guatemala in 1986 did not change their attitude toward Guatemalan authorities. They did not accept the conditions of repatriation offered by the government of President Cerezo. However, these repatriation initiatives motivated the refugees toward a proactive engagement that eventually resulted in negotiations with the Guatemalan government and state representatives, mediated by the Catholic Church and UNHCR. The process of peace negotiations clearly revealed deep doubts and mistrust among the refugees. This was reflected in their insistence on the ban on any military presence in the returnee communities and the exemption from military service, as well as on monitoring by UN forces and international accompaniers. However, at the same time, this process revealed a struggle by the refugees to become a community of citizens through the extension of state institutions and through new administrative techniques of community organization. The latter is reflected in the way they planned their new settlement.

Constructing a "Site of Governance"

We have seen that the construction of La Quetzal was the result of years of detailed planning, assisted by different development agents, the most important being NGOs. As in the case of the villages in Nentón, Huehuetenango, described by Stepputat (2001), the design of the new settlement was made in the image of the town. Before the return, a *plan de urbanización* was designed by an international NGO, but this was not imposed on the villagers. On the contrary, the design of the hamlet is an expression of their desire to create a formal site of governance. After only a few days, a temporary school and a health clinic were functioning in the returnee village, long before the construction of houses started. More formal school buildings were constructed later, as was the current clinic. A venue for public assemblies was soon in place, as was the two-story building to house offices and other cooperative bodies. Later, a bus station and a sports field were built. A park has been planned but is still to be completed. Making and implementing plans is an important element in the returnees' concept of progress and of "being organized."

Organization is one of the key labels used by the returnees to differentiate themselves from their neighbors. In the previous chapters we have seen several demonstrations of their capacity to orchestrate communal actions, the most important being the occupation of the Guatemalan consulate in Chetumál, which led to the acceleration of the process of return, and the occupation of the offices of CONAP to get the access road to the community repaired. This, as well as similar actions, was pursued in the language of rights, equality, and order, and in alliance with international agencies guaranteeing their security.

Other less dramatic actions and negotiations have taken place over the years. In most cases, state institutions have been persuaded or pressed to comply with the peace agreements. The returnees in these cases have also been supported by NGOs or other aid or solidarity organizations. Their proactive attitude and approach have been of key importance for the development and enjoyment of rights that they have obtained, compared to those who have been repatriated and those that stayed in Guatemala, who are dispersed or unaware of the benefit of the agreements.

Perhaps more significant than ad hoc mobilizations are the more long-term processes of organization. When people talk about organization they also often refer to the bureaucratic way of organizing. The cooperative, with its 16 committees and more than a hundred bureaucratic positions, is the ultimate example, but we have seen that all public activities are organized in a similar way. This indicates that the construction of a new community in Guatemala has been strongly influenced by the new forms of organization and new ideas about what a modern democratic state should be, learned while its members were in exile and interacted with NGOs and international institutions. The language used and the bureaucratic positions established are clear evidence of this.

A different example of active involvement in state formation by the returnees is related to education. Wilson (2001) has argued that, for the bureaucracy of the modern state, the school has become the emblem of the state, an institution that relies on ideas about state, nation, and citizen. It is at school that the children learn to become citizens by saluting the flag, standing to attention at hearing the national anthem and learning about national history, geography and ceremonial events (2001: 313). Unlike what Wilson describes from Peru where education has been promoted by the central state to integrate members of the peripheral population, the education system of the returnees was developed by non-state agents in the periphery and incorporated into the central state system through negotiations.

Since the establishment of the camps, education has been defined as a privileged road to personal and social development for the refugees, introduced and promoted by the aid agencies shortly after the establishment of the camps in Mexico. At the beginning, the children had Mexican teachers, but very soon the preparation of education promoters, recruited among the refugees, was initiated by UNCHR and other international agencies, first with the objective of having Guatemalan teachers in the camps, later to prepare teachers for the return.

After the return, educational services have improved both quantitatively and qualitatively. Today they comprise preprimary and secondary in addition to primary education. During the first years the promoters received their salaries from FONAPAZ, a government agency established to assist the peace process, since they were not recognized by the Ministry of Education. Through the national organization of rural teachers, AMERG, who negotiated with the government, they were recognized by the ministry on the condition that they complete a competence-building program, a two year program designed to be combined with their current teaching obligations. By the end of 2000 the program was completed and the first teachers were officially recognized by the Ministry of Education.

This is considered an important achievement not only for the teachers, but also for the returnee community, who are proud of their system of education. The quality of education in La Quetzal is certainly better than in other communities in the region. The number of promoters per pupil is higher than in other communities and promoters are local residents, most of them cooperative members or *pobladores* or married to one, and highly committed to the development of their community. Lack of commitment and presence is a general problem in many other rural areas in the Petén, where the teachers normally live in a faraway town and "arrive in the community on Tuesday and leave on Thursday." The achievements in education in La Quetzal are widely recognized in the area, and the school, especially the *ciclo básico*, receives children from other communities in the region.

A similar process has taken place with regard to health care. Here the negotiations for inclusion have been more complicated because the local health care system is differently organized from and far better than what is common in the Petén. According to my informants, the Ministry of Health has been reluctant to accept it, because it fears demands for similar services from other communities. The returnees, on the other hand, believe that if they agree to adapt their system to the government standards this will mean deterioration. These negotiations were not completed when I finished my fieldwork.

The case of the Guatemalan returnees illustrates a process of state-making from the margins, where NGOs and international organizations have played a central role. This clearly illustrates a point elaborated by Trouillot, that in the globalized world of today, the production of state effects are never obtained solely through national institutions or in government sites (2001: 132). In Guatemala, as in the South more generally, NGOs as well as trans-state institutions are central actors in creating ideas about the state, which, in turn, are used by citizens in alliance with international actors to reshape state institutions.

Contradictory Notions of the State

From this analysis, we have seen that the returnees' ideas and images of the state are complex and at times contradictory. They change over time, depending on the changing historical patterns of state-society relations. These relations have certainly been characterized by antagonism and resistance, as suggested by Smith. This was especially salient during the years of violence and exile. However, we have also seen that they are characterized by active involvement aimed at becoming included as full-fledged citizens of the Guatemalan state. Non-state actors have been instrumental in bringing about the preconditions for the creative engagement of the returnees with state institutions. First, the Catholic Church organized new settlements and cooperatives in Ixcán in the 1970s, providing organizational training, language, and forms of reflection, though these were largely limited to male cooperative and church leaders. Representatives of this "new" Catholic Church introduced the settlers not only to a new religious ethic but also to a new economic ethic of justice and development. When the armed conflict accelerated in the late 1970s, the settlers were caught in the crossfire between the army and the guerrilla. There was little room to maneuver, since most of them happened to live in areas singled out for the scorched-earth campaign by the Guatemalan army.

Crossing the border to Mexico was an eye-opening experience for the refugees in more than one sense, and exile gradually became a learning process regarding the conditions and forms of services that the modern state should provide. This became particularly salient during the negotiations for their collective return.

Today these returnees hold contradictory notions of the state. On the one hand, they see the state as violent and repressive—and this view is reflected in their avoidance of or resistance to certain state practices and institutions. Pertinent examples are their negotiated exemption from military service, and the rule prohibiting members of the armed forces from entering the returnee communities. A further example was the presence of international verification and monitoring during the first years after return. These attitudes build on the decades of nonrecognition and exclusion produced by the violent forms of state repression in their villages. On the other hand, the returnees also see the state as benevolent and productive. It is the body with which one negotiates rights, somehow representing of the will of the people; it is also a provider of services, and the returnees strive to become included. This can be seen in the way their new community has been set up—spatially, in the image of a small town, and organizationally, in the image of modern bureaucracy.

The majority of the returnees are actively engaged in this modernizing experience, a point that does not fit in well with the idea of the all-penetrating state. These efforts, based on a discourse of recognition and rights, in turn presuppose the appropriation of ideas of human dignity and equality acquired during the years of exile. Without the invaluable support of non-state agencies, the returnees would not have gained the negotiating power that they exercise today. The organizational capacity and fighting spirit that characterize the returnees have been developed and maintained through their alliance with the international aid community. This alliance has proven an invaluable resource in their work to contribute to the creation of a new nation-state, symbolized in the schoolyard by the flag, the anthem, and the name Jacobo Arbenz.

Chapter 10
The Struggle Continues

Even though most returnees are actively engaged in the construction of their new community and proud of what they have achieved, especially in health and education, but also within the cooperative, there is an increasing anxiety about the future. This is primarily associated with their economic situation.

While the returnees were well prepared both psychologically and materially for a certain period of difficulties and scarcity, they did not imagine that this period would be so protracted. The constraints on the exploitation of their common land resources associated with their location in the Maya Biosphere Reserve have been much more overwhelming than they had imagined. Individual access to land has been more limited than many of them expected, since 80 percent of the estate is located within the core area, where there is a total ban on agriculture.

Timber extraction was allowed and people had great expectations about what the timber should bring. A forest management plan was prepared, but it took almost four years of difficult struggle and negotiations to get the plan approved before they could start felling trees. The economic output has not been as high as people expected and little has been distributed to the members. Due to a number of bureaucratic difficulties, the timber was sold to a private company that operates as an intermediary, and according to some of my informants, on rather exploitive terms. If and when the plans for direct sale and local processing of timber are implemented, the product sold will have greater value and will create badly needed local employment.

There is also a gap between expectations and actual economic output of the income-generating activities of the cooperative. Even though most of them appear to have economic potential, there is still some way to go. The annual accounts presented at the general assembly in 2000 were rather disappointing. A number of projects gave little surplus and a few no surplus at all, in spite of the enormous effort put into them by many people. Some projects failed because they were unrealistic or badly planned. This was, for example, the case of a project for ecotourism that eventually was abandoned. Limited experience and capacity in project management and implementation was also a problem. Since the returnees have been a favorite target of NGOs and international aid agencies, there has been a tendency to depend too much on external advisors, who in many cases represent agendas determined by people and conditions extrinsic to the local conditions, agendas which they sometimes succeed at making attractive to the returnees.

Moreover, the system of compulsory elections to cooperative positions is also problematic because they do not always place the right person in the right position. Based on a rather narrow interpretation of equality and justice regarding cooperative participation, assignment of most positions is determined by the number of votes a member receives, without taking into consideration his particular interests and capacities. For example, the person elected president of the education committee in 1999 was illiterate. Only after a long discussion was he permitted to alternate between his position and the position of one of the others elected to this committee. The returnees seem to be trapped in a vicious cycle, characterized by resistance to accept positions and collective responsibilities due to lack of sufficient benefits, which in turn is at least to a certain degree a consequence of a lack of efficient management and a dearth of motivated and responsible leaders (van der Vaeren 2000: 301).

There is a continuous tension between household interests and needs and collective ones, and some people argue that their farming suffers from their collective obligations. The steady expansion of the cooperative and its corresponding claim on the time and efforts of its members worry a number of people, because this expansion is not reflected in an improvement in family incomes and welfare. One critic questioned the investment policy of the cooperative in a general assembly in late 1999, calling it "hypercapitalist," and denounced what he called the "disregard of the welfare needs of the people." This has generated an internal discussion that will hopefully lead to some changes.

After almost six years back in Guatemala (early 2001), the returnees continue as poor peasants. They grow enough corn to eat and some to sell, but cash incomes are still too low to cover basic needs, let alone living conditions comparable to what they had in the refugee camps in Mexico. They are still in search of income-generating activities to be managed at the household level, including crops with high commercial value and stable prices. They remember with nostalgia the cardamom and coffee they used to grow in Ixcán that received a high price in relation to weight. They are also expecting increased income from timber.

In the meantime incomes from other sources than agriculture are very limited locally, and temporary migration to is Mexico increasing, especially among young, unmarried people unable to continue their studies in town. The alternative is to marry and settle as a *poblador* in La Quetzal, which many young people find rather unattractive, because it implies limited access to both resources and important decision-making. The possibility of obtaining membership in the cooperative is limited, since new members are accepted only when old ones resign or leave.

This point reminds us of the difference between the community of La Quetzal and the cooperative Unión Maya Itzá. The cooperative has expanded to a variety of areas of economic, social, and political life; it has become the backbone of the community and the site where the most important decisions about its future are taken. However, fewer than half the adult population are cooperative members; most women and the *pobladores* are not. This is a source of tension between the cooperative and the different *sectores*, especially the education promoters and the women, with women's participation in community life decreasing. This exclusionary practice needs to be addressed if they are to achieve the real participatory democracy they sought when they returned to Guatemala.

In conclusion, the returnees are still in a process of transition toward "communitarian development." They have not yet been able to create an economic base to overcome poverty at the household level, which creates increasing anxiety, frustration, and disappointment for many people. The same is the case for "participatory democracy." While there is a tendency to over-participation within the cooperative, creating a new bureaucratic setup for every new activity, the contrary is the case regarding involvement in community activities outside the cooperative. Communitarian development still faces a number of challenges: how to balance household needs with community needs; how to develop new forms of economic and social unity and equality, while maintaining cultural diversity; and how to achieve a sustainable livelihood with an acceptable standard of living without destroying the tropical rain forest. The long-term outcome remains to be seen.

Postscript

Since I finished my fieldwork, the general environment in Guatemala has deteriorated. The climate throughout the country is polarized, confrontational, violent, and full of despair. This seems to have affected most sectors of the population, which continues dealing with unjust systems characterized by the privileges of minority elites that resist change. Furthermore, there has been a shocking increase in drug trafficking, while the quantity of drugs confiscated has decreased. This has accelerated political decomposition and led to increased violence. It has exposed clandestine groups which, with the government's protection, are linked to drug and human trafficking as well as money laundering.

I have not had the opportunity to follow the development of La Quetzal in detail during these years. However, from what I can judge from a distance the returnees continue their struggle for a better future in spite of the troubled general situation in the country. In 2001 the cooperative joined the Association of Forest Communities of Petén, an entity established in 1995 to promote socioeconomic development and improved quality of life through sustainable management of the forest within the Maya Biosphere Reserve. Through concessions allocated to a community, its inhabitants gain access to the harvest of non-timber products such as leaves, wood, fruits, and medical plants for local consumption as well as products, for example, for manufacture and exports. During the same year the cooperative was evaluated by Smartwood, an independent international certifier, and obtained a certificate which guarantees that their timber products are harvested in a sustainable way. These changes are hopefully leading to increased income from the forest and an improvement in the economic conditions of the households.

The returnees in La Quetzal have also made political advances with a certain international impact. They have played an active role in mobilizing resistance against the plans for constructing dams in the Usumacita River, which would cause the flooding and displacement of La Quetzal and a number of other communities in the western part of the Petén. In March 2002 the cooperative hosted an international meeting, with the participation of women and men representing 98 organizations from 21 countries, to protest against these plans. Later the same year the president of the cooperative—and one of my key informants—Santos Choc made a conference tour to the U.S. to gain support for the protest movement against the construction of dams for hydroelectric power, which is part of the Plan Puebla Panama (PPP).[1] All these are changes that contribute to providing hope for an enduring transformation toward peace and development in a country still characterized by injustice, violence and corruption.

Notes

Chapter 1. Introduction: Guatemalan Returnees in the Aftermath of Violence

1. La Quetzal is the name given by local people. The official name is El Quetzal, after the national bird of Guatemala. The feminization of the name is due to the fact that people refer to *La finca* (farm) Quetzal, omitting *finca*.

2. The first collective return to Guatemala took place in January 1993 in a village called Victoria 20 de Enero, located in Ixcán, a department of El Quiché.

3. The FAR guerrilla (Fuerzas Armadas Rebeldes) continued to operate in the Petén until after the Accord on the Definitive Cease-Fire had been signed in December 1996.

4. My project was also part of a research and teaching collaboration between the University of San Carlos and the University of Oslo, financed by the Norwegian Council of Universities Committee for Development Research and Education.

5. No other region in Guatemala has experienced such dramatic destruction and dislocation as Ixcán, giving it the grim distinction of having produced more refugees than any other single area. In terms of the number of refugees, the Ixcán is followed by the western section of the Petén (Manz 1988: 127).

6. The most relevant for my study are AVANCSO 1992; Manz 1988, 2004; Falla 1992; Stoll 1993; Warren 1993; Jonas 1994; Wilson 1995; Le Bot 1995; Zur 1998; Schirmer 1998; Green 1999.

7. The CPRs comprised people who decided to remain in the country, hiding in the jungle or in the mountains. The CPRs were located in three areas: CPR-Ixcán located in the jungles of this region, CPR de la Sierra located in the Ixil area of the county of El Quiché, and CPR-Petén located in the northern-western jungle areas of this county. In the early 1980s some 50,000 people lived in the CPRs. By 1992, when they started to negotiate their resettlement, the number was reduced to less than half. The CPRs have now been resettled on land acquired through negotiations with the government (CIDH 1993).

8. URNG is a coalition of the three guerrilla groups: EGP (Ejército Guerrillero de los Pobres), FAR (Fuerzas Armadas Rebeldes), and ORPA (Organización Revolucionaria de Pueblo en Armas) and the communist party PGT (Partido Guatemalteco de Trabajo), established in 1982.

9. Guatemala's political-administrative divisions comprise 22 *departamentos*—the Petén is one of them—divided into 331 municipalities. *Departamento* is translated as "county," the closest approximation in English.

10. The Maya Biosphere Reserve (MBR) comprises 1.6 million hectares (4 million acres) covering about 40 percent of the Petén. It is divided into three zones that have different degrees of environmental protection. Core Zone areas (784,000 hectares/1.9 million acres) are set aside for absolute protection of biodiversity. No human settlements are allowed, and only research and ecotourism are permitted. The core areas are the national parks and nature reserves (biotopes) located within the MBR. The Multiple-Use Zone consists of sparsely settled areas that surround the Core Zone areas. Some oil and timber industry is allowed, as is sustainable use of forest resources by local people. The Buffer Zone is a 15-km (9-mile) wide band of land that separates the MBR from the southern part of the Petén, and in which all kinds of industrial and agricultural practices are allowed (Beletsky 1998).

11. All of them were associated with the research project on Forced Migration and Social Reconstruction in the Petén, Guatemala, which was part of a wider program of collaboration between the University of Oslo, Norway, and the University of San Carlos, Guatemala City (Wilson 2003; Nesheim et al. 2006).

Chapter 2. Migrating in Search of Land and a Better Future

1. In Guatemala the modern era of planned colonization dates from 1945, when the government of Juan José Arévalo (1945–51) began settlement projects in Poptún, in the south of the Petén. In the late 1950s and early 1960s several projects were implemented on the Pacific coastal plains. In the 1960s interest returned to the northern lowlands of Ixcán and the Petén (Melville and Melville 1971; Fletcher et al. 1970; Dennis et al. 1988).

2. For more thorough analyses of these processes see Melville and Melville 1982; Smith 1990; Berger 1992; Le Bot 1995.

3. Resettlement could not solve the acute man/land problem in Guatemala. According to an evaluation carried out in Ixcán Grande, such projects were too complicated, too costly, and too slow. Moreover, there was not enough public land available for this purpose (Hough 1982).

4. The Northern Transversal Strip (Franja Transversal del Norte) is a strip of virgin jungle stretching from the Atlantic Coast through the south of the Petén to Ixcán and the northern part of Huehuetenango. The project comprised colonization and commercialization along a new highway to be built between east and west. Even though this project was aimed at poor people, some military personnel acquired large tracts of land here (Painter 1987: 18, quoted in AVANCSO 1991: 34).

5. The agency was established through a decree in Congress. From the beginning until its dissolution in the early 1990s, FYDEP was controlled by the armed forces (van der Vaeren 2000).

6. Casasola based his argument on a FAO study that indicated that much of the region's soil was inadequate for crop production and would be unable to support more than 150 000 people by the year 2000 (Casasola, quoted in Berger 1992: 148).

7. It should be noted that INTA only issued provisional titles to the land, to be converted into permanent ones after twenty years (van der Vaeren 2000: 115).

8. He refers to the Law Against Vagrancy enacted in 1934 by the government of General Jorge Ubico (1931–44). This law obliged landless peasants to work a certain number of days on the lands of others. The number of days worked had to be registered in a particular document called *Libreta de Jornaleros.*

9. 1 manzana = 16 cuerdas, 1.74 acres.

10. The municipality of Nentón is one of the Chuj dominated areas in the county of Huehuetenango.

11. *Tierra fría* (cold land), is often used when talking about the Highlands in the northwest parts of Guatemala (Huehuetenango and El Quiché) with its cold climate.

12. She refers to the expenditures associated with the engagement and wedding ceremonies.

13. When my informants use the word *lengua/s* (tongues/languages) they refer to Mayan languages. Speaking a *lengua* is the main criteria for being classified as indigenous.

14. *Costumbres* (customs) is used to refer to rituals and other behaviors associated with Mayan traditions.

15. *Cofradía* is the saints' brotherhood associated with the gerontocratic authority structure in traditional Mayan communities. Through the colonial *cargo* system revolving around the worship of Catholic saints, authority is vested in elders— *principales*—who rule the community through rotating civil and religious offices designed to promote the common good and ensure the survival of the community qua community (Farris in Zur 1998: 37). For descriptions of the traditional cargo system, see Wagley 1941 and Reina 1966.

16. 1 caballería = 64 manzanas = 111.36 acres.

17. She refers to Kjell Laugerud García, president from 1974 to 1978.

18. This is something she had told me several times, and something she is proud of. I met no other women her age who said they had married out of love and their own choice.

Chapter 3. The Escalation of Violence in Ixcán and the Petén

1. See also Gramajo 1995: 177–201.

2. In an interview with Chief Commander of EGP Rolando Morán conducted by Marta Harnecker y Mario Menéndez, Morán explains the different phases in EGP's warfare (EGP 1982).

3. Payeras, who had a Ph.D. in philosophy from Leipzig, considered himself a writer and poet by vocation who by the plight of his people had been "compelled to follow the path the revolution has taken—the difficult and exacting path of guerrilla warfare" (CENSA 1983: 43). According to Arias (1998) the difference between the two categories ("poet" and "guerrillero") was never very pronounced in Central America, especially from the early 1960s on.

4. In contrast to the previous quotations that have been taken from the English translation of Payeras's book, this is my own translation of the original Spanish version. I did not find the English version precise enough.

5. The Truth Commission has confirmed that the guerrillas applied this tactic of "armed propaganda" with a very high civilian death toll, especially among the Mayan population. Although acknowledging the army's clear and sole responsibility for the massive violations, the Commission is convinced that guerrilla actions had a bearing on the way these events occurred (CEH 1999).

6. According to Falla (1992: 28) her uncle saved his life by leaving through a secret aperture in the house.

7. The literal translation of *cabrones* is cuckolds. I use sons of a bitch because that is the meaning here.

8. She refers to plastic sheets used to protect themselves against the rain. *Corte* is a patterned cotton cloth, traditionally handwoven, today often industrially made.

9. He refers to the religious practices associated with the Catholic Charismatic Renewal movement (Chesnut 2003).

10. *Susto* is the result of shock or fright, believed to cause the blood to circulate slowly; symptoms are extreme fatigue, lack of appetite, elevated temperature, thirst, and weeping (Nesheim et al. 2003: 15).

11. This was the case of El Arbolito, Palestina, Josefinos, Las Dos Erres, and Macanché (Amnesty International 1995)

12. This massacre took place in June 1981 and some 50 persons were killed (Amnesty International 1995).

Chapter 4. Witnesses, Victims, and Perpetrators of Violence

1. In an interview published in 1990, EGP Chief Commander Rolando Morán states that the age of the combatants was 14–22 years (Perales 1990).

2. The Patrullas de Autodefensa Civil (Civil Self-Defense Patrols) mostly referred to as PACs were created by the army in 1982 to fight real or alleged enemies of the state. More than 1,000,000 men, most of them indigenous, served in the patrols at the height of their power during the 1980s (Schirmer 1998: 91).

3. This *hoyo* is also referred to in the testimonies registered by Falla (1992).

4. He refers to the highway running from the Atlantic Coast through the south of the Petén to Ixcán and the northern part of Huehuetenango, constructed in the early 1970s.

5. Payeras gives a detailed description of the execution by the guerrilla of EGP insurgent Fonseca. He returned to his group, escaping from army imprisonment, to receive his punishment for giving information about the guerilla (1982: 83–94).

6. For the destiny of those who stayed under military control in this area, see Manz 1988.

7. The Accord on the Definitive Cease-Fire was signed by the government and the URNG on December 4, 1996, and brought to a standstill armed confrontations in areas surrounding the returnee communities.

8. Every Thursday the cooperative put up a TV set outside the shop to show a video. *The Daughter of the Puma* is a political thriller that tells the story of a young Guatemalan Indian girl who witnesses a massacre in her village and is separated from her brother. She and her parents flee to a refugee camp in Chiapas. Determined to find her brother, the girl clandestinely goes back to Guatemala. With the protection of her guardian spirit, the Puma, she endures a nightmarish journey and memories of persecution. The film is based on a novel by Monica Zak (1988) and inspired by a true story.

9. He is referring to one of the three branches of the refugee organization Comiciones Permanentes (CCPP) called *vertientes*, in charge of organizing the collective returns.

10. He refers to a meeting held by the URNG during their election campaign in 1999.

Chapter 5. Exile and Return

1. Most camps were located in three geographical areas along the border, the Trinitaria and Comalapa area, the Margaritas area, and the Selva area (Sánchez Martínez 1999: 47). Most of my informants settled in the latter.

2. In 1983, a group of states comprising Colombia, Mexico, Panama, and Venezuela known as the Contadora Group (named after the island off the coast

of Panama where its first meeting took place) launched an international effort to assist in the search for peace throughout Central America.

3. El Señor Sánchez has written about how he experienced the reception of the refugees that Rosalía refers to (Sánchez Martínez 1999).

4. Sánchez Martínez (1999) and Carrera Lugo (1999) give a more detailed description of the relocations to Quintana Roo and Campeche respectively.

5. These were settlements established in the areas of greatest conflict to serve army control interests. Houses were located extremely close to each other, making it impossible to keep domestic animals or grow fruits and vegetables. Critics denounced them as concentration camps (Taylor 1998: 30).

6. In November 1994, MINUGUA (United Nations Mission for the Verification of Human Rights and the Compliance of the Obligations of the Global Agreement on Human Rights in Guatemala) began its work.

7. In the refugee camps, Stepputat (1994) observed that "organization" had a negative connotation as opposed to "freedom." In La Quetzal the connotation is positive and used in opposition to individualism.

8. CCPP created the Vertiente Norte in 1993 after having evaluated the first return to Ixcán (January 1993) and concluded that future returns should be directed to three different areas of the country. Vertiente Noroccidental and Vertiente Sur were responsible for organizing the returns to Ixcán and the southern coast respectively.

Chapter 6. Constructing a New Community

1. The Agreement on Resettlement of the Population Groups Uprooted by the Armed Conflict (17 June 1994).

2. This does not mean that all the board members are in office for only one year. They are expected to stay for two years. Withdrawal after one year has to be approved by the general assembly and requires a good reason.

3. *Xate* is a wild plant gathered in the jungle and sold for export. Florists use it to accompany flowers when making bouquets. After having been cut it stays fresh for two to three weeks without water.

4. The first three years of secondary school. Five years are required to qualify for tertiary education.

5. AMERG was established in Mexico in the early 1990s as the Unión de Maestros Educativos Refugiados en Mexico. Today it has a membership of several hundred in the returnee areas of Ixcán, the Petén, and the southern coast. AMASAR (Asociación Maya de Salud Rural) was established in August 1996. Among its objectives were the creation of a national alliance of health promoters and the establishment of links with the state.

6. The difficulties associated with the technical studies and the diversity of their results, especially regarding the territorial survey, are accounted for in detail by van der Vaeren, who was directly involved in the process as an NGO advisor (van der Vaeren 2000: 213–30).

7. Centro Maya attempts to take the lead in the development of ecologically sound food production systems and other economic alternatives for use outside the protected zones in the Petén. Established in 1991, Centro Maya includes the Rodale Institute, the Tropical Agricultural Research and Training Center (CATIE), the University of San Carlos, and the Institute of Agricultural Science and Technology (ICTA). The goal of Centro Maya is to increase food production in the Petén while preserving the tropical forest.

8. Those who completed a two-year training program (*programa de profesionalización*) were recognized as teachers by the Ministry of Education by mid-2000; the rest are still in training positions.

Chapter 7. Community and Identity

1. Those who fled from the Petén became *revueltos* in the refugee camps when they mixed with people from different indigenous groups. Before that they were simply Ladinos.
2. This does not mean that there actually are 64 households in each neighborhood. Normally the number is lower, since not all the lots are suited for building a homestead.
3. For a detailed discussion of the Q'eqchi' concept of *tzuultaq'a*, see Wilson 1994, 1995.
4. *Tamal* is made of corn paste, sometimes filled with meat or cheese, wrapped in the leaf of a corn or banana plant before being cooked.
5. She refers to municipalities in the county of Huehuetenango. Leticia seem to believe that Chuj is a dialect of Q'anjob'al.
6. The Pan-Mayan movement is a post-conflict phenomenon, even though Mayan activists have made themselves heard since the 1970s. Educated Mayans have worked to create a social movement focused on the cultural revitalization and unification of indigenous in opposition to the Ladino. The Maya movement is not a unified one, and the priorities are diverse and sometimes contradictory. For information about the Pan-Mayan Movement see Fischer and McKenna Brown 1996; Warren 1998; Warren and Jackson 2002.

Chapter 8. Changing Gender Relations

1. Two other refugee women's organizations, Mama Maquín and Madre Tierra, were created in the returnee camps by women returning to Ixcán and the south coast respectively.
2. She is referring to the local mayor, often referred to as *juez de paz* (peace-judge) since his most important task was to arbitrate in community conflicts.
3. The *dieta* also includes other restrictions, mainly related to work and food.

Chapter 9. The Returnees and the Guatemalan State

1. The state has recently been rediscovered as an object of inquiry by a broad range of scholars as well as by development practitioners (Abrams 1988; Steinmetz 1999; Shore 2001; Trouillot 2001). Social anthropologists have contributed with studies of what the state looks like to those seeing it from a variety of local vantage points (Nugent 1994; Hansen and Stepputat 2001). For a more comprehensive discussion of the state community relations among the returnees see Stølen (2005).

Chapter 10. The Struggle Continues

1. PPP is a multi-billion-dollar series of industrialization projects intended to connect Mexico with Central America physically and commercially.

Bibliography

Abrams, Phillip. 1988. "Notes on the Difficulty of Studying the State." *Journal of Historical Sociology* 1, 1.

Aguayo, Sergio. 1985. *El éxodo centroamericano: Consecuencias de un conflicto.* Mexico City: SEP.

Aguayo, Sergio, Hanne Christensen, Laura O'Dogherty, and Stefano Varese. 1987. *Social and Cultural Conditions and Prospects of Guatemalan Refugees in Mexico.* Geneva: UNRISD.

Allan, Tim, ed. 1996. *In Search of Cool Ground: War, Flight and Homecoming in Northeast Africa.* London: James Currey.

Americas Watch Committee. 1989. *Guatemala: A Nation of Prisoners.* New York: Americas Watch.

Amnesty International. 1995. *Guatemala: Victims of 1982 Army Massacre at Las Dos Erres Exhumed.* AI Index: AMR 34/24/95.

Andersen, Nicolas. 1982. *Guatemala: Escuela revolucionaria de nuevos hombres.* Mexico City: Editorial Nuestro Tiempo.

Antze, Paul and Michael Lembek, eds. 1996. *Tense Past: Cultural Essays in Trauma and Memory.* New York: Routledge

Arias, Arturo. 1993. "Changing Indian Identity: Guatemala's Violent Transition to Modernity." In *Guatemalan Indians and the State 1540–1988*, ed. Carol Smith. Austin: University of Texas Press.

———. 1998. *La identidad de la palabra: Narrativa guatemalteca a la luz del nuevo siglo.* Guatemala City: Artemio Edinter

AVANCSO (Asociación para el Avance de la Ciencias Sociales en Guatemala). 1992. *Dónde está el futuro? Procesos de integración en comunidades de retornados.* Cuadernos de investigación 8. Guatemala City: AVANCSO.

Ball, Patrick, Paul Kobrak, and Herbert F. Spirer. 1999. *State Violence in Guatemala, 1960–1996: A Quantitative Reflection.* Washington, D.C.: AAAS.

Beletsky, Les. 1998. *Belize and Northern Guatemala (Tikal).* San Diego: Academic Press.

Berger, Susan A. 1992, *Political and Agrarian Development in Guatemala.* Boulder, Colo.: Westview Press.

Boff, Leonardo and Clodovis Boff. 1986. *Liberation Theology: From Dialogue to Confrontation.* San Francisco: Harper and Row.

Bourdieu, Pierre. 1977. *Outline of a Theory of Practice.* Cambridge: Cambridge University Press.

Bowman, Glenn. 2001. "The Violence in Identity." In *Anthropology of Violence and Conflict*, ed. Bettina E. Schmidt and Ingo W. Schröder, 25–46. London: Routledge.

Burgos, Elizabeth. 1983. *Me llamo Rigoberta Mencú y así me nació la conciencia*. Barcelona: Editorial Argos Vergara.

Camino, Linda A. and Ruth M. Krulfeld.1994. *Reconstructing Lives, Recapturing Meaning: Refugee Identity, Gender, and Culture Change*. Amsterdam: Gordon and Breach.

Campbell, John R. and Alan Rew, eds. 1999. *Identity and Affect. Experiences of Identity in a Globalising World*. London: Pluto Press.

Carrera Lugo, Laura. 1999. "Creación de nuevos asentamientos en Campeche y el programa multianual." In *Presencia de los refugiados guatemaltecos en Mexico*, ed. UNHCR and COMAR. Mexico City: UNHCR & COMAR.

Cedillo, Manuel. 1999. "Retornos del Vertiente Norte 1995–1998." In *Presencia de los refugiados guatemaltecos en Mexico*, ed. UNHCR and COMAR. Mexico City: UNHCR & COMAR.

CEH (Comisión para el Esclarecimiento Histórico). 1999. *Guatemala. Memoria del Silencio: Informe para el esclarecimiento histórico*. Guatemala City: CEH.

CENSA. 1983. *Listen Compañeros: Conversations with Central American Revolutionary Leaders*. San Francisco: CENSA/Solidarity Publications.

Chesnut, Andrew R. 2003. "A Preferential Option for the Spirit: The Catholic Charismatic Renewal in Latin America's New Religious Economy." *Latin American Politics and Society* 45, 1.

CIDH (Comisión Interamericana de Derechos Humanos). 1993. *Cuarto informe sobre la situación de derechos humanos en Guatemala*. Washington, D.C.: CIDH.

COINDE (Consejo de Instituciones de Desarrollo). 1993. *Diagnóstico sobre refugiados, retornados y desplazados*. Guatemala City: Fondo de Cultura Editorial.

Colom, Yolanda. 1998. *Mujeres en la Alborada*. Guatemala City: Editorial Artemio Editer.

Comisiónes Permanentes de Representantes de Refugiados Guatemaltecos en Mexico. 1989. *El Retorno de los refugiados guatemaltecos en el extranjero: Ponencia de las CCPP presentada a la Comición Nacional de Reconciliación para el Diálogo Nacional*.

Connell, Robert. 1987. *Gender and Power: Society, the Person and Sexual Politics*. Stanford, Calif.: Stanford University Press.

Costello, Patrick. 1995. *Guatemala: Displacement, Return, and the Peace Process*. Writenet country papers—Guatemala.

Crosby, Alison. 1999. "To Whom Shall the Nation Belong? The Gender and Ethnic Dimensions of Refugee Return and Struggle for Peace in Guatemala." In *Journeys of Fear: Refugee Return and National Transformation in Guatemala*, ed. Liisa L. North and Alan B. Simmons, 176–95. Montreal: McGill-Queen's University Press.

Daniel, E. Valentine. 1996. *Charred Lullabies: Chapters in an Anthropology of Violence*. Princeton, N.J.: Princeton University Press.

Delli Sante, Angela 1996. *Nightmare or Reality: Guatemala in the 1980s*. Amsterdam: Thela

Dennis, Phillip, Gary Elbow, and Peter Heller. 1988. "Development Under Fire: The Playa Grande Colonization Project in Guatemala." *Human Organization* 47, 1: 69–76.

Earl, Duncan M. 1994. "Constructions of Refugee Ethnic Identity: Guatemalan Mayas in Mexico and South Florida." In *Reconstructing Lives, Recapturing Meaning. Refugee Identity, Gender, and Culture Change*, ed. Linda A. Camino and Ruth M. Krulfeld, 207–34. Amsterdam: Gordon and Breach.

EGP. 1982. *Entrevista al comandante en jefe del Ejército Guerrillero de los Pobres: Rolando Morán hechas por Marta Harnecker y Mario Menéndez.* Benson Collection, University of Texas, Austin.

Egan, Brian. 2002. "'Somos de la tierra': Land and the Guatemalan Refugee Return." In *Journeys of Fear: Refugee Return and National Transformation in Guatemala,* ed. Liisa L. North and Alan B. Simmons, 95–111. Montreal: McGill-Queen's University Press.

Eriksen, Thomas Hylland. 1991. "The Cultural Context of Ethnic Differences." *Man* 26: 127–44.

———. 1993. *Ethnicity and Nationalism: Anthropological Perspectives.* London: Pluto Press.

Espinoza Leyva, José and Rafael Figueroa. 1999. "Las comisiones permanentes: Su formación, organización de los refugiados guatemaltecos en Mexico." In UNHCR and COMAR, *Presencia de los refugiados guatemaltecos en México.* Mexico City: UNHCR & COMAR.

Fagan, Richard R. 1983. *The Future of Central America: Policy Choices for the U.S. and Mexico.* Stanford, Calif.: Stanford University Press.

Falla, Ricardo. 1992. *Masacres en la selva: Ixcán, Guatemala (1975–1982).* Guatemala City: Editorial Universitaria.

Featherstone, Mike.1990. *Global Culture: Nationalism, Globalization and Modernity.* London: Sage.

Fischer, Edward F. 1996. "Induced Cultural Change as a Strategy for Socioeconomic Development: the Pan-Mayan Movement in Guatemala." In *Maya Cultural Activism in Guatemala,* ed. Edward F. Fischer and R. McKenna Brown, 51–73. Austin: University of Texas Press.

Fischer, Edward F. and R. McKenna Brown. 1996. "Introduction: Maya Cultural Activism in Guatemala." In *Maya Cultural Activism in Guatemala,* ed. Edward F. Fischer and R. McKenna Brown, 1–18. Austin: University of Texas Press.

Fledderjohn, David C. and David C. Thomson. 1982. *Final Report: Northern Transversal Strip Land Resettlement Project.* Washington, D.C.: Agricultural Cooperative Development International.

Fletcher, Lehman B., Eric Graber, William C. Merrill, and Eric Thorbecke. 1970. *Guatemala's Economic Development: The Role of Agriculture.* Ames: Iowa State University Press.

Franco, Leonardo 1999. "Un episodio controvertido en la historia del refugio: La reubicación a Campeche y Quintana Roo." In UNHCR and COMAR, *Presencia de los refugiados guatemaltecos en Mexico.* Mexico City: UNHCR & COMAR.

Freyermuth, Graciela and Nancy Godfrey. 1993. *Refugiados guatemaltecos en Mexico.* Mexico City: Impresora Kavers.

Fried, Jonathan L., Marvin G. Gettleman, Deborah T. Levenson, and Nancy Peckenham 1983. *Guatemala in Rebellion: Unfinished History.* New York: Grove Press.

Fuglerud, Øyvind. 2000. "Tenke globalt—handle lokalt: Om 'etnisk implosjon' på Sri Lanka." *Norsk Antropologisk tidsskrift* 11, 3: 27–239.

Gallagher, Dennis. 1989. "The Evolution of the International Refugee System." *International Migration Review* 23: 579–98.

Garst, Rachel. 1993. *Ixcan: Colonización, desarrollo y condiciones de retorno.* Guatemala City: COINDE.

Gramajo Morales, Hector Alejandro. 1995. *De la guerra . . . a la guerra: La difícil transición política en Guatemala.* Guatemala City: Fondo de Cultura Editorial.

Green, Linda 1999. *Fear as a Way of Life: Mayan Widows in Rural Guatemala.* New York: Columbia University Press.

Gutiérrez, Gustavo. 1988. *A Theology of Liberation*. London: SCM Press.
Hage, Ghassan. 1997. "At Home in the Entrails of the West: Multiculturalism, 'Ethnic Food' and Migrant Home-building." In Helen Grace, Hage Ghassan, Lesley Johnson, Julie Langsworth, and Michael Symonds, *Home/World: Space, Community and Marginality in Sydney's West*. Anandale: Pluto Press.
Hansen, Thomas Blom and Finn Stepputat, eds. 2001. *States of Imagination: Ethnographic Explorations of the Postcolonial State*. Durham, N.C.: Duke University Press.
Hammond, Laura. 1999. "Examining the Discourse of Repatriation: Towards a More Proactive Theory of Return Migration." In *The End of the Refugee Cycle? Refugee Repatriation and Reconstruction*, ed. Richard Black and Khalid Koser, 227–44. New York: Berghahn.
Harbury, Jennifer. 1997. *Searching for Everardo: A Story of Love, War, and the CIA in Guatemala*. New York: Warner Books.
Higgins, Nicholas P. 2004. *Understanding the Chiapas Rebellion: Modernist Visions and the Invisible Indian*. Austin: University of Texas Press.
Hirschon, Renée. 1998 (1989). *Heirs of the Greek Catastrophe: The Social Life of Asia Minor Refugees in Piraeus*. Oxford: Berghahn.
Hough, Richard L. 1982. *Land and Labor in Guatemala: An Assessment*. Washington, D.C.: AID/Development Associates.
Indra, Doreen, ed. 1999. *Engendering Forced Migration: Theory and Practice*. New York: Berghahn.
Jansen, Stef and Staffan Löfving, eds. (forthcoming). *Struggles for Home: Violence, Hope and the Movement of People*. New York: Berghahn.
Jonas, Susanne. 1994. *La Batalla por Guatemala*. Guatemala City: FLACSO.
Jonas, Susanne, Ed McCaughan, and Elizabeth Sutherland Martínez. 1984. *Guatemala Tyranny on Trial: Testimony of the Permanent People's Tribunal*. San Francisco: Synthesis Publications.
Kaldor, Mary and Basker Vashee, eds. 1997. *Restructuring the Global Military Sector*. Vol. 1, *New Wars*. London: Pinter.
Kauffer, Edith Françoise. 1997. "Chiapas y los refugiados de la década de los ochenta: de la conformación de la frontera al desarrollo de un espacio fronterizo." *Perspectivas Históricas/Historical Perspectives/Perspectives Historiques* 1 (July–December): 89–124.
Ker, Ian. 2002. "What Did the Second Vatican Council Do for Us?" *Catholic Herald*, October 11, 2002.
Kirmayer, Laurence J. 1996. "Landscapes of Memory: Trauma, Narrative, and Dissociation." In *Tense Past: Cultural Essays in Trauma and Memory*, ed. Paul Antze and Michael Lembek, 173–98. New York: Routledge
Koser, Khalid and Richard Black. 1999. "The End of the Refugee Cycle?" In *The End of the Refugee Cycle? Refugee Repatriation and Reconstruction*, ed. Khalid Koser and Richard Black, 2–17. New York: Berghahn.
Krohn-Hansen, Christian. 1994. "The Anthropology of Violent Interaction." *Journal of Anthropological Research* 50, 4: 367–81.
Larkin, Mary Ann, Fredrick C. Cuny, and Barry N. Stein. 1989. *Repatriation Under Conflict in Central America*. Washington, D.C./Dallas: CIPRA and Intertect Institute.
Lash, Scott and Jonathan Friedmann, eds. 1992. *Modernity and Identity*. Oxford: Blackwell.
Le Bot, Yvon. 1995. *La guerra en las tierras mayas: Comunidad, violencia y modernidad en Guatemala (1970–1992)*. Mexico City: Fondo de Cultura Económica.
Long, Lynellyn D. and Ellen Oxfeld, eds. 2004. *Coming Home? Refugees, Migrants, and Those Who Stayed Behind*. Philadelphia: University of Pennsylvania Press.

Long, Norman, ed. 1989. *Encounters at the Interface: A Perspective on Social Discontinuities in Rural Development.* Wageningen: Wageningen Agricultural University.

Long, Norman and Alberto Alberto. 2000. *Anthropology, Development and Modernities: Exploring Discourses, Counter-Tendencies and Violence.* London: Routledge.

Lovell, Nadia, ed. 1998. *Locality and Belonging.* London: Routledge.

Macías, Julio César.1999. *La guerrilla fué mi camino.* San Salvador: Editorial Piedra Santa

Mahony, Liam. 1998. "Struggle to Return—Return to Struggle." *New Routes* 1, 98.

Malkki, Liisa H. 1992. "National Geographic: The Rooting of People and the Territorialization of National Identity Among Scholars and Refugees." *Cultural Anthropology* 7, 1: 13–45.

———. 1995. *Purity and Exile: Violence, Memory, and National Cosmology Among the Hutu Refugees in Tanzania.* Chicago: University of Chicago Press.

———. 1997. "Speechless Emissaries: Refugees, Humanitarianism and Dehistorization." In *Siting Culture: The Shifting Anthropological Object,* ed. Karen Fog Olwig and Kirsten Kastrup, London: Routledge.

Manz, Beatriz. 1988. *Refugees of a Hidden War: Aftermath of Counterinsurgency in Guatemala.* Albany: State University of New York Press.

———. 1994. "Epilogue." In Ricardo Falla, *Massacres in the Jungle: Ixcán, Guatemala (1975–1982).* Boulder, Colo.: Westview Press.

———. 2004. *Paradise in Ashes: A Guatemalan Journey of Courage, Terror, and Hope.* Berkeley: University of California Press.

Markowitz, Fran and Anders H. Stefansson, eds. 2004. *Homecomings: Unsettling Paths of Return.* Lanham, Md.: Lexington Books.

May, Rachel. 2001. *Terror in the Countryside: Campesino Responses to Political Violence in Guatemala, 1954–1985.* Research in International Studies, Latin America Series 35. Athens: Ohio University Press.

Melhuus, Marit and Kristi Anne Stølen, eds. 1996. *Machos, Mistresses and Madonnas: Contesting the Power of Latin American Gender Imagery.* London: Verso

Melville, Thomas and Marjorie Melville. 1971. *Guatemala: The Politics of Land Ownership.* New York: Free Press

———. 1982. *Tierra y poder en Guatemala.* San José: Editorial Universitaria Centroamericana.

Millet, Artimus. 1974. "The Agricultural Colonization of the West Central Petén: A Case Study of Frontier Settlement by Cooperatives." Ph.D. dissertation, Department of Geography, University of Oregon.

Montejo, Victor. 2002. "The Multiplicity of Mayan Voices: Maya Leadership and the Politics of Self-Representation." In *Indigenous Movements, Self-Representation and the State in Latin America,* ed. Kay B. Warren and Jean E. Jackson. Austin: University of Texas Press.

Morrisey, James. 1978. "A Missionary Directed Resettlement Project among the Highland Maya of Western Guatemala." Ph.D. dissertation, Department of Anthropology, Stanford University.

Moser, Caroline O. N. and Fiona C. Clark. 2001. *Victims, Perpetrators or Actors? Gender, Armed Conflict and Political Violence.* London: Zed Press.

Nash, June C. 2001. *Mayan Visions: The Quest for Autonomy in an Age of Globalization.* London: Routledge.

Nesheim, Ingrid, Shivcharn S. Dhillion, and Kristi Anne Stølen. 2006. "Traditional Knowledge of Plant Resources in a Resettlement Community, La Quetzal, Petén, Guatemala." *Human Ecology* 34, 1.

Nolin Hanlon, Catherine. 1999. "Guatemalan Refugees and Returnees: Place and

Maya Identity." In *Journeys of Fear. Refugee Return and National Transformation in Guatemala*, ed. Liisa L. North and Alan B. Simmons, 213–36. Montreal: McGill-Queen's University Press.

Nordstrom, Carolyn. 1997. *A Different Kind of War Story*. Philadelphia: University of Pennsylvania Press.

Nordstrom, Carolyn and Antonius Robben. 1995. *Fieldwork Under Fire: Contemporary Studies of Violence and Survival*. Berkeley: University of California Press.

Nugent, David. 1994. "Building the State, Making the Nation: The Basis and Limits of State Centralization in 'Modern' Peru." *American Anthropologist* 96: 333–69.

————. 2001. "Before History and Prior to Politics: Time, Space, and Territory in the Modern Peruvian Nation-State." In *States of Imagination*, ed. Thomas Blom Hansen and Finn Stepputat, 257–83. Durham, N.C.: Duke University Press.

Ordóñez Morales, César Eduardo. 1993. *Eslabones de frontera: Un análisis sobre aspectos de desarrollo agrícola y migración de fuerza de trabajo en regiones fronterizas de Chiapas y Guatemala*. Tuxtla Gutiérrez: Universidad Autónoma de Chiapas.

Ortner, Sherry B. and Harriet Whitehead. 1981. *Sexual Meanings: The Cultural Construction of Gender and Sexuality*. Cambridge: Cambridge University Press.

Painter, James. 1989. *Guatemala: False Hope, False Freedom*. London: Latin American Bureau.

————. 1993. "Between Two Armies in the Ixil Towns of Guatemala" (Book Review). *Journal of Latin American Studies* 27, 1 (February 1995): 252–53.

Payeras, Mario.1982. *Los dias de la selva*. Guatemala City: Piedra Santa.

————. 1983. *Days of the Jungle: The Testimony of a Guatemalan Guerrillero, 1972–1976*. New York: Monthly Review Press.

————. 1996. *Asedio a la utopía*. Guatemala City: Luna y Sol.

Perales, Iosu. 1990. *Guatemala insurrecta: Entrevista con el comandante en jefe del Ejército Guerrillero de los Pobres*. Madrid: Editorial Revolución.

Pérez Hernández, Ricardo Epifanio. 1999. "Mayas de Guatemala Refugiados." In UNHCR and COMAR, *Presencia de los refugiados guatemaltecos en Mexico*. Mexico City: UNHCR and COMAR.

Ramírez, Chiqui. 2001. *La guerra de los 36 años: Vista con ojos de mujer de izquierda*. Guatemala City: Editorial Oscar de León Palacios

Rapport, Neil and Andy Dawson, eds.1998. *Migrants of Identity in a World of Movement*. New York: Berg.

Reina, Rubén E. 1966. *The Law of the Saints: A PocoMam Pueblo and Its Community Culture*. Indianapolis: Bobbs-Merrill.

Richards, Julia Becker and Michael Richards. 1996. "Maya Education: A Historical and Contemporary Analysis of Mayan Language Education Policy." In *Maya Cultural Activism in Guatemala*, ed. Edward F. Fisher and R. McKenna Brown, 208–21. Austin: University of Austin Press.

Riches, David. 1986. "The Phenomenon of Violence." In *The Anthropology of Violence*, ed. David Riches. Oxford: Blackwell.

Riess, Steffanie. 2000. "Return Is Struggle, Not Resignation; Lessons from the Repatriation of Guatemalan Refugees from Mexico." *Journal of Humanitarian Assistance*, http://www.jha.ac/articles/u021.hmt

Rivero, Julio de. 2001. "Reinventing Communities: The Resettlement of Guatemalan Refugees." *Forced Migration Review* 11: 8–11.

Rodríguez Sehk, Penélope. 1986. "La vírgen-madre: Símbolo de la feminidad Latinoamericana." *Texto y Contexto* 7: 73–90.

Salvadó, Luis Raúl. 1988. *The Other Refugees: A Study of Non-Recognized Guatemalan Refugees in Chiapas, Mexico.* Washington, D.C.: HMP/CIPRA, Georgetown University.

Sánchez Martínez, Faustino. 1999. "Recepción y autosuficiencia de refugiados en Quintana Roo 1984–1989." In UNHCR and COMAR, *Presencia de los refugiados guatemaltecos en México.* Mexico City: UNHCR & COMAR.

Sánchez Meraz, Antonio. 1999. "Llegada de los refugiados." In UNHCR and COMAR, *Presencia de los refugiados guatemaltecos en México.* Mexico City: UNHCR and COMAR.

Schirmer, Jennifer. 1998. *The Guatemalan Military Project: A Violence Called Democracy.* Philadelphia: University of Pennsylvania Press.

———. 2003. "Whose Testimony? Whose Truth? Where Are the Armed Actors in the Stoll-Menchú Controversy?" *Human Rights Quarterly* 25, 1: 60–73.

———. 2005. "Paradise in Ashes: A Guatemalan Journey of Courage, Terror and Hope" (Book review). *American Ethnologist* 32, 2.

Schmidt, Bettina and Ingo W. Schröder. 2001. "Introduction: Violent Imaginaries and Violent Practices." In *Anthropology of Violence and Conflict*, ed. Bettina E. Schmidt and Ingo W. Schröder, 1–24. London: Routledge.

Schwartz, Norman B. 1990. *Forest Society: A Social History of Petén, Guatemala.* Philadelphia: University of Pennsylvania Press.

Shore, Chris. 2001. "Nation and State in the European Union." In *Times, Places, Passages: Ethnological Approaches in the New Millennium*, ed. Réka Kiss and Attila Paládi-Kovács. Plenary Papers of 7th SIEF-Conference, Budapest.

Sivard, Ruth. 1996. *World Military and Social Expenditures.* Washington, D.C.: World Priorities.

Smith, Carol A. 1990. *Guatemalan Indians and the State: 1540 to 1988.* Austin: University of Texas Press.

Sosa, Mario. 2001. "Comunidad y sistema de clasificación étnica: El caso de las CPRs-Ixcán." Tesis de Maestría en Antropología Social y Cultura, Universidad de San Carlos, Guatemala City.

Steinmetz, George, ed. 1999. *State/Culture. State Formation After the Cultural Turn.* Ithaca, N.Y.: Cornell University Press.

Stepputat, Finn. 1989. *Self-Sufficiency and Exile in Mexico: Report on a Field Study Among Relocated Guatemalan Refugees in South-East Mexico, August–November 1988.* Geneva: UNRISD.

———. 1994. "Repatriation and the Politics of Space: The Case of the Mayan Diaspora." *Journal of Refugee Studies* 7, 2/3: 175–85.

———. 1999. "Repatriation and Everyday Forms of State Formation in Guatemala." In *The End of the Refugee Cycle? Refugee Repatriation and Reconstruction*, ed. Richard Black and Khalid Koser, 210–26. New York: Berghahn.

———. 2001. "Urbanizing the Countryside. Armed Conflict, State Formation, and the Politics of Place in Contemporary Guatemala." In *States of Imagination: Ethnographic Explorations of the Postcolonial State*, ed. Thomas Blom Hansen and Finn Stepputat, 284–312. Durham, N.C.: Duke University Press.

Stoll, David. 1993. *Between Two Armies in the Ixil Towns of Guatemala.* New York: Columbia University Press.

Stølen, Kristi Anne. 1991. "Women, Gender and Social Change." In *Gender and Change in Developing Countries*, ed. Kristi Anne Stølen and Mariken Vaa, 1–12. Oslo: Norwegian University Press.

———. 1996. "The Gentle Exercise of Male Power in Rural Argentina." *Identities: Global Studies in Culture and Power* 2: 385–406.

———. 1998. "Honour and Shame in the New World: Gender Relations among Argentine Farmers." *Anthropological Journal on European Cultures* 7, 2: 59–86.

———. 2000. "Creating a Better Life: Participatory Communitarian Development Among Guatemalan Returnees." SUM Working Paper 2000.3. Oslo: University of Oslo.

———. 2004. "The Reconstruction of Community and Identity Among Guatemalan Returnees." *European Review of Latin American and Caribbean Studies* 77.

———. 2005. "Contradictory Notions of the State: The Case of the Guatemalan Returnees." In *State Formations: Anthropological Perspectives*, ed. Christian Krohn-Hansen and Knut Nustad, 142–70. London: Pluto Press.

Taylor, Clark. 1998. *Return of Guatemala's Refugees: Reweaving the Thorn.* Philadelphia: Temple University Press.

Torres, Gabriela.1999. "The Unexpected Consequences of Violence: Rethinking Gender Roles and Ethnicity." In *Journeys of Fear: Refugee Return and National Transformation in Guatemala*, ed. Liisa L. North and Alan. B. Simmons, 155–75. Montreal: McGill-Queen's University Press.

Trouillot, Michel-Rolph. 2001. "The Anthropology of the State in the Age of Globalization." *Current Anthropology* 42, 1.

UNHCR and COMAR. 1999. *Presencia de los refugiados guatemaltecos en México.* Mexico City: UNHCR & COMAR.

Vaeren van der, Pierre. 2000. *Perdidos en la selva.* Amsterdam: Thela.

Watanabe, John M. 1993. "Enduring Yet Ineffable Community in the Western Periphery of Guatemala." In *Guatemalan Indians and the State: 1540 to 1988*, ed. Carol Smith, 183–204. Austin: University of Texas Press.

Wagley, Charles. 1941. *Economics of a Guatemalan Village.* Memoir 58. Menasha, Wis.: American Anthropological Association.

Warner Daniel. 1994. "Voluntary Repatriation and the Meaning of Return to Home: a Critique of Liberal Mathematics." *Journal of Refugee Studies* 7, 2–3: 160–74.

Warren, Kay B. 1993. "Interpreting *la Violencia* in Guatemala: Shapes of Kaqchiquel Resistance and Silence." In *The Violence Within: Cultural and Political Opposition in Divided Nations*, ed. Kay B. Warren, 25–56. Boulder, Colo.: Westview Press.

———. 1998. *Indigenous Movements and Their Critics: Pan-Mayan Activism in Guatemala.* Princeton, N.J.: Princeton University Press.

———. 2002. "Voting Against Indigenous Rights in Guatemala: Lessons from the 1999 Referendum." In *Indigenous Movements, Self-Representation, and the State in Latin America*, ed. Kay B. Warren and Jean E. Jackson. Austin: University of Texas Press.

Warren, Kay B. and Jean E. Jackson, 2002. "Introduction: Studying Indigenous Activism in Latin America." In *Indigenous Movements, Self-Representation, and the State in Latin America*, ed. Kay B. Warren and Jean E. Jackson. Austin: University of Texas Press.

Wilkinson, Daniel. 2002. *Silence on the Mountain: Stories of Terror, Betrayal, and Forgetting in Guatemala.* Boston: Houghton Mifflin.

Wilson, Anne Karine P. 2003. "En la tierra de uno: Returnerte flyktninger og identitet i La Quetzal, Guatemala." Oslo: Centre for Development and the Environment (DT02–2003).

Wilson, Fiona. 2001. "In the Name of the State? Schools and Teachers in an Andean Province." In *States of Imagination: Ethnographic Explorations of the Post-*

Colonial State, ed. Thomas B. Hansen and Finn Stepputat. Durham, N.C.: Duke University Press.

Wilson, Richard. 1994. "Anchored Communities: Identity and History of the Maya Q'eqchi'." *Man* 28: 121–38.

Wilson, Richard. 1995a. *Maya Resurgence in Guatemala: Q'eqchi' Experiences*. Norman: University of Oklahoma Press.

Wilson Richard. 1995b. "Between Two Armies in the Ixil Towns of Guatemala." (Book Review). *Journal of the Royal Anthropological Institute* 1, 1 (March 1995): 217–18.

Wollny, Hans. 1991. "Asylum Policy in Mexico: A Survey." *Journal of Refugee Studies* 4: 219–36.

Womack, John, Jr. 1999. *Rebellion in Chiapas: An Historical Reader*. New York: New Press.

Zak, Monica. 1988. *Pumadottera*. Oslo: Norske Samlaget.

Zinser, Adolfo Aguilar. 1991. "Repatriation of Guatemalan Refugees in Mexico: Conditions and Prospects." In *Repatriation Under Conflict in Central America*, ed. Mary Ann Larkin, Fredrick C. Cuny, and Barry N. Stein, 47–114. Washington, D.C./Dallas: CIPRA/Intertect.

Zur, Judith N. 1998. *Violent Memories: Mayan War Widows in Guatemala*. Boulder, Colo.: Westview Press.

Index

209; health promoters and health care, 135–36, 141, 142, 148, 215 n.5; labor and production, 146–50; land distribution and ownership, 138–40, 145; leisure and entertainment, 150–52; local institutions and meetings, 142–44; Maya Biosphere Reserve, 12, 129, 145–46, 207, 210, 212 n.10; name, 211 n.1; neighborhoods, 11, 160, 216 n.2; neighbors' views, 1–2; organizational capacity, 138, 153, 203; peasant homesteads, 12; project management problems, 207–8; public buildings, 11–12, 138, 202–3; *sectores* and community-level organization, 140–42; security anxieties, 135; social organization, 137–44; structure, 11–12; women's participation/ exclusion, 143, 174–84, 197–98, 209. See also *sectores*, La Quetzal community; Unión Maya Itzá cooperative

La Quetzal community, construction of, 134–53; arrival in jungle (emergency phase), 134–37, 178; challenges, 129, 134–35; early services, 135–36; forest clearing, 134–35, 136; formal "site of governance," 202–5; hardships and isolation, 137; motives for return, 130–33; negotiation of land purchase, 129; political/social character of return, 130; road negotiations, 137; setting and selecting area, 11–12, 128; working brigades, 129, 135

La Quetzal identity, 2, 154–72; anthropological notions of ethnicity and identity, 8–9; and bilingual education, 170–72; Castellanos and "reinvention of ethnicity," 158; cultural markers and ethnicity, 154; dress, 159, 167; ethnic differentiation, 156–57; ethnic markers other than language, 158–59; indigenous surnames, 159; interethnic/mixed marriages, 160, 165–68, 189–91; interethnic mixing, 2, 154–56, 159–60; language, 142, 156–58, 168–69; neighborhoods, 11, 160, 216 n.2; nuclear households, 165; Pan-Mayan movement, 158, 170–72, 216 n.6; Q'eqchi' traditionalism, 160–65; *sectores* and ethnicity, 142, 156–57. See also Q'eqchi' Indians

Laugerud García, Kjell Eugenio (President Kjell), 38, 39

Law Against Vagrancy, 212 n.8
Law of Agrarian Reform, 23
Le Bot, Yvon, 43
liberation theology, 21–22
Los Angeles cooperative, 23
Luís, Padre. See Gurriarán, Luís

Madre Tierra (refugee women's organization), 216 n.1
Malkki, Liisa, 8
Mam Indians: interethnic marriages, 165–66; language, 142, 156, 170; surnames, 159
Mam Manz, Beatriz, 4, 51
Mama Maquín (refugee women's organization), 216 n.1
marriage practices, 186–89; arranged marriages, 186–89, 198; and fiestas, 187, 188; interethnic/mixed, 160, 165–68, 189–91; protection of female virginity/chastity, 191; Q'eqchi', 163, 164, 189
matazona (killing zone), 3, 45
Maya Biosphere Reserve. See MBR
Mayalán cooperative, 23, 29–30, 59–61
Mayan languages, 2, 142, 156; and bilingual education, 170–72; and ethnic differentiation in La Quetzal, 142, 156; public contexts, 169; switching with Spanish, 169
Mayan religion: and Catholic Church, 36–37, 161–62, 171; *cofradías*, 35, 162, 213 n.15; planting rituals, 161–62; Q'eqchi' *costumbres*, 34–37, 161–64, 189, 213 n.14
Maya Q'eqchi' Don Bosco teacher training college (Cobán), 158
Maya Tikal (youth organization), 127–28, 141
MBR (Maya Biosphere Reserve): forest management, 145–46, 207, 210; land use constraints, 12, 145, 207, 210; and La Quetzal, 12, 129, 145–46, 207, 212 n.10
Mejía, Gen. Victor, 170
Mexican Commission for Aid to Refugees. See COMAR
Mexican government: attitudes on refugees, 116–17, 121; enforcement of borders, 113–17; immigration authorities, 113–18, 121–23; refugee relocation, 121–23. See also refugee camps in Mexico